SAMS
Teach Yourself

Lotus Notes 7

in 10 Minutes

Jane Kirkland
Dorothy Burke

 SAMS   *800 East 96th Street, Indianapolis, Indiana, 46240 USA*

Sams Teach Yourself Lotus Notes 7 in 10 Minutes

Copyright © 2006 by Sams Publishing

International Standard Book Number: 0-672-32800-3

Library of Congress Catalog Card Number: 2005902432

Printed in the United States of America

First Printing: October 2005

08   07   06   05   4   3   2   1

Trademarks

All terms mentioned in this book that are known to be trademarks or service marks have been appropriately capitalized. Sams Publishing cannot attest to the accuracy of this information. Use of a term in this book should not be regarded as affecting the validity of any trademark or service mark.

Warning and Disclaimer

Every effort has been made to make this book as complete and as accurate as possible, but no warranty or fitness is implied. The information provided is on an "as is" basis. The authors and the publisher shall have neither liability nor responsibility to any person or entity with respect to any loss or damages arising from the information contained in this book.

Bulk Sales

Sams Publishing offers excellent discounts on this book when ordered in quantity for bulk purchases or special sales. For more information, please contact

U.S. Corporate and Government Sales
1-800-382-3419
corpsales@pearsontechgroup.com

For sales outside of the U.S., please contact

International Sales
international@pearsoned.com

PUBLISHER
Paul Boger

ACQUISITIONS EDITOR
Loretta Yates

DEVELOPMENT EDITOR
Melanie Palaisa

MANAGING EDITOR
Charlotte Clapp

PROJECT EDITOR
Andy Beaster

INDEXER
Erika Millen

PROOFREADER
Elizabeth Scott

TECHNICAL EDITOR
Rob Kirkland

PUBLISHING COORDINATOR
Cindy Teeters

INTERIOR DESIGNER
Gary Adair

COVER DESIGNER
Aren Howell

PAGE LAYOUT
Toi Davis

GRAPHICS
Tammy Graham

Contents at a Glance

Table of Contents

About the Authors

Jane Kirkland has authored Lotus Notes books (as Jane Calabria) with Dorothy Burke and Rob Kirkland for many years. She is the series editor for the Macmillan Computer Publishing series of Lotus Notes and Domino R5, R6, and R7 books. She is a CLP Notes Principal Application Developer with a principal certification as an application developer. She is also a Certified Microsoft User Specialist at the Expert level in Word and Excel. She and her husband, Rob Kirkland, own Stillwater Enterprises, Inc., a consulting firm located near Philadelphia. Jane and Rob are preeminent Lotus Notes authors, and Rob lectures and trains on the topic of Lotus Notes and Domino as well as IBM WebSphere Application Server, IBM Portal, and IBM Lotus Workplace. Jane is also the publisher and author of *Take A Walk Books*, an award-winning series of nature discovery books for kids. Learn more about her "other life" at www.takeawalk.com.

Dorothy Burke is a Certified Lotus Notes Instructor (CLI) and a CLP Notes Principal Application Developer. She teaches Domino application development and has been an independent consultant and trainer since 1988. Dorothy is the editor for Jane's *Take A Walk* series.

Together, Jane and Dorothy have coauthored more than 20 books, including topics such as Microsoft Word, PowerPoint, and Excel and Lotus Notes and Domino from releases 4.6 to 7. Their recent Lotus Notes and Domino titles include Que's *Ten Minute Guide to Lotus Notes 6*, *How to Use Lotus Notes 6*, *Teach Yourself Lotus Notes 5 in 10 Minutes*, *How to Use Lotus Notes R5*, *Teach Yourself Lotus Notes R5 in 24 Hours*, and *Teach Yourself Lotus Notes and Domino R5 Development in 21 Days*. All of Jane and Dorothy's books maintain reviews with high ratings at Amazon and other online booksellers. Their books have been translated into more than eight languages throughout the world. Their books remain some of the most popular Lotus Notes and Domino development books on the market today.

About the Development Editor

Melanie Palaisa has been a technical writer and development editor for more than 15 years. She has been the development editor for several Que and Sams series, including the *Ten Minute Guides, Complete Idiot's Guides, 6 in 1, Easy, Special Edition Using*, and *Sams Teach Yourself.*

She has joined Jane and Dorothy as the development editor for several books, including *Microsoft Works 6-in-1, Microsoft Office 97 6 in 1, Using Microsoft Word 2000, Que's Ten Minute Guide to Lotus Notes 4.6, Ten Minute Guide to Lotus Notes Mail 4.6*, and *Sams Teach Yourself Lotus Notes 5 in 24 Hours*. Melanie is also the development editor for Jane's *Take A Walk* children's books.

About the Technical Editor

Rob Kirkland is an IBM Certified Professional and IBM Certified Instructor for Lotus Software and an IBM Certified System Administrator and IBM Certified Instructor for Websphere Application Server v5.x. He is an associate of The RockTeam in southeast Pennsylvania, providing Lotus Domino and IBM WebSphere training and consulting services to companies in the Delaware Valley. Rob is the primary author of *Domino System Administration* (ISBN 1562059483), the acclaimed "bible" of books on that topic. Rob is also co-owner of Stillwater Publishing, publisher of the award-winning *Take A Walk* series of children's nature adventure books.

Acknowledgments

Our publisher remains a leader in Lotus Notes and Domino books and their commitment to providing quality books in a timely fashion to the Notes/Domino community has made working with their dedicated staff exciting. We thank them for the opportunities they provide us and the information they make available to Lotus Notes and Domino users at all levels of expertise.

We Want to Hear from You!

As the reader of this book, *you* are our most important critic and commentator. We value your opinion and want to know what we're doing right, what we could do better, what areas you'd like to see us publish in, and any other words of wisdom you're willing to pass our way.

As an associate publisher for Sams Publishing, I welcome your comments. You can email or write me directly to let me know what you did or didn't like about this book—as well as what we can do to make our books better.

Please note that I cannot help you with technical problems related to the topic of this book. We do have a User Services group, however, where I will forward specific technical questions related to the book.

When you write, please be sure to include this book's title and author as well as your name, email address, and phone number. I will carefully review your comments and share them with the author and editors who worked on the book.

Email: feedback@samspublishing.com

Mail: Paul Boger
               Publisher
               Sams Publishing
               800 East 96th Street
               Indianapolis, IN 46240 USA

For more information about this book or another Sams Publishing title, visit our website at www.samspublishing.com. Type the ISBN (excluding hyphens) or the title of a book in the Search field to find the page you're looking for.

Introduction

Welcome to *Sams Teach Yourself Lotus Notes 7 in 10 Minutes*

This book focuses on the basics of Lotus Notes and Domino; introduces general groupware, Notes, and email concepts; and shows you some advanced features of the program. You can work through the book lesson by lesson, building on your skills, or you can use the book as a quick reference when you want to perform a new task. Features and concepts are presented in tasks that take 10 minutes or less to complete.

If you are new to Notes, start at the beginning of the book. If you've used Notes before, you might want to skip the first few lessons and work from there. Use the Table of Contents and select the lessons that cover features of the program you haven't yet used. If you travel with Lotus Notes on your laptop, the compact size of this book is perfect for fitting into your laptop or notebook case.

Who Should Use This Book

Sams Teach Yourself Lotus Notes 7 in 10 Minutes is for anyone who

- Has Lotus Notes 7 installed on his PC or laptop

- Needs to learn Notes 7 quickly

- Wants to explore some of the new features of Lotus Notes 7

- Needs a task-based Lotus Notes 7 tutorial

- Requires a compact Notes 7 reference guide

Conventions Used in This Book

In telling you to choose menu commands, this book uses the format menu title, menu command. For example, the statement "choose File, Properties" means "open the File menu and select the Properties command."

In addition, *Sams Teach Yourself Lotus Notes 7 in 10 Minutes* uses the following icons to identify helpful information:

 New or unfamiliar terms are defined in "plain English."

 Look here for ideas that cut corners and confusion.

 This icon identifies areas where new users often run into trouble and offers practical solutions to those problems.

From Here...

For Lotus Notes press releases, technical information, and new product information, visit the Lotus website. The following Lotus site contains information relevant to the Notes client:

- **www.Lotus.com**—The Lotus home page, where you can find information on all Lotus products and services, including support and access to other Lotus Notes sites.

LESSON 1
What's New in Lotus Notes 7

In this chapter, you see a quick view of the the new features of Lotus Notes 7. This is also your roadmap to where you can learn more about these new features in this book. This chapter assumes you have previous experience with Lotus Notes. In this chapter we discuss:

- The new features of the Desktop

- The new features of Mail

- The new features of the Calendar

- The new features of Instant Messaging and Web Conferencing

New Features of the Desktop

The new features of the Desktop include:

- **Close All Windows**—You can now close all open windows in Notes by choosing **File, Close All Open Window Tabs** from the menu. This is covered in Chapter 2, "Getting Started."

- **Exit Prompt**—Notes 7 prompts you when you attempt to exit. To disable this prompting, choose **File, Preferences, User Preferences**. Under **Additional Options** select **Do not prompt when exiting from Notes/Domino Designer/Domino Administrator**. Click **OK**.

- **Right-Click menus**—Notes 7 has enhanced some context-sensitive menus accessible by right-clicking the mouse.

- **Saving the state of window tabs**—You can now save the state of window tabs when you exit Notes. By doing so, the next time you open Notes you'll see the same window state. To enable this feature choose **File, Save Window State** from the menu. To learn more about this new feature, see Chapter 19, "Customizing Notes."

New Features of Mail

New enhancements to Lotus Notes Mail help you create, sort, follow up, save, and locate mail items more efficiently.

- **Faster follow up formatting**—You can now drag and drop an email message to the Follow Up view. You can also access the follow up menu by clicking on a Follow Up item with your right mouse button. To learn more about Follow Up, see Chapter 4, "Managing Mail."

- **Sort by Subject**—You can now sort by Subject in all of your mail views by clicking on the Subject header of the mail view.

- **Find the folder where a document is stored**—To locate which folders a document is stored in, go to your Inbox and click the **Folders** button on the Action bar. Choose **Discover Folders** and a new dialog box displays the list of folders that contain the document you've selected. To switch to one of those folders click **Open Folder**. From this dialog box you can also add or remove the document from folders.

- **Auto Save**—If you've ever had a power failure or computer lockup while writing a lengthy email in Notes, you'll love this new feature. Now Notes can automatically save your work as you create it. To enable this feature, create a local Auto Save database by choosing **File, Preferences, User Preferences** from the menu. Under **Startup Options** select **AutoSave Every 15 minutes** and click **OK**. To learn more, see Chapter 19.

- **Mark messages to show whether your name is in the "To" or "cc" field**—To help you determine how much of the responsibility to reply to a message is yours, you can display icons in your mail views which indicate whether your name appears in the "To" or "cc" field of an email. To enable this new feature, open your mail database and choose **Actions, Tools, Preferences** from the menu. Under **Mail** click the **Message Marking** tab. Click the **Recipients** tab. Select your icon display preferences. To learn more about this new feature, see Chapter 8, "Setting Mail and Calendar Preferences."

New Features of the Calendar

- **Calendar Clean Up**—The calendar Clean Up tool helps you easily delete past calendar and To Do items. For more information see Chapter 9, "Using the Calendar."

- **Calendar Auto Feature**—Notes 7 allows you to automatically accept a meeting even when there is a calendar conflict. To learn how to set the auto feature, see Chapter 10, "Working with Meetings and Group Calendaring."

- **Calendar and To Do MiniViews**—To keep track of Calendar and To Do items without having them appear in your Inbox, use the new MiniView. The MiniView displays all notices you have not yet responded to, responses that include comments, and the date of the To Do item or meeting as well as any mail messages you have flagged for follow-up action. When you first install Notes 7 you'll see a **Configure** button on the left side of your Calendar under the Date Picker. To configure and use the MiniView in Notes 7, see Chapter 4, Chapter 9, and Chapter 11, "Working with To Do Items."

- **All Calendar Entries View**—This view replaces the Meetings view of previous versions of Notes. This new view can display all meeting invitations, meeting workflow documents such as responses to invitations, updates, or notices about your meetings and other Calendar entries including holidays. To open the All Calendar Entries view, click the **All Calendar Entries** tab in the Calendar. To learn more about this new view, see Chapter 9.

New Features of Instant Messaging and Web Conferencing

Two new features of Instant Messaging and Web Conferencing are available only if your company is running an instant messaging and conferencing server and the features are only available for Windows versions of Lotus Notes.

- **Show instant messaging status for names**—Given conferencing capabilities, you can use instant messaging to chat with people or include them in instant meetings. This feature is enabled by default. To learn more about this feature, see Chapter 18, "Instant Messaging."

- **Instant Meetings**—Instant meetings can take place when you have Instant Messaging and Web Conferencing capabilities. The Instant Meetings feature of Notes allows people to chat through text messages, communicate using computer audio or audio and video, and use a whiteboard or share computer screens during the meeting. To learn how to use this feature, see Chapter 18.

In this chapter, you learned about some of the new features of Notes 7 and where in this book you can learn more about those new features. In the next chapter, you learn how to log into and navigate the Notes Client.

LESSON 2
Getting Started

In this chapter, you learn about some Lotus Notes concepts and get famil-iar with the Notes client user interface. This chapter gives you a brief explanation of Lotus Notes, what it is and how it works, instructions for navigating around Lotus Notes, and instructions on how to protect your Notes Desktop by locking your password.

Understanding the Notes Client

Lotus Notes is based on client/server technology, which enables you to access, share, and manage information over a network. The network can consist of five or ten computers in your office building, cabled together, or it can consist of 30,000 computers located all over the world, connected to one another in various ways. The software you're running on your PC is called the *Lotus Notes 7 Client*. It requests and receives information from the server called the "Domino" server and can also be a client to non-Domino servers.

While working in Lotus Notes, all information, including your email, is stored in Domino applications, or databases. Notes *applications* are a col-lection of one or more *databases* that are designed to perform a specific function or work process (workflow). It is not unusual for people to use the terms *application* and *database* interchangeably. Your mail database, stored on the Domino server, is secure and only you (and possibly your Domino administrator) have access to that database unless you change the settings and allow others to have access. Other databases, such as the Help database, are accessible to many people, and many people can access such databases simultaneously.

The connection you have to the Domino server is similar to the connection you might have to your file server at work. Often, you store work that you have created in other software programs (such as Microsoft Word) on the file server on your network at the office. For example, you might save your Word documents on your F: drive, which is actually space that is dedicated to you for storing files on the file server.

Lotus Notes applications typically support or automate business functions by helping you create, collect, share, and manage almost any kind of information. Notes applications can incorporate information from external sources (such as spreadsheets), export data to external databases (such as DB2), or contain documents (such as Word).

This book assumes that you're working in your office, connected to a Domino server; however, most of the procedures and tasks in this book are similar, whether you're in your office or working from home. If you're not attached to your network when you start Notes, the Choose Location dialog box might appear. Choose **Home** as your location and continue to work through this chapter, or go to Chapter 17, "Using Notes Remotely," and see the section "Connecting." Windows XP users may find an icon for "Lotus Notes" at the top of their startup menu. This is a special icon that starts the user's default email application. Clicking this icon will start Notes and navigate directly to the email Inbox.

When you start Notes for the very first time, you might see the Lotus Notes setup screen, in which case you should select the option that says "No thanks, just give me the defaults" so that you see the default Welcome page as shown in Figure 2.1.

Through hotspots and bookmark buttons, the Welcome page provides access to mail, calendars, Address Books, and To Do lists. The Welcome page is customizable and you can add your favorite websites or newsgroups. From here, you can also search databases or websites, take a tour of Notes, and see what's new in Lotus Notes 7 Client. Table 2.1 describes the elements of the Notes window.

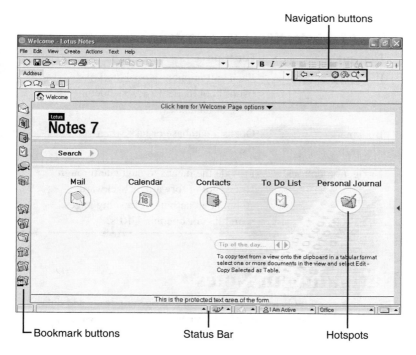

Navigation buttons

Bookmark buttons   Status Bar   Hotspots

FIGURE 2.1   The Lotus Notes Welcome page is your starting point
to access your mail, the calendar, and all features of Notes.

Table 2.1   Notes Window Elements

Element	Function
Status bar	Presents information about the selected item, shows error messages (if any), displays your location, and indicates when you have new mail.
Hotspots	Text or picture that you click to perform an action or follow a link.

continues

continued

Table 2.1   Notes Window Elements

Element	Function
Bookmark buttons	Each button opens a bookmark page or a list of bookmarks to access documents, sites, or databases.
Bookmark	Opens a database or task when you click the bookmark.
Navigation buttons	Provide the means to navigate through Notes, going forward or backward, stopping an activity, refreshing pages, searching, or opening URLs.

Navigating in Notes

There are several tools for moving around and opening tasks and databases in Notes. They include hotspots such as those on the Welcome page, navigation buttons, and bookmarks.

The hotspots on the Welcome page are pretty self-explanatory: Click on the Mail hotspot to open your mail database, or click on the Calendar hotspot to view your calendar.

Navigation buttons are located in the toolbars (see Figure 2.1). When you point at one of the buttons, a tip appears to tell you the name of the button and the keyboard shortcut that performs the same function. Table 2.2 provides a short explanation of each button.

Table 2.2   The Navigation Buttons

Click Here	Name	Description
⇦ ▾	Go Back	Returns to the previous page, document, or task. Click the arrow on the right to see a drop-down menu of places you can go back to; select one to go there.

Table 2.2   The Navigation Buttons

Click Here	Name	Description
	Go Forward	Takes you to the task, page, or document that was displayed prior to your clicking Go Back. Click the arrow on the right to see a drop-down menu of the places you can go forward to; select one to go there.
	Stop	Interrupts the current program activity.
	Refresh	Refreshes the current document, page, or view with the latest data.
	Search	Opens the Search bar in the current view. Click the arrow on the right to display a drop-down menu of search choices. You can search the current view, document, or page; your Notes domain; or the Web.

Bookmark buttons are located on the left of the Welcome page. From here you can also open your Mail, Calendar, and To Do list (just as you can by clicking a hotspot). Bookmark buttons link to databases, bookmark pages, or even web pages. Bookmark buttons are customizable; you learn how to add bookmarks throughout this book. Table 2.3 describes the default bookmark buttons that are found on the Welcome page.

Table 2.3   The Default Bookmark Bar Buttons

Click Here	To
	Opens your **Mail** database. From here you can view your Inbox, create new mail, and so forth. You learn about the mail database in Chapter 3, "Email Basics."

continues

continued

Table 2.3   The Default Bookmark Bar Buttons

Click Here	To
	Opens the **Calendar** where you manage your appointments, access the calendars or free time of other people (given permission, of course), invite people to meetings, accept invitations, and so forth. You learn about calendar functions in Chapter 9, "Using the Calendar."
	Opens your personal **Address Book**, where you keep information about your contacts. You learn more about address books in Chapter 12, "Using the Address Books."
	Opens your **To Do** list. You learn how to work with To Do tasks in Chapter 11, "Working with To Do Items."
	Opens your **Sametime Connection**, so you can see your Instant Messaging Contact list. You learn more about instant messaging (chat) in Chapter 18, "Instant Messaging."
	Opens the **Replication** page, which is the tool you use when you are working from a remote location or disconnected from the server. Learn about the Replication page in Chapter 17.
	Opens the **Favorite Bookmarks** page. Favorites contains links to the databases and pages you visit frequently, such as your mail, address book, calendar, and to do list.
	Opens the **Databases** bookmark page. If you upgraded to Notes 7 from Notes 4.x, all the data bases you had on your workspace now appear on this bookmark page. To add a new bookmark to the page, drag the window tab onto the bookmark page.

Table 2.3   The Default Bookmark Bar Buttons

Click Here	To
	To remove a bookmark from a page, right-click the bookmark and select **Remove Bookmarks**.
	Opens the **More Bookmarks** bookmark page, where you add any additional bookmarks that you want to use.
	Opens your **History** page, where you can see web pages and database pages you've previously viewed. If you are opening Notes for the first time, this folder will not contain any web pages.
	Opens the **Internet Explorer Links** page. If you have Internet Explorer installed, the bookmarks for the web browser appear here.
	If you have Netscape Navigator installed, you will see a bookmark for **Netscape Navigator Links**. If you have both of these programs installed, you see one bookmark for each program.

When a bookmark opens a task such as a database, a document, or mail, it opens the task in a new window and creates a new window tab (see Figure 2.2). Opening a new window for each task is similar to the way a word processing document works—it opens a new window for each document you have open, or for each document you are creating. To move from window to window, click on its window tab. In Figure 2.2, several tasks are open and several window tabs are displayed. Each window tab has a close button. Close a window by clicking the close button on its tab, or click the **Close All Open Window Tabs** button on the Universal toolbar to close all your open windows at one time.

To create a bookmark from an open window or document, drag from the window tab onto the Bookmark bar or into a folder that is located on the Bookmark bar. You can also create a bookmark for files on your PC such as Word documents or Excel spreadsheets by dragging the file from the file system to the Bookmark bar.

Window tabs　　　Close All Open
　　　　　　　　Window Tabs button　　　　　　　　　　　　　Close button

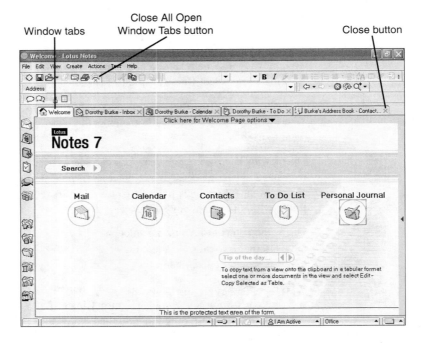

Figure 2.2　Here, the Welcome page is the active page. Note that the Welcome window tab is highlighted. Other open windows include the Inbox, Calendar, To Do, and Address Book, all of which are represented with window tabs. Window tabs are also referred to as task buttons.

Using Toolbars

Some people prefer to click on buttons to perform program functions in lieu of accessing the menu. Like most programs that are designed to run under Microsoft Windows, buttons can be found on the window's toolbar. Toolbars are context sensitive, and they change depending upon the task you are performing in Notes. For example, one set of buttons appears when you are reading a document, and another set appears when you are editing a document. You can turn off context-sensitive toolbars (although we don't recommend it) by choosing **File, Preferences, Toolbar**

Preferences, and then turning off the **Show Context Sensitive Toolbar** check box.

When you hold a mouse over one of the toolbar buttons, a brief description of the icon appears. You learn how to customize, change the position of, and create sets of Toolbars in Chapter 19, "Customizing Notes."

Using Properties Boxes

As you work with databases, documents, text, and other Notes objects, you need to set attributes for the selected item. This is usually done in a **Properties box**. Although it resembles a dialog box, you work differently with a Properties box. A Properties box displays only the properties of a specific item, such as selected text or a database. Properties contain information about an item such as its name, location, settings, design, size, and so on. When you make a selection in a Properties box, it takes effect immediately—even though the Properties box remains onscreen as you work. You won't see an OK or Cancel button.

Properties boxes contain tabbed pages that offer various options for the item you have selected. Figure 2.3 shows the properties box for selected text in a document.

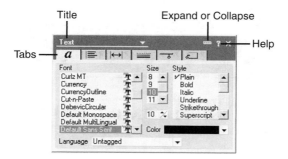

FIGURE 2.3   Use a Properties box to change the properties or attributes of selected items.

Properties boxes have many of the same elements that dialog boxes have: drop-down lists, list boxes, text boxes, and check boxes, for example.

However, Properties boxes also contain the additional elements described in Table 2.4.

Table 2.4   Properties Box Elements

Element	Description
Title	The Properties box title displays the selected item, as in *Document* or *Text*. To change the item in the Properties box, use the drop-down list in the title bar.
Tabs	Named flaps that represent pages of options related to the selected element.
Help	Click this button to launch context-sensitive help.

Because a Properties box can remain onscreen while you work, you might want to reposition it on your screen. To move a Properties box, click the title bar and drag it to a new position.

 Click the **Collapse** icon on the title bar of a Properties box to collapse it. Collapsing hides all but the title bar and the tabs, and it frees up space on the workspace. When the box is collapsed, the icon becomes the Expand icon. Click the **Expand** icon to expand the Properties box back to its original view and size.

Changing and Locking Your Password

The first time you use Lotus Notes, your system administrator will supply a password for you to use. You want to change your password so that no one else can access your mail and other databases. The ability to access information in Notes is based upon the use of your password and a file stored on your computer called your User ID file. To access information in Notes, a user needs both knowledge of the password and a copy of the

User ID file on their computer. The User ID file is discussed in Appendix A, "Understanding Security and Access Rights." Here, we discuss changing and locking your password.

A password can have any combination of keyboard characters, as long as the first character is alphanumeric. Be careful when capitalizing your password, because Notes passwords are *case sensitive*, and *PASSWORD* is different from *password*.

Use the following steps to change your password:

1. Choose **File, Security, User Security** from the menu.

2. Enter your current password in the box (see Figure 2.4) and click **OK**.

FIGURE 2.4   As you enter your password, you see a series of X's.

3. When the User Security dialog box appears (see Figure 2.5), click **Change Password**.

4. Enter your current password and click **OK**.

5. In the Change Password dialog box, enter your new password. You'll have to enter this new password twice. Be sure to type it correctly because you can't see the characters you type. A good choice for a password uses upper- and lowercase, alpha and numeric characters. It should also be a word not found in the dictionary; for example, "wildcat" is not a good choice for a password.

6. Click OK.

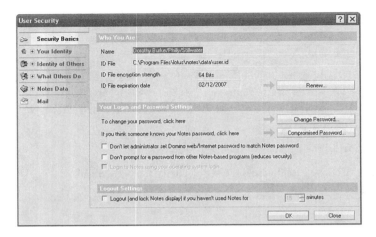

FIGURE 2.5 The User Security dialog box is where you set many of your user preferences in Notes. When changing your password, keep in mind that your password requires a minimum of eight characters and no spaces. Also remember that your password is case sensitive.

 Rather than figuring out your own password, you can have Notes make up one for you. Click the **Generate Password** button in the Change Password dialog box. This allows you to select from a list of randomly created passwords. Select one from the list and click **Choose Selected Password**—but remember to memorize it first!

Always protect your password. Don't share it with anyone, and don't write reminders to yourself that you leave in obvious places (such as the Post-It note on your monitor).

Don't give your password to others, and never give your User ID file to others! If someone copies your User ID file, changing your password will not stop him from accessing your mail because the password is stored in the User ID file. For further security, it's also a good idea to change the password that was assigned to you by your Notes administrator. Typically, the administrator assigns a password that is easy for him (and you) to remember so that you can get up and running on Notes. It's not unusual for that password to be the same password that is assigned to all Notes users. Shortly after you become familiar with Notes, take the time to change your password—and keep it to yourself!

Locking Your ID

When you start Lotus Notes you enter your password. Once your password has been entered and authenticated by Notes, you can leave Notes running on your computer and you won't be prompted to enter your password again—unless you close and reopen Notes. If you walk away from your desk with Lotus Notes running, you stand the risk of others accessing your personal information and your mail. You may want to lock your ID in Notes, which will require you to reenter your password after a certain (determined by you) amount of time.

To lock your ID, choose **File, Security, Lock Display** from the menu, or press **F5**. Lotus Notes will display a large splash screen and no one can see your mail or other databases unless they enter your password. If you keep Notes open all day and you work with sensitive data or are in a high-traffic area, you can set Notes to automatically lock your ID for you after a specified time period of inactivity. To set up this automatic lock, choose **File, Preferences, User Preferences** from the menu to open the User Preferences dialog box. Enter the number of minutes in the "Logout (and lock Notes display) if you haven't used Notes for ____ Minutes" field. Click the checkbox in front of this field and enter your preferred number of minutes. Click **OK**. You can customize the logout screen as described in Chapter 19.

Exiting Notes

When you're finished with Notes, you can close the program in several different ways:

- Choose **File, Exit Notes**.

- Double-click the application's Control menu button.

- Click the application's Control menu button, and choose **Close** from the menu.

- Press **Alt+F4**.

- Click the Close (**X**) button at the right end of the Notes title bar.

You will be prompted to be sure you really want to exit. Click **Yes** to exit. If you don't feel you need this prompt, check **In the future, exit without prompting** before you close the dialog box.

In this chapter, you learned how to start Notes, navigate the Notes window, use Properties boxes, change your password, and exit Notes. In the next chapter you learn about reading and sending mail.

LESSON 3
Email Basics

In this chapter, you learn about sending mail, reading your incoming mail, and replying to your mail.

Opening Your Mail Inbox

Mail, like all information found in Lotus Notes, is stored in a database. The stored mail includes copies of messages you've received and sent, as well as some specialized documents such as calendar entries and tasks. To open your mail database, click on the mail hotspot on the Welcome page or click the **Mail** bookmark.

When you first open a Lotus Notes database (such as Mail), the display is split into two large panes called the Navigation pane and the View pane. The titles of the available views are displayed in the pane on the left (the Navigation pane), and more specific information is displayed in the pane on the right (the View pane).

The Navigation Pane

The Mail Navigation pane (see Figure 3.1) lists views and folders, such as the Inbox, Drafts, Sent, Follow Up, Junk Mail, and Trash, as well as containers named Views, Folders, and Tools, which contain other views and folders.

Views and folders   Incoming mail   Action bar

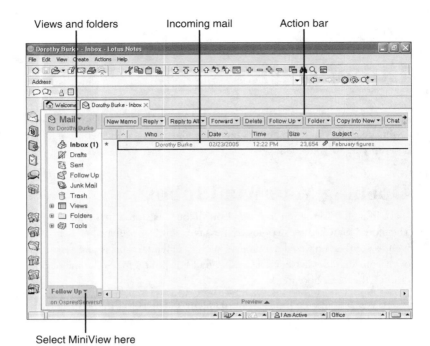

Select MiniView here

FIGURE 3.1   The Mail Navigation pane with the Inbox selected.

You can change the size of the Navigation and View panes to see more of one side or the other. Point to the line that separates the two panes until your mouse pointer turns into a two-headed arrow, separated by a black line. Drag that line to the left or right. You can also resize the columns in the View pane. Use the method that was just described for resizing panes, but drag the lines between columns.

At the bottom of the Navigation pane, you can display a MiniView. There are three possible MiniView options:

- Follow Up shows any messages you have flagged for follow up (learn more about using Follow Up in Chapter 4, "Managing Mail").

- New Notices displays all Calendar notices to which you have not yet responded (see Chapter 9, "Using the Calendar").

- To Do shows outstanding To Do items (see Chapter 11, "Working with To Do Items").

To change the MiniView display, click the arrow next to Follow Up (or whatever the current choice is) and select the option you want to see. To expand/collapse the MiniView display, click just to the right of the MiniView tab.

The View Pane

As you make choices in the Navigation pane, documents change in the View pane. For example, when you click on Inbox, your incoming mail messages are visible in the View pane. When you click on Sent, however, your outbound mail messages are visible.

Click on the Inbox to see your incoming mail messages. You can see who sent the message, the date it was sent, and the size and subject of the message. All unread messages have a red star in the selection bar to the left of the message (see Figure 3.1).

 If you don't see mail, make sure that you have clicked the Inbox at the top of the Navigation Pane. If you are new to Notes, it's entirely possible that no mail has been sent to you, so no documents are listed in the View pane.

Table 3.1 describes the views that are found in the Mail Navigation pane.

TABLE 3.1   Mail Database Views

View	Description
Inbox	Displays mail that has been sent to you.
Drafts	Displays mail messages you've elected to save as drafts instead of sending, which allows you to edit or make changes to the message before you send it.
Sent	Displays copies of messages you have sent if you chose to keep a copy of the message when you sent it.
Follow Up	Displays copies of messages you have marked for follow up, so you know that you still have to do something about the message.
Junk Mail	Any mail you block from your Inbox using the Mail Tools appears in this view until you decide what you want to do with it—delete it or move it back to the Inbox or a folder.
Trash	Displays messages that are marked for deletion until you empty the trash or permanently delete the message.
Views	Click the + sign next to Views to access the All Documents and Mail Thread views as described below.
All Documents	(Available when you click the + next to Views) Displays all messages, including those you've sent, received, saved in folders, saved as drafts, and so on. The subject line of reply messages are indented, so it is easy to see the relationship between messages and their replies.
Mail Threads	(Available when you click the + next to Views) A list of mail messages organized by conversation, with an initial message listed

TABLE 3.1   Mail Database Views

View	Description
	first and the responses to that message listed directly below it.
Folders	Contains the folders that you create to organize your mail. When you first open Lotus Notes, this folder is empty. Learn more about creating and using folders in Chapter 4.
Tools	Click the + sign next to the Tools icon to reveal the Archive, Rules, and Stationery views.
Archive	(Available when you click the + next to Tools) Contains a view of documents that have been archived, or saved in a way that compacts the size of the database. Archiving is beyond the scope of this book; however, we recommend you read the Lotus Notes Help database regarding archiving and discuss archive settings and preferences with your System Administrator.
Rules	(Available when you click the + next to Tools) Displays a list of mail rules you have created. When you first open Lotus Notes, this view shows no rules. Learn more about rules in Chapter 5, "Using Mail Tools."
Stationery	(Available when you click the + next to Views) Displays a list of custom stationery you have created and saved. If you are new to Notes, this shows no stationery. You learn more about stationery in Chapter 5.

The Mail Threads view is one of the most useful, yet most overlooked views in Lotus Notes. It can help you to determine if you've responded to an email, or if someone has responded to an email you sent to them. But it's important to understand that the Mail Threads will only work when you answer an email using the "reply" feature and your mail recipients use the "reply" feature when answering your email. Replying to mail is discussed later in this chapter.

The Action Bar

The Action bar (see Figure 3.1) contains command buttons to assist you with your current task. For example, when you select a mail message in the View pane, you can click one of these buttons to delete a message or to reply to a message. Like the menu bar and toolbars, the Action bar buttons change depending on the task you are performing. If your screen isn't wide enough to display all the buttons on the Action bar, a pair of arrows appears on the right side; click an arrow to see additional buttons. You can move the action bars by dragging them. You can also right-click the Action bar to display a menu showing which Action bars are currently displayed, and change them if you wish.

Selecting and Marking Mail

Before you can read, delete, print, or take any other action on a mail message, you must first *select* it. One message is already selected when you open your mailbox. To select a message, click once on the message in the View pane. A selected message has a heavy black rectangle around the name, date, and subject of the message.

To select a different message in the list, click on it or use the up and down arrows on your keyboard to move to it. To select multiple messages, click in the column to the left of the "Who" column (this column is called the "selection margin"). This places a checkmark in that column; then any action you take will be applied to all checked documents, such as clicking the Delete button or the Print button.

You can also use the menu command **Edit, Select All** to select all the messages in the view, and you can use **Edit, Deselect All** to remove all the checkmarks from the messages in the view.

If you accidentally select a document, you can deselect it by clicking on the check mark again.

 If you want to select multiple messages, place your mouse cursor in the selection bar to the left of the messages. Click and hold down the mouse button and drag down the selection bar. This places check marks next to all the messages you drag past. You can deselect messages the same way.

After you select mail messages, you can delete them, move them to folders, print them, and so forth. To delete them click the Delete button on the Action bar, and the marked messages will be removed from the Inbox and put in the Trash view. By default, the memos in the Trash folder are removed from the database after 48 hours. You will learn how to use folders and print from views in other lessons in this book.

Reading and Previewing Your Mail

To read a mail message, double-click the message in the View pane or press the **Enter** key on a selected message. Figure 3.2 shows an open mail message.

Every mail message, or memo, contains the following elements:

- **Heading**—The heading contains the name of the person who sent the message, as well as the date and time it was sent. You might also see a domain name, company name, or other information next to the sender's name.

- **To:**—The To: line shows the name of the person to whom the message is being sent. Again, the domain name might be included. If the message is coming to you, your name is displayed in the To: line.

- **cc:**—The cc: (carbon copy) line displays a list of anyone who received a copy of the message, as determined by the sender.

- **bcc:**—The bcc: (blind carbon copy) line contains a list of anyone who received a blind copy of the message, as determined by the sender; however, only the sender sees the entire contents of the bcc: field. For example, if Jane sends an email and lists Dorothy and Rob in the bcc: field, Dorothy will see only her name in that field, and Rob will see only his name in the field, but Jane (the originator of the email) sees both names in that field.

- **Subject**—The subject describes the topic of the message, as defined by the sender of the message.

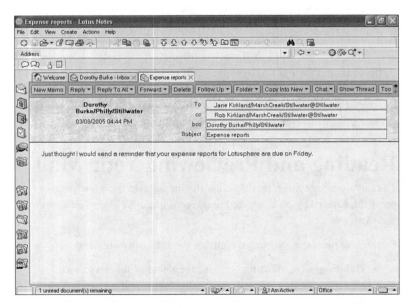

FIGURE 3.2 When you create a mail message you use the Mail Memo form.

The rest of the email message form is the body field. The mail body field in Lotus Notes is a *rich text field*, which means that you can read and create text with attributes such as bold and italics, and you can view and create images in your email. If you cannot view an entire message onscreen at once, use the vertical scroll bar, or use the Page Up, Page Down, and arrow keys on your keyboard to navigate.

You can press **Ctrl+End** to go to the end of a long message or **Ctrl+Home** to go to the beginning of a message.

Information that is stored in Lotus Notes is stored in fields. A *rich text field* is the only type of field that can accept multiple data types: text, numbers, graphics, file attachments, and so forth. It is also the only kind of field in which you can assign text and paragraph attributes such as changing the font, bolding or italicizing text, or changing the spacing between paragraphs and creating numbered lists.

When you finish reading a message, press the **Esc** key to return to your Inbox, or click on the **X** at the top right of the message window tab.

Understanding Read Marks

You can tell with a glance at your Inbox which messages you've read and which you haven't read or opened. Mail messages you haven't read appear in red and have a red star located in the selection bar to the left of the mail message. After you open and read the message, the star disappears, and the mail message appears in black. Figure 3.3 shows both read and unread messages in the Inbox, as well as messages that are marked, or selected.

Marked message

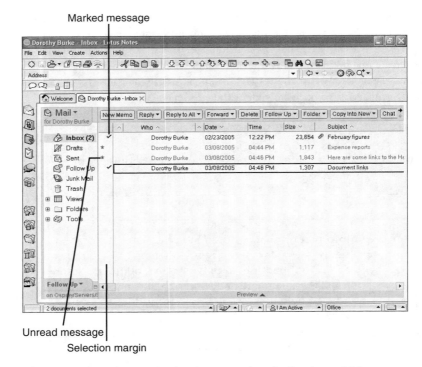

Unread message
Selection margin

FIGURE 3.3   Red stars display in your Inbox indicating which messages have not been opened (read), and checkmarks appear next to messages that have been marked (or selected).

Using the Preview Pane

The *Preview pane* enables you to read most of your messages from the Inbox view without opening them in a new window. To see the Preview pane, click on the Preview triangle at the bottom of your View pane; the Inbox view splits into three panes (see Figure 3.4).

Next   Next Unread

Previous / Previous Unread

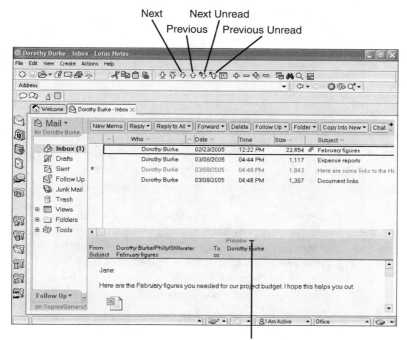

Click here to open or close the Preview pane

FIGURE 3.4 The Preview pane enables you to read most mail messages quickly. If you prefer, press the Enter key to view your mail message, and use the Navigate View buttons on the toolbar to navigate through your mail.

Once the Preview pane is open, you can resize it by placing your cursor at the top of the pane, and when the cursor turns into a double-headed arrow, drag the mouse up or down the screen to obtain the size pane you prefer.

With the Preview pane activated, the mail message that is selected in the View pane is the message that displays in the Preview pane. To navigate through mail while using the Preview pane, you can do the following:

- Use the up and down arrow keys on your keyboard

- Use the Navigate View buttons (Next, Previous, Next Unread, Previous Unread) on the toolbar

- Use your mouse to select a mail message

 By default, Lotus Notes does not consider previewed mail as having been read. Unread marks continue to display until you open individual mail messages. You can change this default setting but be warned; by changing the default if you use your keyboard arrow keys to quickly pass over messages in your inbox, each one you pass will be marked as "read" even though you didn't take the time to read the actual message, but merely cursored over it. To change this default, choose **File, Preferences, User Preferences** from the menu. In the **Additional Options** box, place a check mark next to **Mark documents read when opened in preview pane**. Click **OK**.

Creating Mail

Notes mail messages use a form called the Mail Memo form (see Figure 3.5) and can contain formatted text, tables, graphics, attachments, graphs, and embedded objects.

You can create mail messages from any area of Notes, even when you are working in other databases. Use one of the following methods to create a mail message from your Inbox:

- Click the **New Memo** button on the Action bar.

- Choose **Create, Memo** from the menu.

To create a memo when the Mail isn't open, choose **Create, Mail, Memo** from the menu.

Filled in by Notes if you pressed the Reply button   Heading

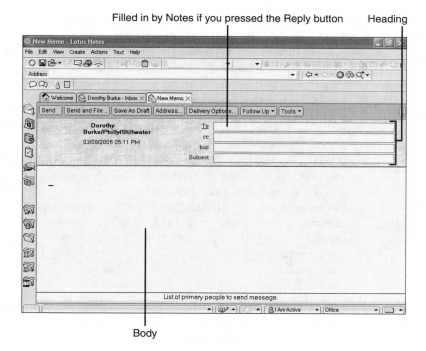

Body

FIGURE 3.5 To display a new Memo like the one shown here, click the New Memo button on the Action bar. If you are responding to an email in your Inbox, click the Reply button, which will also display a new mail memo but with the To: field filled in.

A blank memo like the one in Figure 3.5 appears. Your name and today's date and time are displayed in the Heading of the email. A separate window tab labeled New Memo displays to the right of the Inbox. The message is split into two parts: The **heading** is the top part and the **body** is the bottom.

Filling in the Heading

The heading of the mail memo consists of fields; you begin your email by filling out those fields. Follow these steps to complete the heading information:

1. Type the name of the person to whom you want to send the memo in the **To** field. To send to multiple recipients, separate the names in the **To** field with a comma.

 As you type, Notes searches your personal address book and a company-wide address book called the "Domino Directory" to find a match for the name you are typing. This feature, called type-ahead, continues to search as you type until it finds the unique name you want. Quick-address searches for both first names and last names. If you don't like this feature, you can disable it in the Mail section of your Location document. See "Connecting" in Chapter 17, "Using Notes Remotely," for more information on Location documents.

2. (Optional) Use the Tab key or your mouse to move to the **cc** (carbon copy) field. Type the name of the person to whom you want to send a copy of the message. The cc field is used to send a copy of a message to someone who is not directly affected by the message, but who needs to know about the contents of the message for informational purposes only. Quick-address works in this field, too.

3. (Optional) Click in the **bcc** field and type the name of the person to whom you want to send a blind carbon copy. The recipients of the message, and those listed in the carbon copy field, do not know that the person who is listed in the blind carbon copy field received a copy of the message.

4. In the Subject field, enter a descriptive title for your message. It is extremely important that you fill in a Subject because it appears in the recipients' Inbox views, telling them the purpose of your message. To create multiple lines within the subject line, press the Enter key.

Don't send an email without including a clear and concise description of your message in the Subject line. It lets your recipients know what the message is about before they open it. If you enter something benign like "read this!" you are taking the chance that people will not read (or even delete without reading) your message, as they may think it's an advertisement or junk mail. Be descriptive and professional, and by helping the recipient determine the contents of your mail without opening it, you are helping yourself to ensure your email will be read.

Addressing Mail

Most Notes clients have two *address books*: the *Personal Address Book*, which is usually stored on your local hard drive or in a network folder reserved for your files, and at least one *Directory* stored on the Domino server. Like everything else in Notes and Domino, these address books are databases. You are the only person who has access to your personal address book, and your last name is usually part of the database name (for example, "Burke's Address Book"). The Directory is accessible to everyone in your company and it usually contains the name of your company (for example, "Stillwater's Address Book") in the title. The Directory is managed by your company's system administrators; you manage the content of your personal address book.

While you're writing a memo, you can use the address books to add people to your **To**, **cc**, and **bcc** fields. This is especially useful if you aren't sure of a person's last name or the spelling of his name. Use the following steps to access the address books from a new mail memo:

1. Click the **Address** button on the Action bar. The Select Addresses dialog box appears, as shown in Figure 3.6. Table 3.2 lists the options in this dialog box.

2. Select the address book you want to access. If you are using the Notes client for the first time, your Personal Address Book is

probably empty at this point, but it can be easily populated using the Copy to Local button. In order to access the company-wide Directory, you have to connect to the Domino server.

3. Select the names of the individuals or groups from the available list of names. To select one person, click on that person's name; to select more than one person, click once in the margin to the left of the person's name to place a checkmark next to their name.

4. Click on **To**, **cc**, or **bcc**, depending on which address field you want to complete. Or you can click the **Copy to Local** button to add this person or people to your personal address book.

5. Click **OK**.

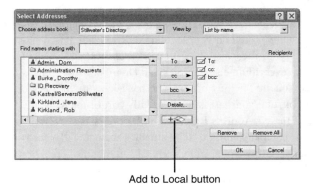

Add to Local button

FIGURE 3.6 Choose your address book and mail recipients in the Select Addresses dialog box. To add a person to your Personal Address Book at the same time as you are using this dialog box to address mail, click the Add to Local button.

TABLE 3.2   The Select Addresses Dialog Box

Prompt	Description
Choose Address Book	The names of all the address books to which you have access.

TABLE 3.2   The Select Addresses Dialog Box

Prompt	Description
Find Names Starting with	Type in the first letter of the name you are looking for to jump to the names that begin with that letter. As you continue to type, Notes narrows suggested entries with each letter you enter. So, if you type J, you'll see names that begin with J; if you type Ja, you'll see names that begin with Ja; and so forth.
View by	Pull-down choices enable you to change the order of the display of the names in the address books. The default setting is List by Name. Other choices include by Notes name hierarchy, Corporate hierarchy, and Categorized by language.
Details	Opens up the Person or Contact Document of the currently selected person in the Directory, where additional information is stored about the individual. If you select a group, the members of the group are displayed.
To>, cc>, bcc>	Fills in the heading fields with the names that are selected.
Remove, Remove All	Removes either just the selected names, or all the names from the Recipients window.

Completing the Message

Type the message you want to send in the lower half of the screen, which is known as the *body* (see Figure 3.5). Unlike the fields in the heading, the text and the paragraphs in the body of the message can be formatted because this is a *rich text field.* You learn more about rich text formatting in Chapter 14, "Editing and Formatting Documents," and more about attachments in Chapter 15, "Working with Attachments."

Using Spell Check

Spell Check compares your text against a stored spelling dictionary of tens of thousands of words. If any of your words aren't in the spelling dictionary, Spell Check tells you that the word is possibly misspelled. In addition to your misspellings and typos, Spell Check also alerts you to proper names and unusual words that might be spelled correctly, but that are not in the spelling dictionary.

Lotus Notes looks in two dictionaries for correctly spelled words. The main dictionary is extensive, covering most of the common words. Proper names, acronyms, and business jargon that are not included in the main dictionary are then looked for in your user dictionary. The user dictionary is one to which you can add words.

Spell Check reports duplicate words, such as *the the,* but it won't look at single-character words such as *a* or *I,* or words that are longer than 64 letters. It also ignores text that doesn't have any letters, such as the number 1,200,543.

Unlike other programs, for example some word processing programs, Spell Check does not operate as you type. You have to initiate it. When you want to check the spelling in your message, you must be in edit mode. Edit mode enables you to change the text in the document in which you are currently working. When you're *creating* a new mail message, you're automatically in edit mode.

To run Spell Check, follow these steps:

1. Choose **Edit, Check Spelling**, or, if you have toolbars displayed, click the **Check Spelling** button. If Spell Check finds a questionable word, the Spell Check dialog box appears, as shown in Figure 3.7.

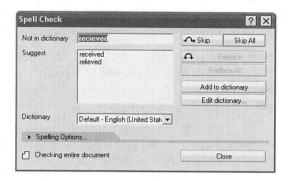

FIGURE 3.7 From the Spell Check dialog box, you can add new entries to your personal dictionary, correct spelling errors, and skip words.

2. When Spell Check finds a word it doesn't recognize, the word appears in the **Replace** box of the dialog box. You can then choose one of the following options:

- **Skip**—Ignores the misspelling and goes on to the next word. Use this option when the word is spelled correctly.

- **Skip All**—Tells Notes to ignore all the instances of this word in the message. This is useful when a correctly spelled proper name crops up several times in a memo.

- **Replace**—Enables you to change an incorrect spelling to a correct one. If the correct spelling of the word shows up in the Suggest box, click the correct guess and then the **Replace** button. If Spell Check provides no suggestions and you know the correct spelling, click in the **Not in dictionary** field and make the correction by deleting or adding characters. Then, click **Replace** to make the change in your message.

- **Replace All**—Tells Notes to replace all the instances of this word with the suggested word you choose.

- **Add to Dictionary**—Adds the selected word to your user dictionary. After the word is added, Spell Check recognizes it as correctly spelled (so make sure you spell it correctly when you add it).

- **Edit Dictionary**—Opens a new dialog box displaying the contents of your personal dictionary. This is very useful when you accidentally add an incorrectly spelled word to your personal dictionary and need to correct or delete that word.

3. After correcting, adding, or replacing words that Lotus Notes Spell Check has questioned, click **Close**.

To further refine your Spell Check, click the arrow by Spelling Options to expand the Spell Check dialog box and provide more options that make Spell Check ignore words that are all in uppercase or that contain numbers.

By default, Spell Check checks your entire mail message. If you want to Spell Check one word or a paragraph, select the word or text with your mouse, and then start the Spell Check using the previously outlined process.

Running Spell Check doesn't guarantee a perfect mail message. If you accidentally type the word *form* when you wanted to type *from*, for example, Spell Check won't catch it because *form* is a word that is in the dictionary. Also, Spell Check doesn't catch incorrect punctuation or missing words.

As previously mentioned, you might mistakenly add a misspelled word to your personal dictionary. To edit your personal dictionary when not running spell check, do the following.

1. Choose **File, Preferences, User Preferences**. In the User Preferences dialog box (see Figure 3.8), click the plus sign next to **International** and click on **Spell Check**. On the right side of the dialog box, click the **Edit User Dictionary** button.

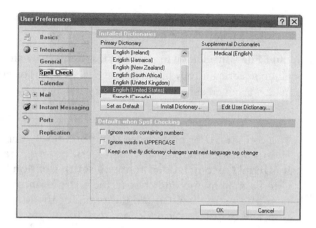

FIGURE 3.8　The User Preferences dialog box is where you can make changes to many of the default settings for Lotus Notes 7.

2.　You can then make any of the following changes:

- To delete the incorrectly spelled word, select it and click **Delete**.

- To change a misspelled word, select it from the list, enter the correct spelling in the small text box at the bottom of the dialog box, and then click **Update**.

- To add a word, enter it in the small text box and click **Add**.

3.　When you finish, click **OK**. Then, click **OK** to close the User Preferences dialog box.

Sending Mail

When you have completed spell check, you can send the message or you can save it as a draft to send later (see Figure 3.9).

To send the message, click the **Send** button or the **Send and File** button in the Action bar:

Send—Sends the message to the recipient's mailbox and, by default, saves a copy of your message in the Sent view.

Send and File—In addition to sending the message, you are given the option of storing a copy of the message in a folder. For more information about creating folders, see Chapter 4.

You can set a user preference to automatically perform a Spell Check on every mail message you create. It is highly recommended that you set this option. Open a mail memo and choose **Tools, Preferences** from the Action bar. On the Basics tab of the Mail section, select **Automatically check mail messages for misspellings before sending.** Click **OK** to close the window.

To save a message as a draft, click the **Save As Draft** button in the Action bar. Your message is stored in the Drafts folder. At a later time, you can open the message by double-clicking the message from the Drafts view. The document is automatically opened in edit mode. When you're ready to send the message choose **Send** or **Send and File** in the Action bar.

If you attempt to close the memo before you send or save it as a draft, a dialog box appears asking whether you want to send, save, or discard your changes. Click the appropriate button to properly close the memo.

Send and File
Send   Save As Draft

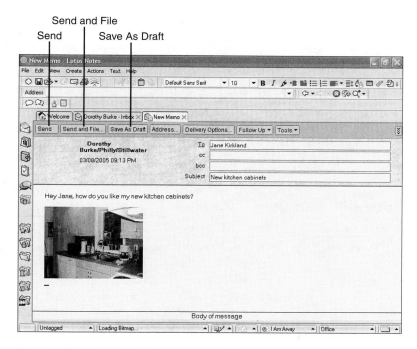

FIGURE 3.9 A completed message can be sent or saved in the drafts folder. The body of the message is a rich text field and can contain formatted text or pictures as shown here.

Choosing Delivery Options

You control how and when each of your mail messages is delivered through the **Delivery Options** button on the Action bar. Delivery Options, as described in Table 3.3, have to be set prior to sending the message. If you are sending mail via the Internet to non-Notes users, some of these features do not work, and they are marked as such with an asterisk (*) in Table 3.3. See Figure 3.10 to see the Delivery Options dialog box, which appears when you click the Options button on the Action bar.

For the most part, you do not need to access Delivery Options for each mail memo you send. The default settings in Notes may be sufficient for efficient sending and receiving of mail. Changing the priority of a mail memo can affect the performance of your Domino servers. Discuss mail delivery options with your supervisor, help desk, or system administrator and ask them to suggest if and when you need to set or change your email delivery options.

Table 3.3   Basic Delivery Options

Option	Description
*Importance	Choices: Normal, High, or Low. If this is set to High, an exclamation mark appears to the left of the message in the recipient's Inbox. The envelope icon to the left of the message in the sender's Sent view is red. Otherwise, no icon appears.
Delivery report	Tells Notes to place a report in your mailbox that indicates how the delivery of your message went. The default option is Only on Failure. Your system administrator might ask you to change this option if you are experiencing mail problems. Otherwise, there is no need to change this option.
Delivery priority	Marks the message as Normal, High, or Low priority. Priority governs how quickly the mail is delivered. When you send a message to a recipient on the same Domino server, it is not necessary to choose a priority—Normal priority delivers it immediately. When you send a Notes message to a different Domino server or to the Internet, High priority causes your Domino server to deliver it immediately,

Table 3.3   Basic Delivery Options

Option	Description
	instead of at the scheduled delivery set by your system administrator. Low priority means that the mail will be delivered in the middle of the night, during off-business hours.
Return receipt	Places a receipt in your mail Inbox that tells you the time and date at which the recipient opens, prints, or deletes the message for the first time if the recipient is a Notes mail user.
*Prevent copying	Prevents the recipient from forwarding, copying, or printing your message. Use this if the information is highly confidential.
Auto Spellcheck	Automatically spell checks the mail memo you are sending.
Do not notify me if recipient(s) are running Out of Office	When a Notes user is using the Out of Office feature of Notes, automatic replies are generated to each sender when this person receives mail. If you check this box in your preferences, Notes will reject any automatic Out of Office replies that would come to you as a response to the mail memo you are sending.
Sign	Adds a unique digital code to your message that identifies you as the sender. The digitial signature also assures the recipient that the content hasn't been altered since the signer signed it.
Encrypt	Encodes the message so that no one but the intended recipient can read it.

continues

continued

Table 3.3   Basic Delivery Options

Option	Description
Save these security options as the default	Click this box and the Sign and Encrypt options you have chosen will be saved as the default for all of your mail messages.
*Mood stamp	Mood stamps create graphics that appear in the Inbox of other Lotus Notes mail users and in the body of the mail memo. To add a mood stamp, select one from the pull-down list. Mood stamps will appear in the box below the pull-down list as you select them, enabling you to see the graphic that will appear in the recipient's Inbox.

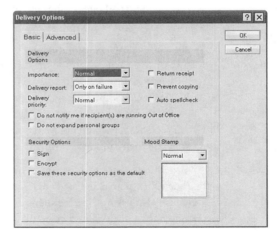

FIGURE 3.10   Set your delivery preferences in the Delivery Options dialog box. Please check with your Domino system administrator before you send mail High priority. It might not be necessary for you to select that option for important mail.

Encryption sounds like you need to put on your magic decoder ring! When you choose to encrypt a message, Lotus Notes scrambles the message, and only the recipient has the key to unscramble it. Because your message travels from your PC to the Lotus Notes server and then to the PC of the recipient, encrypting the message prevents anyone who might be working at the Lotus Notes server from reading your message.

 Lots of new Notes users think that the Flame mood stamp indicates that a message is "hot" (important). In the true Net Etiquette sense, flaming is an indicator that you are truly angry with someone and is considered insulting. You might want to think twice about using this mood stamp. Try setting the Importance to High instead.

You can find less frequently used delivery mail options by choosing the **Advanced** tab of the Delivery Options dialog box. For example, you can set mail expiration dates and request where and when you want replies to messages to be sent. The Advanced Delivery Options are not used as frequently as the Basic Delivery Options. For most of your mail, you can leave advanced options set at their default. For additional help with the Advanced Delivery Options, see the Lotus Help database.

Replying to Mail

To reply to a mail message, select the message to which you want to reply in the View pane, or open the message. Click the **Reply** or the **Reply to All** button in the Action bar. Each of these buttons has the same choices on its pull-down menus, beginning with **Reply**. The difference between the two buttons is that the **Reply** button sends your reply to the sender only; the **Reply to All** button sends your reply to the sender and anyone he included in his To and cc fields.

Follow these steps to reply to mail:

1. Click the **Reply** or **Reply to All** button and choose Reply from the pull-down list. The New Reply window appears. When you reply to mail, Notes fills in the header information of your mail message. You can make changes to the header information if you want.

2. To send a copy of the message to new parties, type the names in the **cc** field. If you used the Reply to All button and the sender had names in the cc field, those names will be filled in.

   To send blind carbon copies, type the names in the **bcc** field.

3. Position the mouse cursor in the message body and begin typing your reply message.

4. Click the **Send** or **Send and File** button on the Action bar.

 Use the **Reply to All** button when replying to mail that originally included others in the header fields. This is a courtesy that saves you time later, when you discover that you have not informed everyone in the original distribution list of your reply.

Use the **Reply with History** option to attach a copy of the original message to the bottom of the reply. Use this option when you want to respond to a lengthy message, providing the recipient with a copy of the original message, or when you just want to make it easy for the recipient to understand your reply by attaching their original email. Keep in mind that **Reply with History** will resend any attachments that you received in this email. If there were attachments in the email you received, you might want to choose the **Reply without Attachment(s)** option, which sends the body of the email but not the attachments.

Choose the **Reply with Internet Style History** if you are replying to an email you received from someone who is not using Lotus Notes. This option strips out headers from the original message as shown in Figure

3.11. This makes a much cleaner history and is easier for non-Notes users to read.

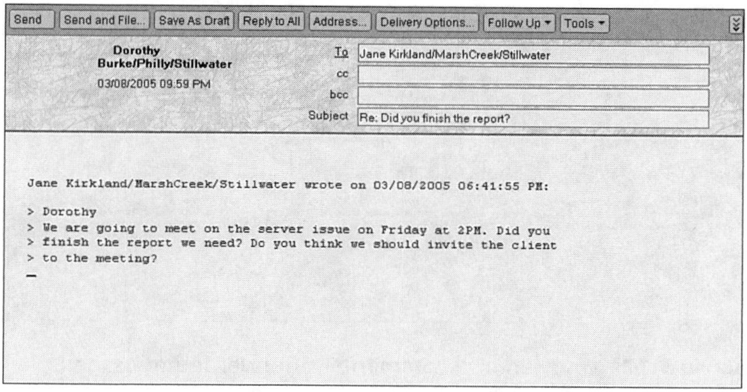

FIGURE 3.11   Using Reply with Internet Style History results in a more compact and easier to read email memo for Internet mail users. Notice the line of text added by Notes, indicating the original author and date sent.

Forwarding Mail

You can forward any mail message (that has not been restricted with the "Prevent copying" feature) to another person, and you even can add your own comments or reply to it. To pass a message on to someone else, click the **Forward** button in the Action bar. Options for this feature are **Forward without Attachments** and **Internet-Style Forward**. These options work similarly to the reply options discussed in the previous section, "Replying to Mail."

When you select a **Forward** option, the New Memo window appears (see Figure 3.12).

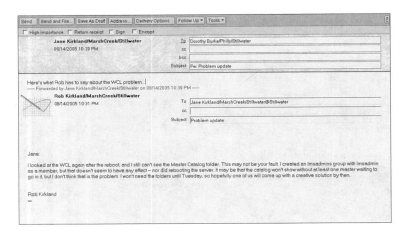

FIGURE 3.12   You can add comments to forwarded messages, explaining your purpose for sending this message.

Forwarding a mail message inserts one mail message into another so that the original header information stays intact. Complete the To and Subject lines and add your comments above the Forwarded by line. Click the **Send** or **Send and File** button in the Action bar to send the message.

Creating a New Mail Memo from Quick Notes

Quick Notes enables you to quickly create a new mail memo, contact, journal entry, or reminder from the Welcome page (see Figure 3.13) if you are using the Basics or Basics with Calendar Welcome page. To enable Quick Notes, click the small blue triangle on the right side of your Welcome page.

Click in these fields to create a mail memo

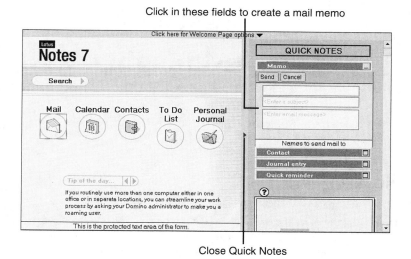

Close Quick Notes

FIGURE 3.13   To close Quick Notes, click the small blue triangle to the left of Quick Notes. Resize the Quick Notes window by dragging the left border of the Quick Notes frame.

To Create a new mail memo from Quick Notes, simply place your cursor in the To, Subject, and message fields and type your information.

In this chapter, you learned how to open and close your mail database, read and navigate your incoming mail messages, and to create, reply to, and send mail. You also learned how to use Spell Check and set delivery options, as well as how to use a new feature of Lotus Notes called Quick Notes. In the next chapter you learn how to sort, manage, and print mail.

LESSON 4
Managing Mail

In this chapter, you will learn some skills that help you organize your mail and keep it up to date.

Sorting Mail

By default, the Inbox view is sorted by date in ascending order, which means that the older messages are at the top of the view and the newer messages are at the bottom. You can change the sort order of the documents in a view by clicking on the view column headers. However, not all the columns in the view can be changed. You can tell *which* columns can be sorted by the triangle on the column head (see Figure 4.1). The sortable column headers have triangles on them. For example, in the Inbox view, the Who column header has an up triangle that indicates that this column can be re-sorted in ascending order (alphabetically, from A–Z). The Date column has a down triangle, which means this column can be re-sorted in descending order (from most recent to oldest). The Size column has a down triangle, indicating that the messages can be re-sorted by size, with the largest messages first.

If the option to sort both ways is available in a view, there are two triangles in the column heading—one points up and the other points down. Once you sort columns, the columns stay in the sort order you placed them in, even if you exit Notes and open it again.

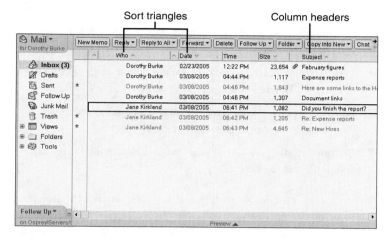

Sort triangles   Column headers

FIGURE 4.1 Sorting columns on-the-fly can help you find messages quickly.

 Would you prefer to have the Subject column appear right after the Who column? You can rearrange the order of the columns in your Inbox. Point to the Subject column header and drag it to the left until you see a dark vertical line at the end of the Who column header. When you release your mouse button, the Subject column header is in its new position right after Who.

Deleting Mail

To keep your Mail database manageable, make it a practice to clear out old messages when you are through with them. It helps to keep your database file at a manageable size. If you think you'll need the message again, archive it or store it in a folder. If you know that you don't need the message anymore, delete it.

You can mark messages for deletion while you're reading them, or you can do it from the View pane. Use the following steps to delete a message while you are in read mode:

1. In the opened message, click the **Delete** button on the Action bar or press the **Delete** key on your keyboard.

2. Lotus Notes marks your open message for deletion and closes the message; your next message appears.

3. Continue reading the rest of your messages, deleting those that you don't want to keep.

To mark messages for deletion while you are in the Inbox or while you are in some other folder or view, you must first select the message or messages you want to delete. This can be done using one of the methods for selecting documents that were described in Chapter 3, "Email Basics." Then click the **Delete** button on the Action bar or press the **Delete** key.

When you delete mail messages, they disappear from the Inbox and move to **Trash**. Deleted mail messages will stay in Trash for a specified period of time, and then be permanently removed from your Mail database after the time limit expires. To see this *soft deletion* time limit, open your Inbox and choose **Tools, Preferences** on the Action bar. The Preferences dialog box opens, as shown in Figure 4.2.

To permanently delete a message from your Mail database, open the Trash view in the Mail Navigator pane. You'll see the messages you marked for deletion, as shown in Figure 4.3.

Click the **Empty Trash** button in the Action bar to delete all the messages in Trash. Alternately, to delete a single item, highlight the item and click **Delete Selected Item**. You will be asked to confirm that you want to delete the message(s). Be careful; once you do this you won't be able to get the message(s) back!

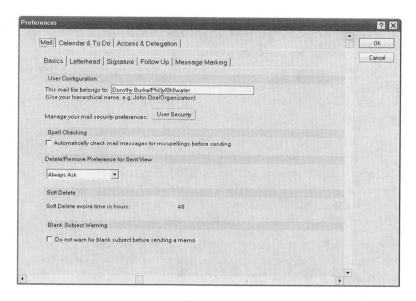

FIGURE 4.2 The number of hours your deleted messages will stay in the Trash is specified under the Soft Delete section. Depending on how your organization has configured your mail, you may even be able to set the time period yourself.

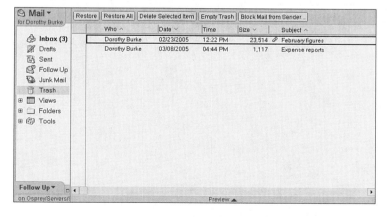

FIGURE 4.3 The Trash displays messages that are marked for deletion in the View pane.

Following Up on Messages

Some of the mail messages you receive may require answers that you can't research at the moment you open them, or ask you to do something that you want to be sure to remember to do later. You need to set some sort of reminder for yourself so you do what is required and then get back to the sender.

There are two ways you can handle these situations. If the memo asks you to complete a task, you may want to add a task to your To Do list. With the memo open or selected in a view, click the **Copy Into New** button on the Action bar and select **New To Do**. You then fill in the To Do item and save it to the list for action later. You'll learn more about the To Do list in Chapter 11, "Working with To Do Items."

The other way to handle this situation is to flag the message for Follow Up. With the message open or selected in a view, click the **Follow Up** button on the Action bar. Choose one of the following options:

- **Quick Flag** immediately adds a green flag to the header of the memo and next to the message in views (see Figure 4.4). It automatically sets the priority of the Follow Up to Normal Priority.

- **Add or Edit Flag** adds a flag to a message or allows you to edit the attributes of the Follow Up if you already flagged it. A dialog box appears (see Figure 4.5) where you set these attributes.

- **Remove Flag** removes the flag you had placed on the memo.

Flag

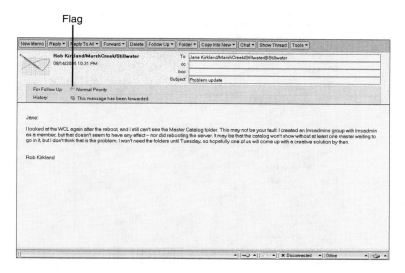

FIGURE 4.4   With an email flagged for Follow Up using Quick Flag, a green flag and the words "Normal Priority" appear in the header area of your copy of the email.

Using Folders

Each time you select another view or folder in the Mail Navigator pane, you see different documents in the View pane, or you see the same documents sorted in a different way. If you want to save a mail message, assign it to an existing folder by dragging it to that folder. Alternately, select the message and choose **Folder, Move to Folder** from the Action bar, and if moving to a folder, select a folder from the list of folders. If you click the **Add** button in the Move to Folder dialog box, Notes will copy the message to the folder you pick but still leave a copy in the current view or folder.

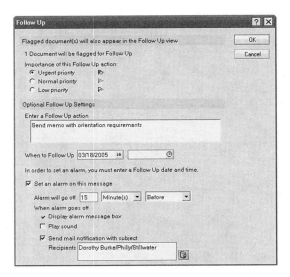

FIGURE 4.5 In this dialog box you set the priority of the Follow Up, enter a description of the action you need to take, select a deadline date and time, and choose whether you want a reminder alarm (either a sound or mail notice).

So how does a folder differ from a view? The content of a view is controlled by the designer of the view; the content of a folder is controlled by you, the user. However, that same memo still shows up in your All Documents view. There aren't two copies of the document in your database, just two ways to access the document. See Chapter 6, "Working with Databases," for more information on views.

Creating and Removing Folders

You can create your own folders in which to save your mail. To create a folder, follow these steps:

1. Choose **Folder, Create Folder** from the Action bar.

2. When you open the Create Folder dialog box, "Untitled" appears in the **Folder name** box until you replace it with your desired

title. Type the name of the new folder directly over the word *Untitled* in the Folder name box. Figure 4.6 shows the **Create Folder** dialog box in which a folder is being created.

3. Select the location for the new folder. The default location is **Folders**, but you can place your new folder within an existing folder by selecting an existing folder—this is called nesting folders. For example, create a folder called Customers, and then create two folders under Customers called Active and Inactive (see Figure 4.7).

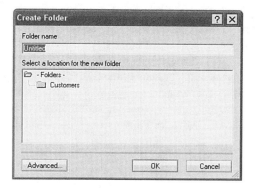

FIGURE 4.6   Type the name of your new folder in the Create Folder dialog box.

 Be careful when deleting documents from your folders because this action deletes those documents from your mail database. When you place a document in a folder or folders, it does not make a new copy of the document for each location; you are actually creating a pointer to that one document in the database. If you no longer want a particular document in a folder, select it and click on **Folder** in the Action bar and then **Remove from Folder** from the pull-down list.

4. To select a design for your folder, click on the **Advanced** button and click the **Copy From** button. The design determines what information from the documents appears in the columns of the folder. By default, the design is the Inbox folder, so the columns and headers you see in the Inbox folder are the same columns and headers you will see in your new folder. However, only the documents you send to that folder will appear when you open the folder. But you might want your new folder to look like your Drafts folder, where the column header information differs from the Inbox folder. When you click the **Copy From** button, select a folder on which to base your new folder and then click **OK**.

5. Click **OK** to save your changes and see your new folder in the Mail Navigation pane (see Figure 4.7).

You can open your new folder at any time by clicking on it; its contents appear in the View pane. You can also move and add messages to folders by clicking and dragging selected documents to folders you have created or by choosing **Folder, Move to Folder** from the Action bar.

FIGURE 4.7 The Mail Navigation pane, showing nested custom folders.

To delete a folder, remove it from the Navigation pane by selecting it and choosing **Actions, Folder Options, Remove Folder** from the menu (not the Action bar). Any memos that are contained in the folder at the time you delete the folder remain in the All Documents view of the Mail database; they are not deleted when you delete the folder.

Printing Mail

You can print one or many mail messages at a time, and as with many Windows products, you can activate the Print command in several ways. However, like deleting and moving documents, if you want to print multiple messages you must first select the messages in the View pane by placing a check mark in the selection bar to the left of the messages. If you want to print just one message, you can print that message from the view or from the opened document. Then print using one of the following methods:

- Click the Print icon on the Toolbar or Hold down the **Ctrl** key while pressing the letter **P**.

- Select **File, Print** from the menu.

- Right-click on the unopened mail message and then click on **Print** at the bottom of the shortcut menu.

All three of the previous options present the Print Document or Print View dialog box (see Figure 4.8), which enables you to select the printer, print a view, print selected documents with various page break and form options, select the pages to print, and print multiple copies. Table 4.1 describes the Print dialog box options in detail.

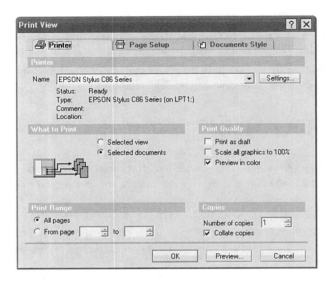

FIGURE 4.8   Set print options in the Print View dialog box, which appears when you select the document(s) from a view. Click the Settings button if you need to make changes to your printer such as selecting a particular tray, printing duplex, and so forth.

At times, it's useful to print a view. For example, you might want to print a list of your customer emails contained in your active customer folder (if you created such a folder). When you print a view, the information displayed is exactly as it is displayed in the view pane, and in the case of mail, it would show you the Who, Date, Size, and Subject fields. To print a view, choose **File, Print** from the menu. In the **What to Print** portion of the Print dialog box, click **Selected View**. Click **OK** to print.

TABLE 4.1   Common Print Options

Option	Description
Printer	Use the drop-down menu to select your printer if you have multiple printers installed.
What to Print	Choose **Selected view** to print the current view, or **Selected documents** to print documents you have selected or a single document which is selected.
Print range	Select **All** to print all pages of the message, or to print a range of pages, select **From page** and enter the beginning and ending page numbers for the document.
Print quality	Choose the **Print as draft** option if you don't need a letter-quality copy (dark text and nice looking graphics). Draft quality enables the printer to print more quickly and uses toner more sparingly. This feature might not work on all printers.
	Choose **Scale all graphics to 100%** if there are pictures in the message and you want them to appear full-sized on the printout.
	Choose **Preview in color** if you wish to see an onscreen preview of your print job in color before you print.
Copies	Enter the **Number of copies** of the message you want to print. Choose the **Collate copies** option when printing multiple copies so your printed documents will be sorted into sets.

After you set your print options, click **OK, Preview,** or **Cancel** to finish and close the dialog box.

In this chapter, you learned how to sort mail, delete mail, flag messages for follow up, print mail and views, and use folders. In the next chapter, you learn how to create stationery, rules, and out of office notices.

LESSON 5
Using Mail Tools

In this chapter, you learn how to use some of the tools your Mail database provides to add graphics to mail headers, create personal stationary, manage junk mail, use the out of office reply, and set rules to handle your incoming mail.

Choosing Letterhead

You can personalize your mail by selecting a graphic to appear beside your name in your mail header. Lotus Notes has several from which to choose.

To select a letterhead, open your mail inbox and choose **Tools, Preferences** on the Action bar. The Preferences dialog box opens. Click on the **Letterhead** tab as shown in Figure 5.1. A list of available letterheads appears in the list box. As you move your cursor over the choices, the graphics appear in the Preview pane. When you find the letterhead you want, click **OK**. The new letterhead will appear on the next memo you create; older mail messages will not change.

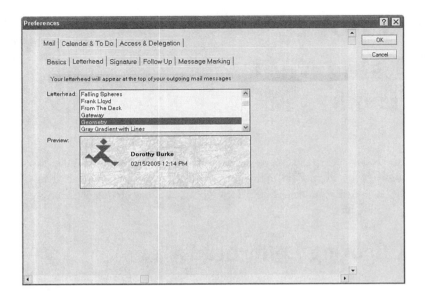

FIGURE 5.1 The Geometry letterhead is selected in the letterhead box and displays in the Preview box next to your name, just as it will appear in your Lotus Notes mail memo.

Creating Stationery

Stationery differs from letterhead in that letterhead simply provides a graphic in your mail memo, whereas stationery can contain a graphic, list of recipients, and information in the body of the mail memo. Use stationery for reports that you generate frequently, such as a customer status report. Stationery is also useful when you want to create a signature or use a graphic for a signature. You can create as many different stationery designs as you like. Stationery is stored in your Stationery view and you can create mail memos using stationery at any time.

There are two kinds of stationery you can create: *Memo* stationery and *Personal* stationery. The Memo stationery uses the Mail Memo template, the same template you use when you create an email in Notes. This template contains only one rich text field—the body field—and has no header or footer fields.

Different from Memo stationery, the Personal stationery template has a total of three rich text fields to support graphics and formatting at the top and the bottom of the document.

Because the Memo stationery uses the Mail Memo template, a quick way to create stationery is to create a memo as you would any mail message, by clicking the **New Memo** button on the Action bar. When you have completed the fields you'd like to save, choose **Tools, Save as Stationery**, from the Action bar. Give the stationery a name and click **OK**. This saves your memo as Memo stationery.

To create Personal stationery, do the following:

1. Open your mail database and click **Tools** in the Navigator pane, then select **Stationery**.

2. Click the **New** button on the Action bar and choose **Stationery - Personal**.

3. The blank stationery form appears. If you have previously selected a letterhead, the letterhead graphic also appears. If you intend to put your own graphics or photos in your stationery, consider removing your letterhead graphic by choosing Plain Text from the list of letterhead choices. It will result in your memos looking like the one in Figure 5.2.

4. Fill in the header information—the To, cc, bcc, and Subject lines—if you want them to remain the same each time you use this stationery. These important fields are part of the purpose of creating stationery. Information you put into these fields is saved with the form.

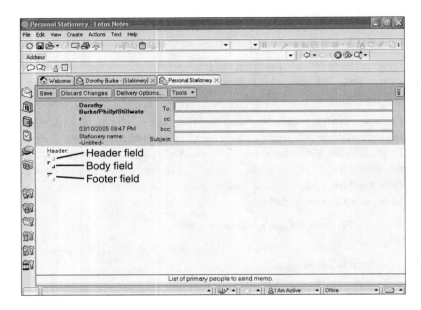

FIGURE 5.2 Blank stationery, ready for your customization. Whenever you create a mail memo using your saved stationery, all fields in the stationery form open in edit mode, allowing you to make changes to this form on-the-fly.

5. Fill in the first rich text field that appears in the body of the memo. This is an optional step; however, if you leave this field blank, it appears as a blank field at the time you create a memo using your stationery. In other words, you can't make this field disappear from the form by leaving it blank. Include any graphics or formatted text. This field name (Header) is misleading, since the *header* area of the memo is the area that you completed in the previous step (number 4). Unfortunately, we think Lotus made a bad call when they named this field Header. The result is that this stationery has two headers: One is the header *area*, the other the header *field*, and they are not at all related. To insert graphics in this field, choose **Create, Picture** from the menu and select a graphic from your personal files on your PC.

6. Fill in the body field (optional). It's the second rich text field contained on this form. Remember, a rich field can contain

formatted text (bold, italics, colors) as well as graphics. It's not a good idea to put too many graphics in your stationery form, though, as this results in large files that may take a long time for people to download when they are retrieving their mail messages from you. This is an optional step, but leaving the field blank does not delete the field from your saved form.

7. Fill in the third rich text field: the footer field. This is an optional step but leaving the field blank does not delete the field from your saved form.

8. Click the **Save** button on the Action bar.

9. A dialog box appears, as shown in Figure 5.3. Enter a name for the stationery in the What Would You Like to Call This Stationery? box, and then click **OK**.

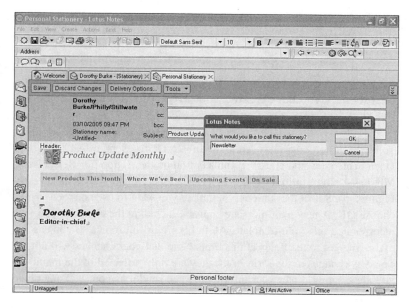

FIGURE 5.3 This Personal stationery contains information that will be used again and again. When saving your stationery, create a descriptive and meaningful name so you can easily identify the correct stationery to use in the future.

Figure 5.3 is an example of a Personal Stationery template with a graphic heading and a table in the body field. With this kind of design leverage, you can use your stationery for many reports, such as weekly expense or sales reports.

The stationery is stored in the Stationery folder (see Figure 5.4).

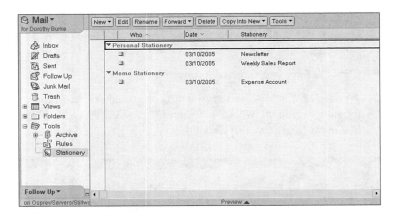

FIGURE 5.4 The Stationery view is the only view that shows a list of stationery you have created and saved. You don't need to be in this view to create new memos with your stationery.

To use your new stationery, go to the Inbox, Drafts, Sent, or All Documents view and click the **Tools** button on the Action bar. Select **New Memo—Using Stationery**. The Select Stationery dialog box appears (see Figure 5.5). Select the stationery template you want to use and then choose **OK**. A new mail message appears, including the elements you incorporated into your template. All fields are in edit mode, so you can make changes to the fields at this time. Note that your changes will not be saved as changes to the form itself; they are only reflected in the memo you are creating. Enter your information and send it as you send any other mail message.

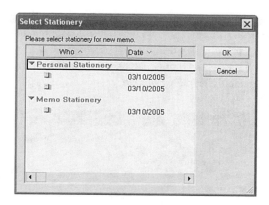

FIGURE 5.5 Choose the stationery for your new memo from the Select Stationery dialog box.

To change your stationery design, select it from the Stationery view and click the **Edit** button on the Action bar. Make your changes and save the document. To delete a stationery, select it in your Stationery folder and press the **Delete** key.

To create *Memo* stationery, follow the preceding instructions for creating Personal stationery, but choose **Memo Stationery** from the **New Stationery** button on the Action bar.

Managing Junk Mail

Spam is a major problem for many email users, often clogging thier Inboxes with unwanted messages. The definition of spam is unwanted, unsolicited, mail, usually sent to sell you something, often sent indiscriminately to mailing lists—otherwise known as junk mail. Most organizations today have some sort of spam-blocker on their mail servers, but even so some mail gets past it. Your anti-virus software is set up to detect possible viruses, so it won't stop this type of mail.

One Notes tool that can help you control spam to a degree, is the Block Mail from Sender tool. This can help you to block mail from a specific sender or a specific domain. But keep in mind that most spammers never do two spams purported to be from the same sender. So this feature isn't a junk mail controller, but can help with those who continue to send you email from the same email address. To block email from a sender, click the **Tools** button on the Action bar and choose **Block Mail from Sender**. The Blocked Senders List dialog box appears (see Figure 5.6).

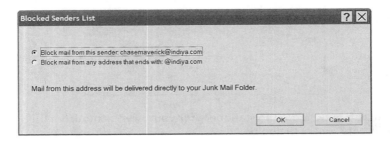

FIGURE 5.6   You can choose to block all mail from the specified sender or all mail from the same domain. In the future, all mail from that address or domain will go to the Junk Mail folder instead of the Inbox.

You choose what you want to block: all the mail from this particular sender or all the mail from the same organization (domain). When you click **OK**, the selected message moves from the Inbox to the Junk Mail view. All future mail from that person or domain will be put directly into the Junk Mail, so you won't have to deal with it in the Inbox.

After the messages are relegated to Junk Mail (see Figure 5.7), you can deal with them individually by selecting the ones on which you want to take action or with all of the messages in Junk Mail. You click on the appropriate button on the Action bar:

- **Delete** removes the selected message and puts it in Trash, ready for deletion. It is still available in the All Documents view and Trash until you empty the trash.

- **Delete All** performs the same action as Delete, but on all the messages in the Junk Mail view.

- **Unblock** stops the blocking on the email address for the selected memo (you will be asked to confirm the removal of the block). Future messages from that address will be delivered into the Inbox. However, the selected message will remain in the Junk Mail unless you drag it back into the Inbox.

- **Manage List** opens the Blocked Senders List dialog box (see Figure 5.8), which displays the addresses of all the senders you have blocked. Select the address of any senders you want removed from the list and click **Remove**. Click **Remove All** to remove all the addresses from the list. Click **OK** to close the dialog box. Future messages from these removed addresses will appear in your Inbox, but current messages will remain in Junk Mail.

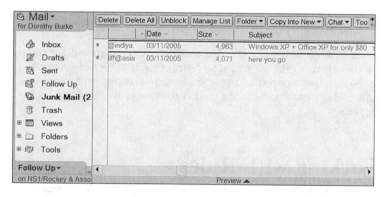

FIGURE 5.7   You can read or preview mail that appears in Junk Mail so you can be sure you really want to block messages from that sender.

FIGURE 5.8 If you regularly use the block option to reduce spam, it will eventually fill up and stop being usable. The only way to make it usable again is to use the Manage List option to remove names. The easiest way to do that is to choose Remove All and start over.

Working with Rules

Rules determine how Notes handles your incoming mail. You create a rule by defining an action that Notes should take upon receiving email addressed to you. Creating rules is a two-step process: First you create the rule and then you activate the rule. Notes acts on any incoming mail that meets the conditions of the rule you create. If conditions are met, Notes then takes the action you define. For example, you can create a rule that tells Notes that when a memo arrives that has the subject "National Convention," it should move the memo immediately upon receipt into your "Convention" folder. Folders display a number next to the folder icon that indicates the number of unread messages contained in the folder, so you can quickly tell when new messages have been moved to a folder. If you have blocked junk mail, you have already created one rule.

Use the following steps to create a new rule:

1. Open your mail database, open the Tools view, and then open the Rules view.

2. Click the **New Rule** button on the Action bar. The New Rule dialog box appears (see Figure 5.9).

3. Under Create Condition, select the elements of the rule's condition: From the first drop-down list, select the item to look at (sender, subject, importance, To, cc, and so on). From the second drop-down list, select the condition "contains", "does not contain", "is", or "is not". In the third box, type or select the value for which you are looking.

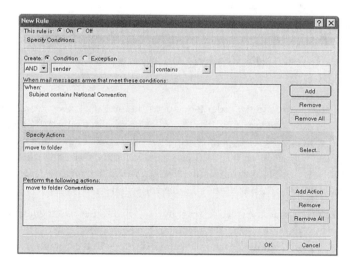

FIGURE 5.9 The New Rule dialog box. When conditions you set are met, Notes takes the action you indicate. If you use rules to move incoming mail into folders, you must remember to check those folders regularly for new mail.

4. Click **Add**.

5. (Optional) To create other conditions for the rule, select **Condition** and then choose **AND** or **OR**—AND to match both conditions, OR to match either. Then enter the second condition. Click **Add**.

6. (Optional) To create a condition under which the rule doesn't apply, select **Exception**. Select or enter the appropriate conditions. Then click **Add**.

7. Under Specify Actions, define what action to take when a memo meets the conditions you set. Click the first drop-down list to select an action such as Move to folder or Delete. If you want to move or copy the memo to a folder, click **Select** to open the folders dialog box where you select a folder, and then choose **OK** (you can also create a new folder). Click **Add Action**.

8. After your conditions, exceptions, and actions are defined, click **OK**.

Rules are evaluated in the order they appear in the list of rules, from the top down. If any rule tests positive, no rules below are evaluated. So the order in which the rules appear is important, as is the composition of conditions and actions in each rule. Create your rules such that one rule won't block the evaluation of another rule. Use the Move Up and Move Down buttons in the Action Bar to re-order the rules in the list.

To make changes to the rule, select it in the Rules folder and then click **Edit** on the Action bar. The New Rule dialog box opens again so that you can change your settings. Make your modifications to the conditions or actions and then choose OK.

If the rule is getting in the way of your mail management or if you are missing an element that you need when the rule runs, turn the rule off before opening it to edit. To turn rules off or on, click on the rule in the Rules view and click the Disable or Enable button on the Action bar. A rule is enabled when a green check mark shows next to its name.

Using Out of Office Notices

The Out of Office notice automatically responds to incoming mail messages while you are away from the office. This is a good tool to use when you are away from the office for long periods of time without access to your mail. Prior to your vacation or absence, create a standard message that is automatically sent as a response to incoming messages, notifying others that you are away. You can even create a unique response message to individuals or groups so that some people receive one response and others receive a different response.

Use the following steps to create an Out of Office message:

1. Open your mail database. Click the **Tools** button and choose **Out of Office** from the menu.

2. The Out of Office dialog box appears. There are four tabs on this dialog box. On the **Dates** tab, add the dates for **Leaving** and **Returning**. Figure 5.10 shows those fields.

3. The Out of Office Message tab provides a place for you to type the Out of Office message (see Figure 5.11) that will be delivered to all people except those who you will list on the Special Message and Exceptions pages. Note that this message will actually be delivered to all people unless you indicate otherwise.

4. (Optional) The **Special Message** tab enables you to provide a message for a special person or a group of people. To select people for this group, click the down arrow button next to the **To** box. When the dialog box appears, select people from your address book, and type your message, as shown in Figure 5.12.

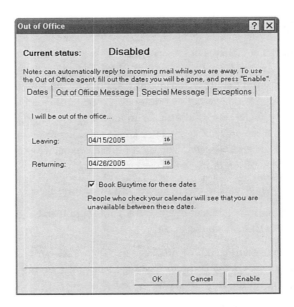

FIGURE 5.10   The Out of Office dialog box with Leaving and Returning dates. The Book Busytime option is selected by default. Leave the check in the box so others will see that you are not available when they are searching for free time on your calendar. You learn about free time in *Chapters 8, 9, and 10.*

5. On the **Exceptions** tab (see Figure 5.13), indicate the people and groups who are not to receive any notification in the **Do not automatically reply to mail from these people or groups** field. Click the drop-down arrow key and select people or groups, type the names directly into the field, or leave the field blank if you have no such exceptions.

6. While you're away, you might also get mail that is addressed to a group of which you are a member, and you won't want Out of Office responses going out to the senders. In this case, enter the names of those groups in the **Do not automatically reply to mail which is addressed to these groups** field.

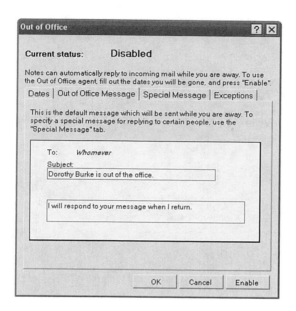

FIGURE 5.11   The customizable basic message is sent as a reply to most emails you receive while you're away.

7. You may be a member of an automatic mailing, to which you don't want Out of Office messages sent. Examples are notices of company meetings, or agents that search databases and notify you with automatic emails. In these cases, you might not know who will be sending the notices, and therefore you can't include them in your exclusions list. However, you can exclude notification by using words or phrases. In the **Do not automatically reply if the subject contains these phrases** field, enter words or phrases (such as *meeting*) you want Notes to look for in the subject line of incoming messages. Note that this applies only to words in the subject line of incoming messages, and that these terms are case sensitive, so you want to enter both *meeting* and *Meeting*. Note too that this does not apply to Internet mailings; for those go to step 8.

FIGURE 5.12   Select the names of those you'd like to receive a special message. Notes supplies the dates for your out of office message and places them just before your special message so you don't need to include dates in the text of your message.

8. Consider selecting the **Do not automatically reply to Internet addresses** field only if you have automatic mail sent to you from websites, list groups, and so forth.

9. Click the **Enable/Disable** button. A dialog box confirms that the agent is enabled. Click the **OK** button. If you receive a message indicating that you should contact a developer or administrator because you are not allowed to run agents, contact your Notes administrator for assistance.

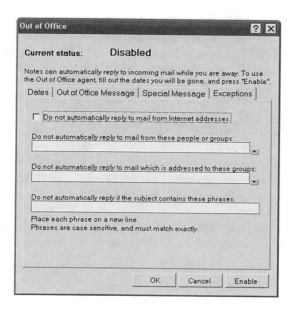

FIGURE 5.13   Enter or select people or groups who are not to receive Out of Office notices.

 The Out of Office agent runs on the server once a day in the early morning hours. Because of this, enabling Out of Office for a one-day absence is not a good idea. Use it for an absence of two days or longer.

When you return to the office you need to disable the Out of Office agent using the following steps:

1. Open your inbox. **Choose Tools, Out of Office** from the menu.

2. When the Out of Office dialog box appears, click the **Enable/Disable** button.

If you are a remote user and you have created an Out of Office message from your remote PC, be certain to replicate your Mail database before leaving for your trip. Otherwise, the server is not notified that this Out of Office agent needs to run. Refer to Chapter 17, "Using Notes Remotely."

In this chapter, you learned how to create and customize stationery. You also learned how to create, enable, and disable an Out of Office message. In addition, you'll now be able to filter out unwanted messages from your Inbox and sort other messages into appropriate folders. In the next chapter, you will learn how to work with Notes utilities and use the Lotus Notes About and Using documents as well as the Help database.

LESSON 6
Working with Databases

In this chapter, you learn how to open databases other than mail, use views, and read the Status bar.

Understanding Local Versus Server

Some databases are *local* databases; the database files are stored on the hard disk of your PC and are available whenever you need them, regardless of whether you are connected to the Domino server. When you make your changes, additions, and deletions in a local database, no one else sees those changes.

Other databases are stored on the Domino server. This enables you and others in your organization to access information centrally and share it. When you are working on a server database, the changes you make can be immediately seen by anyone else who is also accessing that database.

If you are a remote user, which means your computer is not connected to the server at all times, the local databases you have might be *replicas* of databases on the server. A replica is a specialized form of copy that maintains a link back to the original on the server. When you make changes to your local replica of the database, you are working on your computer with a database that is saved on your hard disk. However, at some point the changes you make to the database are transmitted to the server, and any modifications to the server version of the database are transmitted back to your replica. This process is called *replication*. When you replicate, your computer and the server only exchange the modified or new database documents—not the entire database file. See Chapter 17, "Using Notes Remotely," to learn more about replication.

Accessing the About and Using Documents

Even though your mail database is where you'll spend a lot of time in Notes, Lotus Notes is much more than email. The primary purpose and function of Notes is to be a collaboration tool—a place for you and your co-workers to come together for discussions, sharing, and editing of documents and information, as well as communication through email. The features and functions of Lotus Notes that you learn in this chapter are common to all databases. The mail and help databases are used for our examples, but what you learn here will apply to any other Lotus Notes databases including those created and provided by your company.

Every database contains two documents intended to convey to you the purpose of the database and how to use the database. Those documents are the *About this Database* document and the *Using this Database* document. The About document is an overview of the database and how it is intended to be used. The Using document is intended to explain how to use given features of the database. However, these documents might be blank in a given database because the composition of the documents is in the discretion of the designer of the database. Assuming these documents are populated, the About document displays when you open a database for the very first time.

To view these documents, you must first open a database. To open a database other than mail from a bookmark, click on the Databases folder icon on the Bookmark bar to display the Databases bookmark page (see Figure 6.1). Click **Browse for a Database** to open the Open Database dialog box and select the database you want to open.

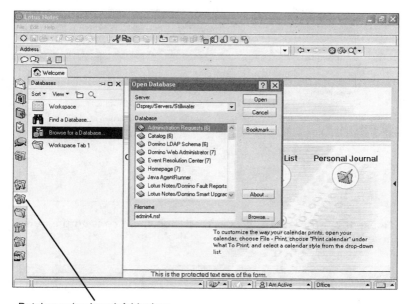

Databases bookmark folder icon

Figure 6.1   Select a database from your PC (local) or from your server. If you don't have the proper access (rights) to open a database, Notes will notify you.

Because it's impossible for us to know what databases are available to you, we're using the mail database for many of our examples. To see the *About* document for a database that you have opened (such as mail), choose **Help, About this Database** from the menu. Figure 6.2 shows the *About this Database* document for a mail database. To close the document, press the **Esc** key.

A database can also contain a *Using this Database* document. The *Using* document provides more detailed information on how to use the database. To access the Using document, open a database or select it on the bookmark page and select **Help, Using this Database** from the menu. To close this document, press the **Esc** key. Figure 6.3 shows the *Using this Database* document for a mail database.

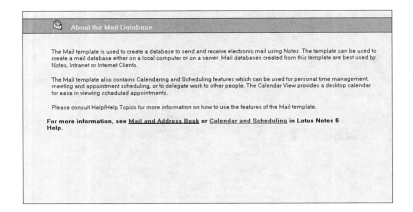

FIGURE 6.2   The About this Database document conveys the purpose of a database.

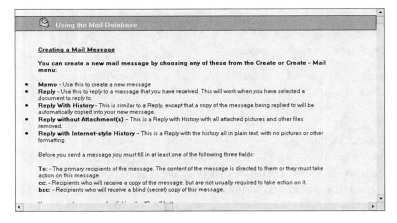

FIGURE 6.3   The Using this Database document provides information on how to use a database.

Working with Views and Folders

When you open a database, Notes displays the contents of the database in a list, called a view. Each line in the database represents one document. Databases often contain more than one view or more than one way of listing information. Some views can be sorted.

Figure 6.4 shows a list of views and folders that are available in the Notes Mail database. From the Mail database, you can send, receive, forward, delete, read, and answer messages. To move from view to view, click the view name in the navigation pane on the left of the mail database workspace.

Often, you can expand or collapse views. A small caret next to the view name (called a *twistie*) or a "+" or "–" sign indicates that you can expand or collapse the view.

A triangle (that's what the Notes Help database calls it, but it actually looks like a caret) next to a column title indicates that you can sort on that column. In Figure 6.4, you can sort the Who column in ascending order and the Date column in descending order.

To open a document, double-click the document in the View pane. To preview a document without opening it, open the Preview pane by dragging up toward the view (see Figure 6.4). Adjust the size of the Preview pane by dragging its top border up or down.

To close a document and return to the database list of views, choose **File, Close** or press the **Esc** key. Repeat these steps to close the database.

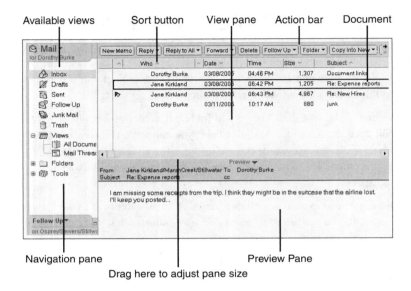

Available views   Sort button   View pane   Action bar   Document

Navigation pane   Preview Pane

Drag here to adjust pane size

FIGURE 6.4 A view lists the documents of a database; many databases contain more than one view.

Reading the Status Bar

The Status bar, located at the bottom of the Notes window, displays messages, icons, and other information you use as you work in Notes. The Status bar is divided into sections; some of these sections display messages, and others lead to a pop-up box or pop-up menu. When a pop-up menu appears, you can select from the menu to make changes in your document or location. Figure 6.5 shows the Status bar.

The Status bar is context-sensitive, and the available features depend on the task you are currently performing and the area of Notes in which you are working. Throughout this book, we refer to available options on the Status bar when they apply to the task you are performing. As you can see in Figure 6.5, each section of the Status bar is a button with a specific function. Table 6.1 describes the Status bar buttons and their functions. You won't see all of these buttons on the status bar at once; remember, the status bar is context-sensitive.

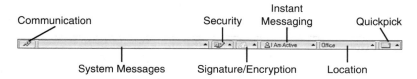

FIGURE 6.5 Use the Status bar for shortcuts and information.

TABLE 6.1 Status Bar Buttons

Button	Description
Communication	Displays a lightning bolt while Notes is accessing the network; otherwise, the button label is blank. Absence of the lightning bolt does not mean you are not connected to the server. The bolt displays only when the server and your workstation are actively talking to each other.
Font	When a rich text field is being edited, this button shows the font name for the current or selected text. You can choose a different font from the pop-up menu.
Font Size	When a rich text field is being edited, this button shows the font size for the current or selected text. You can choose a different font size from the pop-up menu.
Language	When a document is being edited, this button displays the language tag name for the current or selected text. A language tag allows you to tag text with a specific language so when the

continues

continued

TABLE 6.1   Status Bar Buttons

Button	Description
	document is spell checked, the spell checker uses the appropriate dictionary for that word. This is helpful if you use a lot of foreign-language words but you write in English. You assign language tags in the Text Properties Box when you are creating the text. The language tag on the status bar lets you know what tags have been assigned. For the most part, the language button on the status bar will read "untagged."
Paragraph Style	When a rich text field is being edited, this button displays the paragraph style assigned to the current or selected paragraph. You can assign a different style to a paragraph by selecting a style from the pop-up menu.
System Messages	Displays system messages about Notes activities or shows progress. This box is never labeled and is always active. Clicking the messages section displays a list of the most recent system messages.

TABLE 6.1   Status Bar Buttons

Button	Description
Security	Displays a symbol that represents your level of access to a database. Click the security button to see a dialog box that lists the groups and roles that define your access to the database.
Signature/Encryption	Shows the signature or encryption settings for the document you have open.
Instant Messaging	Displays your current instant messaging status. Click the button to change your status.
Location	Displays your current location. Click the button to see a pop-up menu with choices to change your location.
Quickpick	Displays a pop-up menu from which you can choose Mail options without having to open the Mail database first. An Inbox on the button means you have new mail.

You can modify the Status bar to add or remove items and set the order in which the Status bar items display. To modify the Status bar, choose **File, Preferences, Status Bar Preferences** from the menu. The Status Bar Preferences dialog box appears, as shown in Figure 6.6. Choose the items you want to display on your Status bar by clicking the check boxes. To remove an item, deselect it.

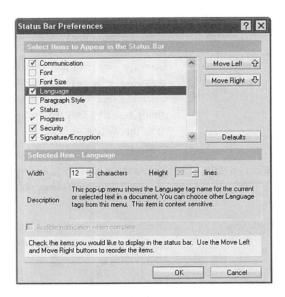

FIGURE 6.6   To change the size of a selected item on the Status bar, use the arrow keys next to the Width or Height preferences. Use the Move Up and Move Down buttons to reorder items on the status bar.

Bookmarking a Database

Opening any database that you have opened before is a simple matter of clicking its bookmark. But what do you do if you want to open a database for which you don't have a bookmark? In that case you can use the Browse for Database feature mentioned earlier in this chapter or you can use the menu commands:

1. Choose **File, Database, Open** from the menu.

2. In the Open Database dialog box (refer to Figure 6.1), specify the computer on which the database is stored by selecting **Local** or the name of a server from the Server drop-down list.

3. From the Database list box, select the name of the database. If you don't see the name of the database on the list, click **Browse** and locate the database file.

4. If you aren't sure which database you need, click **About** to see the About this Database document.

5. To open the database, click **Open**. If it is the first time you have opened the database, the About this Database document displays. Press **Esc** to continue. After you've opened the database, point to the window tab and drag it to a bookmark page to create a bookmark for the database.

 When you are in the Open Database dialog box, you can create a bookmark for the selected database. Click the **Bookmark** button. The Add Bookmark dialog box opens, and you can specify where you want the bookmark—on the Bookmark bar or in one of the Bookmark folders—and then click **OK**. The Open Database dialog box stays open so that you can select other databases and add them to your bookmarks. Click **Cancel** to close the dialog box.

Deleting Databases

Here's the first rule in deleting databases: Don't try to delete databases on the server. In most cases, you wouldn't have the authority to do so but you might be able to delete your mail database. If you want a database removed from the server, contact your system administrator to get assistance and to be sure you are deleting the database you really want to delete.

Deleting a database is not the same thing as removing the database bookmark from your bookmark pages. If you want to remove a database from your bookmarks, right-click on the database icon and choose **Remove Bookmark**. When you do this, the database disappears from your list of bookmarks. However, the database file still exists on your computer or on the server.

Deleting databases on your own computer is mostly within your control. If you truly want to get rid of a database file on your hard disk, select the bookmark and choose **File, Database, Delete**. When the warning appears that the action can't be undone, click **OK**.

In this chapter you learned how to open and bookmark a database and use views and folders. You also learned how to read the *About* and *Using this Database* documents, as well as how to read the Status bar. In the next chapter, you learn how to search and index databases.

LESSON 7
Searching and Indexing Databases

In this chapter you learn how to index and search a database.

Index a Database

For Notes to find information within a database, that database must be indexed. The Notes administrator usually indexes any databases on the server except for your Mail, and then the server updates each index nightly. You won't be able to index databases unless you have Manager or Designer access to the database.

For any local databases or your mail database, you are responsible for the indexing. You create a full-text index only once per database, and Notes takes care of updating the index thereafter.

How do you know when a database has a full-text index or when you need to create one? One way is to check the Database properties box. View the Database properties box for an open database by choosing **File, Database, Properties** from the menu. For a database that's not open, right-click the bookmark, and choose **Database, Properties** from the shortcut menu.

Select the **Full Text** tab in the Database properties box (that's the one with the magnifying glass on the tab). If the database needs to be indexed, "Database is not full text indexed" appears at the top of the Full Text page (see Figure 7.1).

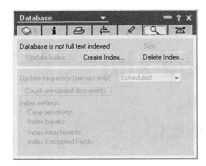

FIGURE 7.1   There is no question that this database needs to be indexed. You can create an index if you have Manager or Designer access. Otherwise, contact your Notes administrator and ask him to create a full-text index.

Another way to see that a database isn't indexed is to open the Search bar for the database. Choose any database view, and select **View, Search This View** from the menu. The Search bar appears above the View pane (see Figure 7.2). It indicates whether the database has been indexed. You'll learn more about the Search bar later in this chapter.

To create a full-text index for a database, follow these steps:

1. From the Full Text page of the Database Properties box, click **Create Index**. Or, from the Search bar in a database, click **More**, and then choose **Create Index**.

2. The Create Full-Text Index dialog box appears (see Figure 7.3). Select the options you want to apply to this index.

Index indicator

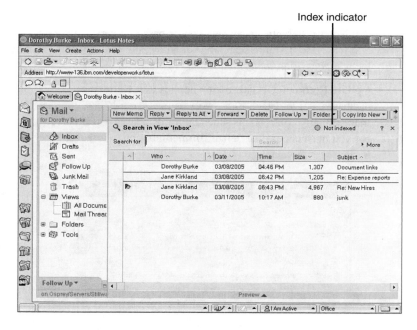

FIGURE 7.2 The Search bar tells you if the Mail database is indexed. "Not Indexed" displays when you need to create an index as shown here.

- **Index Attached Files**—Select this to be able to search all documents, including the attachments. Select **Without Using Conversion Filters** for a faster, but less comprehensive search (it searches just the ASCII text of the attachments). Choose **Using Conversion Filters on Supported Files** for a slower but more comprehensive search.

- **Index Encrypted Fields**—With this selected, Notes searches all words in fields, including the encrypted fields.

- **Index Sentence and Paragraph Breaks**—Select to be able to search for words in the same sentence or paragraph.

- **Enable Case-Sensitive Searches**—Selecting this option means that Notes differentiates between words based on the capitalization (case), so if you're searching for *Home*, the results won't include *HOME* or *home*.

- **Update Frequency**—This option applies to server copies of databases, not to databases on workstations. Your Notes administrator actually controls this schedule for databases on the server, but you must choose the default **Immediate** option to index local copies of databases.

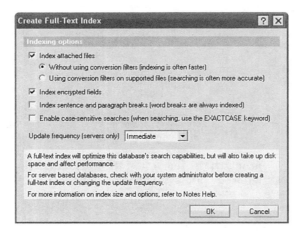

FIGURE 7.3   Be aware that each option you select increases the size of the index and therefore the overall size of the database. However, each additional option you select increases the accuracy of your searches.

3. Click **OK**. Your request for indexing is queued to the server. It may take a few minutes before Notes creates the index. When indexing is complete, the Database Properties and the Search bar show that the database is indexed.

Search a Database

The best way to search a database is to search from a view. Open a database view and click the **Search** icon to display the Search bar. Enter the text you want to search for in the Search For text box (commonly called the "search box") and then click **Search**.

The results of the search display in the View pane (see Figure 7.4). The documents are listed in order of relevance (the gray bar in the left margin is darker at the top to indicate greater relevance).

 The Search icon has a drop-down menu, which allows you to search a database, do a Domain search, find people (search an address book), find a database, or open Internet search engines, such as Excite, Lycos, or Yahoo!.

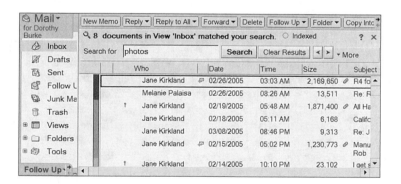

FIGURE 7.4   The most relevant document (the one that exactly matches your search, or the document that contains the most occurrences of your search words) is at the top of the list.

The Search icon is context sensitive. You can search from a view or from a document while in read or edit mode. When you click the search icon with a document in read or edit mode, a dialog box appears to help you search for text within that document.

When you open one of the documents listed in the search results, every instance of the searched-for text is highlighted in the document (see Figure 7.5).

FIGURE 7.5   Searching from a view, the search text was "photos," so every occurrence of "photos" is highlighted in the resulting documents when opened from that view.

To close the Search bar and your search results, click the **Close** button (×) on the Search bar or click the Search icon. To clear your search and return to your original view, or to keep the Search bar open, click the **Clear Results** button on the Search bar.

 You might not even have to engage the Search bar if the view you're searching is categorized or the first column is set in alphabetical order. You can use Quick Search instead. Just type a letter or word, and click **OK**. Notes searches the first column in the view and stops at the first instance of that letter or word. Using Quick Search, Notes does not search fields in the documents other than those that show in the first column of the view.

Set Search Conditions and Options

It's easy to be too specific or too general when searching for information, and in that case, you won't get the results you need. If you're too general, you may get too many documents returned in your view, making it difficult to sift through. Using search conditions and options will refine your search.

Use Options

There are three options to chose from when searching. The first is **Word Variants**, which expands the search to include variations from the root word (when searching for "bowl" it also looks for "bowling," "bowls," "bowler," and so on). The second is **Fuzzy Search**, which allows some room for misspellings (such as when you type "Philadlphia," but it still finds "Philadelphia"). The third is **Search within Results**, which allows you to filter down within a search you've already run.

To activate these options when the Search bar is open, click **More**. The Search bar expands (see Figure 7.6). Select **Use Word Variants** or **Fuzzy Search** or both. Enter the text you are searching for in the Search box and click **Search**.

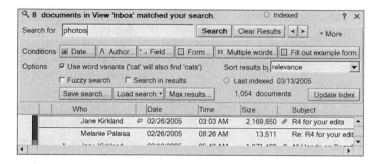

FIGURE 7.6   When you expand the Search bar, you see not only the Options, but the Condition buttons.

Use Conditions

A condition sets criteria that must be met for a document to "match" the search. You use conditions in combination with your search text.

With the Search bar displayed, click **More** to expand the Search bar. Click the appropriate condition button to set the criteria for the search.

Table 7.1 lists the buttons and describes what they do. When the condition is set, click **Search**.

TABLE 7.1   Search Condition Buttons

Button	Limits Search To	Instructions
Date	Documents that were created or modified in relation to a specific date or time period	Choose **Date Created** or **Date Modified** from the Search for Documents Whose field. Select how the date is to be related to the date value (is on, is before, and so on). Specify the number of days or date. Click **OK**.
Author	Documents that were created or modified (or not) by the specified author(s)	Choose **Is any of** or **Is not any of** in the **Search For Documents Whose Author** field. Then, type in user names (separate names with commas), or click the Author icon and select one or more names from the Names dialog box. Click **OK**.
Field	Documents that contain a specified value in a particular field	Select the field from the **Search For Documents Whose** field drop-down list. Choose how you want to evaluate the field from the list (contains, is on, is equal to, and

TABLE 7.1   Search Condition Buttons

Button	Limits Search To	Instructions
		so on). Specify the value for which you are searching. Click **OK**.
Form	Documents that were created using one of the forms in the list box	From Condition, select **By Form**. Select the form from the **Search for documents which use form** list. Click **OK**.
Multiple Words	Documents that contain or don't contain specified words or phrases	In **Search For**, choose whether to search for all or any of the words or phrases you list. Then, in the text boxes, enter the words or phrases for which you want to search. Click **OK**.
Fill out Example Form	The documents that contain specified values in the fields of your example form	Select the form to use as an example and then fill in the fields where your search words would appear. Notes searches all the forms in your database. To limit the search to only documents created with a specific form, add a "by Form" condition, specifying that example form.

The condition appears next to the search text (see Figure 7.7). It's possible to use more than one condition, although you should try searching using one condition first before further refining the search.

Condition token

FIGURE 7.7 A condition token appears next to your search text after you define the condition. Double-click the token to open a dialog box and edit the condition. To delete the token, click it once, and then press Delete.

Refine Searches with Operators

An *operator* is a word or character that you type in the Search box to further define the search. For example, typing AND between two words in the search box means you want to find documents where both words appear. Table 7.2 lists popular operators and their variations available for you to use. For a full list of operators, search the Notes Help database for *search operators*.

TABLE 7.2   Search Operators

Operators and Variations	Description
And AND &	Finds documents that contain all the words or conditions combined with the operator. Example: Man AND Woman
* (asterisk)	A wildcard that represents any extension of letters, more than

TABLE 7.2 Search Operators

Operators and Variations	Description
	one character per asterisk (doesn't work with dates or numbers). Example: *ow, ho*, *ho*
CONTAINS Contains = (equal sign)	Specifies that the field before the operator must contain the text that follows the operator. Example: [title] = Favorite. Surround your field names with square brackets.
EXACTCASE Exactcase	Finds documents that contain words where the case matches exactly the example in the Search box. The database's case-sensitive option must have been selected when the full-text index was created. Example: EXACT CASE Notes
Field FIELD *[fieldname]*	Finds documents in which the specified field contains the specified value, using the syntax *FIELD fieldname CONTAINS value*. Example: FIELD LName CONTAINS Dobbs
NOT Not !	Makes query negative. Examples: Man AND NOT Woman, Not [LName] CONTAINS Dobbs, FIELD LName CONTAINS NOT Dobbs
PARAGRAPH Paragraph	Finds documents in which the words around PARAGRAPH are

continues

continued

TABLE 7.2   Search Operators

Operators and Variations	Description
	in the same paragraph and then ranks the documents by how close the words are. The database's indexing option must be on. Example: desk PARAGRAPH computer
Or OR | ACCRUE , (comma)	Finds documents that contain either of the conditions or words in combination with the operator. ACCRUE works a little better when sorting results by relevance. Example: Man OR Mouse
? (question mark)	A wildcard that represents any extension of letters—one question mark per character (doesn't work with dates or numbers). Example: ?ow, ho??
" " (quotes)	Place quotes around *and, or, contains*, and so on to have those words treated as words and not as operators. You can also surround a series of words or a pharase with quotes to have the search engine search for that exact string.
SENTENCE Sentence	Finds documents in which the words around SENTENCE are in the same sentence and then ranks the documents by how close the words are. The database's indexing option must be on.

TABLE 7.2 Search Operators

Operators and Variations	Description
	Example: desk SENTENCE computer
TERMWEIGHT Termweight	Gives weight to search words when documents containing the words are found. Use any value between 0 and 65537, with the higher number being most important in ranking. Example: TERMWEIGHT 50 manual OR TERMWEIGHT 75 automatic
= (equal to) < (less than) > (greater than) <= (less than or equal to) >= (greater than or equal to)	Numeric operators for use in searching for numbers or dates in number or date fields. Example: FIELD CreateDate > 1/1/1999

Display Search Results

Unless you dictate otherwise, search results display in order of relevance. To sort the resulting documents in a different order, click **More** on the Search bar. From Sort Results By, select the option you want to use:

- **Relevance**—Sorts the resulting documents according to the number of matches in the document, with the document having the highest number appearing at the top of the list.

- **Last Modified**—Sorts the resulting documents by the date modified, with the latest being at the top of the list.

- **First Modified**—Sorts the resulting documents by the date modified, with the earliest being at the top of the list.

- **Keep Current Order (sortable)**—Leaves the documents in the order they appear in the view (only available if the current view provides column sorting).

- **Show All Documents (sortable)**—Displays all documents in the current view but marks the documents that meet the search criteria as selected (can be sorted if column sorting is active in view).

 Too many documents displayed in the results? Limit the number of resulting documents displayed by clicking **Max Results**, entering the number of documents you want to see as search results, and then clicking **OK**.

Save and Load Searches

If you perform the same search frequently, you can save the search criteria, so you don't need to enter all the conditions and options each time you search.

To save the search criteria, enter any necessary text in the Search box, select the options you need, set the conditions, and specify the display option you want. Then, click **Save Search**. Give the search a name (see Figure 7.8), and then click **OK**.

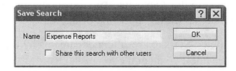

FIGURE 7.8   Enter a name to use when you want to call up this search criteria again.

Later, when you want to use the search you created, you click **More** in the Search bar and then choose **Load Search**. Choose the name from the drop-down list, and click **Search**.

 If you have access privileges in the database to create a private folder, create one to hold your search results. Choose **Edit, Select All** to select all the documents that resulted from the search. Copy the documents into your folder. If you drag the selected documents into your new folder, Notes moves them into the folder and they will no longer appear in your Inbox, so be sure to copy, not move.

In this chapter you learned how to index and search databases. In the next chapter you learn how to set mail and calendar preferences.

LESSON 8
Setting Mail, Calendar, and To Do Preferences

In this chapter, you learn how to set your preferences for your mail database and your calendar. You'll also learn how to control access to and delegate tasks for mail and calendar.

Specifying Mail Preferences

Mail preferences determine how your mail works—who can read your mail, whether mail should be encrypted automatically, whether all your outgoing mail is signed by you, and so on.

Complete the following steps to set your mail preferences:

1. Open your mail database.

2. Click the **Tools** button on the Action bar and choose **Preferences**. The Preferences dialog box appears (see Figure 8.1). When the Mail tab is selected, the following five subtabs appear: Basics, Letterhead, Signature, Follow Up, and Message Marking.

3. Click the **Basics** tab. The **This Mail File Belongs To** field automatically displays your full Notes name. (If it displays a name other than yours, tell your Notes administrator or help desk immediately.) Other options on this tab include:

- To have Notes automatically check the spelling of your mail messages, enable **Automatically Check Mail Messages for Misspellings Before Sending**.

- When you try to delete a message from the Sent view in your mail, you need to set one of the options under **Delete/Remove Preference for Sent View**: **Always Delete** removes the mail from the mail database (all views), **Always Remove** removes the mail from the Sent view but leaves it in the All Documents view, and **Always Ask** prompts you to make a choice each time you delete mail from the Sent view.

- **Soft Delete Expire Time in Hours** displays the number of hours a deleted message will remain in your Trash view until it is automatically deleted from your mail. Depending on your level of access to your mail database, this may be a read-only field.

- Enable **Do Not Warn for Blank Subject Before Sending** a Memo if you want to turn off the automatic alert that occurs when you attempt to send mail without adding a subject.

4. Click the **Letterhead** tab. Select the default letterhead of your choice. A preview is provided at the bottom of the screen. When you change letterhead, memos created with your previous choice of letterhead do not change. New memos you create after selecting a letterhead here use the new letterhead. You can change letterhead as often as you like.

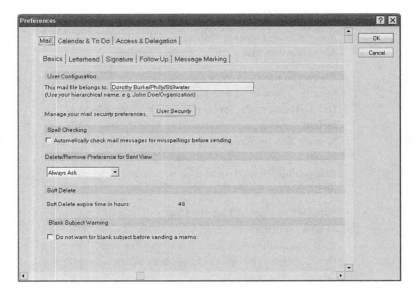

FIGURE 8.1 The Preferences dialog box is divided into three sections—Mail, Calendar & To Do, and Access & Delegation—which display as tabs on the first row of the Preferences box.

5. Click the **Signature** tab. Select **Automatically Append a Signature to the Bottom of My Outgoing Mail Messages** if you want your signature added to all your mail memos. A signature can be a piece of text or an HTML file. Don't confuse this signature with electronic signatures, which are a security feature as described in Appendix A, "Understanding Security and Access Rights." To create a text signature, choose **Text** and enter the signature text in the **Signature** box. To use an existing file as your signature, select File and enter the name of the file (or click **Browse** and select the file).

Signatures that you create as text cannot be formatted, because the Signature feature of Notes does not allow that. However, if you attach an HTML file, formatting is preserved. If you want a scripted signature, create a signature in your word processing program and format it to your liking. Save it as an HTML file and attach it in the Signature file box.

Hypertext Markup Language (HTML) is the coding used to format documents used on the Web.

6. Click the **Follow Up** tab. The options on this tab set the defaults for the Flag for Follow Up dialog box. You can set the default for flag priority, follow up date, follow up time, and alarms (see Chapter 4, "Managing Mail," for more information on flagging messages for follow up).

7. Click the **Message Marking** tab. You use message marking to help identify mail that is important to you. There are two tabs—Senders and Recipients.

   • On the **Senders** tab you can set up to three color combinations to identify mail from specific senders. Enter or select the name(s) whose mail you want to color code in one of the Sender names' boxes. Then select a background and/or text color. Mail from these senders will appear in your mail views with the designated coloring.

   • On the **Recipients** tab, you specify what icons you want to see next to your incoming mail in mail views. Enable any or all of the options: **Display a Solid Circle When I Am the Only Recipient in the To Field, Display a Half-circle When My Name Is One of UP TO This Many Names in the To Field** (and specify the number), or

Display an Empty Circle When My Name Is in the cc Field. If you receive mail under any other name (such as an Internet name), enter that name in the box at the bottom of the screen. When you belong to a group and mail is addressed to that group, the icons will not display for that email.

8. Click **OK**.

Setting Calendar Preferences

As you did with your mail, you set up how you want to use the features of the calendar using the calendar preferences. You learn more about using the calendar in the next chapter, but you can set calendar preferences even if you aren't yet familiar with the use of the calendar. For example, in the calendar preferences you set up your free time schedule and determine who can see your schedule. The default free time is Monday through Friday, 9 a.m. to 12 p.m. and then 1 p.m. through 5 p.m. If your regular work schedule is different than those hours or your lunch hour is different, you'll want your calendar to reflect that. You also specify when and how you want to be reminded of upcoming calendar events, set defaults for calendar entries, choose how time intervals display on your calendar, decide how to process meeting invitations, and specify who can view or manage your calendar.

Complete the following steps to set your calendar preferences (if you did not close the Preferences dialog box after choosing your mail preferences, skip to step 3):

1. Open your mail database.

2. Click the **Tools** button on the Action bar and choose **Preferences**.

3. Click the **Calendar & To Do** tab.

4. Click the **Basics** tab to set the defaults for the calendar. From the drop-down list, select the type of calendar entry you want to automatically appear when you create a new calendar entry. Set the default length for appointments (in minutes) and meetings by specifying the number of minutes in the second box. In the **Anniversaries Repeat For** box, enter the number of years for which you want an anniversary to be entered on your calendar. Finally, if you want to enter any personal categories for use in the calendar, type the category text in the **Personal Categories** text box.

5. Click the **Display** tab. To set the length of day you want to see in the calendar pages, indicate when you want the calendar day to start by selecting a time in the **Beginning of the Work Day** field. Do the same for the ending time in the **End of the Work Day** field. Select a number of minutes from the **Each Time Slot Lasts** drop-down list to decide how far apart the times on your calendar should display, as in 60-minute increments, 30-minute increments, and so forth. Choose the **Days Displayed in a Work Week** by clicking in the checkbox next to the days in the list. You can also choose to start your month view with the current week by selecting the **Start Monthly View with Current Week** field. If you don't want meetings to appear in the All Documents view of Mail select the **Don't Display New Calendar Entries and Notices in the All Documents View of Mail**. If you don't want meeting invitations to appear in your Sent View of mail, select **Don't Display New Meeting Invitations in the Sent View of Mail**. If you would like to have your meeting invitations removed from your Inbox after you respond to them, select **Remove Meeting Invitations from Your Inbox After You Have Responded to Them**. You can also specify **Types of Meeting Notices to Be Shown in Your Inbox** by selecting **All**, **All except responses**, or **None** from the drop-down list. Where can you keep track of these meetings if you choose not to show them in your Inbox? You can display them in the MiniView that appears in the lower portion of your mail and calendar navigation pane. Enable **Put C&S documents into a Special New Notices MiniView for Processing**.

The *MiniView* doesn't display until you configure it. In the Navigation pane of the Calendar, click the **Configure** button under the date picker and then click **OK** to activate the MiniView. Using the down arrow at the top of the MiniView, you can change between **New Notices, To Do,** or **Follow Up.**

6. Click the **Scheduling** tab (see Figure 8.2), if it's not already displayed. On the **Your Availability** tab, check the days you want to include in your free time schedule (the time you are available for meetings). For each day you check as being available for meetings enter the times when you are normally available. You can also set the **Time Zone** for these hours. On the **When Adding an Entry to Your Calendar** tab, select the option **When Adding Appointments, Accepting Meetings, Scheduling a Meeting** if you want Notes to check for conflicts when you schedule or accept a meeting. If you select this option, you may also enable **Note a Conflict If Entry Occurs Outside Available Hours Described on the Your Availability** tab. There are also options for what you will see in the Scheduler when you are setting up a meeting. You can choose to see **Schedule Details for Each Participant** or **Suggested Best Times for Meeting**. You may also opt to **Show 24 Hours on Meeting Scheduler Display**.

7. Click the **Alarms** tab. Select **Enable the Display of Alarm Notifications** if you want Notes to alert you to upcoming events that you have entered in your calendar. When you select this field, the dialog box shows new fields, and a list of calendar entry types. Select the types of calendar entries about which you want to be reminded. Then enter the number of minutes or days in advance you want to receive the reminder. If you want to be alerted by a sound, select a **Default Sound** from the drop-down list (if your computer has sound capabilities).

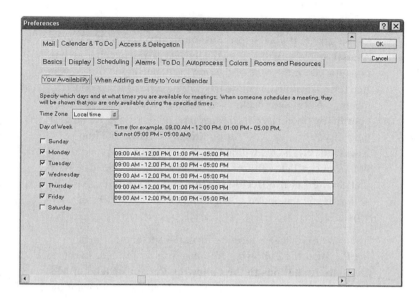

FIGURE 8.2 The Preferences dialog box with the Calendar Scheduling tab selected. Here you indicate which days and times should be considered your default free time.

8. Click the **To Do** tab. When you create a To Do item, it appears on the Calendar unless you enable **Do not Display To Do Entries in the Calendar**. To display incomplete To Do entries on the current day in the Calendar, select **Allow Notes to Update To Do Status and Dates for Incomplete Entries**.

9. Click the **Autoprocess** tab to determine how you want to process meeting requests. You must manually respond to all requests for meetings unless you choose **Enable Automatic Responses to Meeting Invitations**. By choosing this, Notes will automatically respond to meeting invitations that arrive in your Inbox. Once you choose this option, you must then select from the following:

When a Meeting Invitation Is Received from—Anyone is a default setting for this field, but you can use the drop-down menu to select a list of people, or a list of exceptions.

You must also tell Notes what actions to take when meeting invitations arrive: If you choose **Automatically Accept If Time Is Available**, Notes will automatically accept any meeting invitations for you if the time of the proposed meeting is free in your free time schedule. If you're busy at the time of the proposed meeting, Notes auto-declines the meeting, but places a memo in your Inbox titled "Declined Meeting Name" so you can accept later. If you choose **And Automatically Decline If Time Is Not Available**, Notes will automatically decline meeting invitations that conflict with free time shown on your calendar. When you choose **Let Me Decide If Time Is Not Available**, Notes will give you the option of attending or not, regardless of your schedule.

You can also delegate meeting invitations to another person. In the **Perform the Following Actions** drop-down field, select **Delegate Invitations to the Following Person Instead of Me**. By choosing this option, Notes forwards all meeting invitations to the person you specify (the person you enter in the Delegate field). This is useful if someone else manages your calendar. The person who invited you to the meeting will receive notice that you have appointed a delegate to this meeting.

Select **Automatically Accept Even If Time Is Not Available** to accept all meetings, whether you have free time or not. You will have to resolve any conflicts if this causes double bookings.

10. Two options are available in the Automatic Inbox Management section: The first is **Prompt to Confirm Deletion**, which results in Notes prompting you when you delete a calendar notice from your Inbox or any view in your Mail Database. The second, **Remove from This View/Folder with Prompting**, results in no prompting by Notes when you make such deletions.

11. Click the **Colors** tab to choose your color preferences for calendar items.

12. Click the **Rooms and Resources** tab. If your organization's directory contains listings for rooms or resources or there is a

reservations database (see your Domino administrator if you want to know more), you can set some defaults for how these items appear when you schedule a meeting, such as a preferred site, a preferred rooms list, and a preferred resources list. You can also determine when you want rooms and resources added to your own preferred rooms and resources lists.

13. Click **OK**.

Controlling Access and Delegation

The Access & Delegation preferences are divided into three tabbed pages: Access to Your Mail and Calendar, Access to Your Schedule, and Shortcuts to Others' Mail. On these pages, you determine who can access your mail (see Figure 8.3), who can access your free time, who can see your calendar entries, who can create calendar entries in your calendar, and so forth. If you make no changes and accept the program defaults, no one can access your mail, everyone has access to your free time (but they can't see the details or names of entries in your calendar), and you have no shortcuts to access the mail databases of other people.

To set Access and Delegation preferences, follow these steps (if the Preferences box is open, skip to step 3):

1. Open your mail database.

2. Click the **Tools** button on the Action bar and choose **Preferences**.

3. Click the **Access & Delegation** tab (see Figure 8.3). On the **Access to Your Mail & Calendar** page, click **Add Person or Group** and select the person or group you want to permit access to your mail or calendar entries under step 1 (see Figure 8.4).

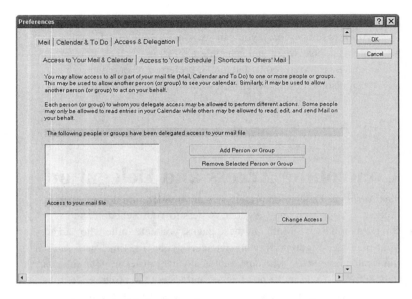

FIGURE 8.3 By the default setting, no one but you has access to your mail. When you add someone to the access list, you'll have the opportunity to designate their level of access.

In step 2, choose how much of your mail file you want to grant access to. See Table 8.1 for an explanation of access levels.

In step 3, choose the level of access you want to give for your mail, calendar, and To Do items. See Table 8.1 for a detailed explanation of level of access. The choices in the drop-down section of step 3 change according to the choices you made in step 2.

In step 4, if you want Notes to automatically forward notices to the person listed in step 1, choose either **Forward Notices Where You Are the Invitee** (when you receive meeting invitations they will automatically be forwarded to the person listed in step 1), or **Forward Notices Where You Are the Chair of the Meeting** (when you receive calendar notices where you are the Chairperson, they will be automatically forwarded to the person listed in step 1).

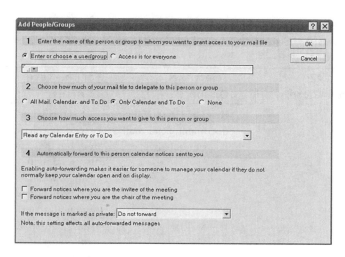

FIGURE 8.4 When you give access to your mail to others, they can see everything in your mail database that is not marked Private.

TABLE 8.1 Select the Level of Access to Your Mail and Calendar

If in #2, You Chose...	Select This Option	For This Level of Access
All Mail, Calendar and To Do	Read any document	Allows the person or group you designate to read your email (but not encrypted mail), calendar entries (but not details of entries marked private), and To Do items (but not those you mark private).

continues

continued

TABLE 8.1   Select the Level of Access to Your Mail and Calendar

If in #2, You Chose...	Select This Option	For This Level of Access
	Read and create any document, send mail on your behalf	The same as the preceding selection, but they can also send mail from your database. When they send mail from your database, the mail is identified to the recipients as a memo created by the delegate, and sent on your behalf (By Jane Kirkland on behalf of Dorothy Burke).
	Read, edit, and create any document, send mail on your behalf	Same as previous, but also allows the delegate to edit your mail.
	Read, edit, create, and delete any document, send mail on your behalf	Same as previous but also allows the delegate to delete any document in your mail database.
	Read and create any document, delete any document they created	Restricts the delegate to deleting only those documents they created in your database.

TABLE 8.1 Select the Level of Access to Your Mail and Calendar

If in #2, You Chose...	Select This Option	For This Level of Access
Only Calendar and To Do	Read any Calendar Entry or To Do	Allows delegate to read your Calendar and To Do items, but not your email and calendar items you marked as private.
	Read, create, edit, and delete any Calendar Entry or To Do	Same as previous but also allows delegate to edit and delete Calendar and To Do items.
None	No options offered	

Allowing others to see your schedule information is different than allowing them to see your calendar entries. By default, when others are scheduling a meeting and they check your availability, they can see if your time is free or not free. There are two sections to the **Access to Your Schedule** page: First, **Who Is Allowed to See Your Schedule Information (When You Are Busy or Available)** is where you give access to individuals or groups to your scheduling information. The default is **Everyone May See Your Schedule Information**. To make changes to the default, choose **No One May See Your Schedule Information** or select an individual or group who may see your schedule information. The second section is **What Schedule Information They May See** and the default here is **Only Information About When You Are Busy or Available.** You can choose **Detailed Information About Your Calendar Entries** if you want everyone to see appointments on your calendar when they are looking for your available time, or choose **Only Information About When You Are Busy or Available, Except the Following People May See Detailed Information** and in the drop-down menu, select the people that you want to see your calendar entries.

You do not have to give out your password for others to access your mail or calendar information if you grant them access through the Preferences dialog box. Never give out your password. When you give people access to your mail database, they can't read encrypted mail sent to you, and you can't read encrypted messages they create on your behalf unless your User ID contains the encryption key used to encrypt the messages. Consult with your Administrator if you need to read each other's encrypted mail or if your designee needs to send encrypted mail on your behalf.

Opening Someone's Mail, Calendar, and To Do

For others to read mail, send mail, set appointments, and use the rights you have just given them, they need to open your mail database, or if you've been given rights to others' databases, you need to open their mail databases. The easiest way to access the calendar and mail to which you have rights is to add a shortcut. To do so, open your mail inbox, and choose **Tools, Preferences**. On the **Access & Delegation** page, choose **Shortcut to Others' Mail**. Use the drop-down menu to choose people from the address book who have given you access to their mail or calendars (see Figure 8.5).

Mail ▼							
Switch to Calendar	ply ▼	Reply to All ▼	Forward ▼	Delete	Follow Up ▼	Folder ▼	Copy into New ▼	Chat ▼	Tools ▼
Switch to To Do		Who ∧		Date ∨	Time	Size ∨	Subject ∧
Open Mail for Joe Doaks/Philly/Stillwater	Rob Kirkland	03/16/2005	08:51 AM	4,956	Sales report for Febr
Open Another Person's Mail	Rob Kirkland	03/16/2005	08:52 AM	4,968	Corrected sales repc
Sent	Rob Kirkland	03/16/2005	09:01 AM	1,533	Link Message: Corre
Follow Up	Rob Kirkland	03/16/2005	09:08 AM	1,769	Link Message: New Please add it to your "Accept Recovery Inf
Junk Mail					
Trash	Rob Kirkland	03/16/2005	09:25 AM	977	Link Message: Hack

FIGURE 8.5   Click the down arrow next to Mail and you'll see the shortcuts you created to access the mail and calendars of others.

Using the Notes Minder

As long as you have your Notes client running, even minimized, you receive notification of any new mail. If you exit Notes, however, you have no idea that a new, and possibly urgent, memo has been delivered to your Mail database.

Notes has a utility that notifies you of new mail and any Calendar alarms, even when you aren't running your Notes client. The utility is called the *Notes Minder*. When Notes Minder is running, an envelope icon displays in the system tray of your Windows taskbar. The current status or number of new mail messages received pops up when your mouse pointer points to the icon. For example, it might read "Mail last checked at 4:45 PM." Double-clicking the icon launches Notes in your Mail file.

Start Notes Minder initially by choosing **Programs, Lotus Applications, Notes Minder** from the Start menu (click Start on the Windows taskbar). Your Notes client does not have to be open. If you want Notes Minder to start automatically when your computer starts, copy its Windows menu icon into the Windows Startup menu. You can do this by dragging it or using copy and paste commands.

Clicking on the Notes Minder icon with the right mouse button pops up a menu (see Figure 8.6).

FIGURE 8.6   Right-clicking the Notes Minder icon displays a pop-up menu.

Select a menu choice to do one of the following:

- **Open Notes** opens the Notes client and displays your Inbox.
- **Check Now** checks the status of your Mail file.

- **View Mail Summary** opens a dialog box that displays the unread messages in your Inbox. Double-clicking one of the messages in the Unread Mail Summary dialog box opens the Notes client and displays that message. To close the dialog box without viewing a mail message, click OK.

- **Properties** displays the Options for the Lotus Notes Minder dialog box (see Figure 8.7). In the Properties box, you set the types of notifications you want to receive (audible, visual, and/or missed alarms). You also specify how frequently you want the Notes Minder to check for incoming mail, or you can disable checking. Click **OK** to close the dialog box.

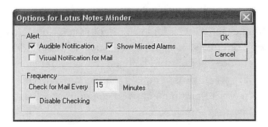

FIGURE 8.7   Specify whether you want to receive audible or visual notification when you get new mail, or both.

- **Enabled** has a check mark when Notes Minder is enabled. You click this menu selection to enable or disable the Notes Minder.

- **Exit** exits the Notes Minder.

In this chapter, you learned how to set your preferences for both mail and the calendar, how to choose letterhead, and how to use Notes Minder. In the next chapter, you learn how to use the calendar.

LESSON 9

Using the Calendar

In this chapter, you explore the Notes Calendar. You learn how to open and select calendar views; make, customize, edit, and convert entries; and print the calendar.

Some Calendar entries affect your free time availability. Managing access to your calendar, who can read it, and who can see when you are available, was covered in Chapter 8, "Setting Mail, Calendar, and To Do Preferences." You might want to revisit that chapter to set your Calendar preferences before using the Calendar. Here we discuss scheduling appointments which is different than scheduling meetings, covered in Chapter 10, "Working With Meetings and Group Calendaring."

Selecting Calendar Views

To open your calendar, select **Calendar** from the Welcome page or click the Calendar bookmark, as shown in Figure 9.1.

Calendar bookmark

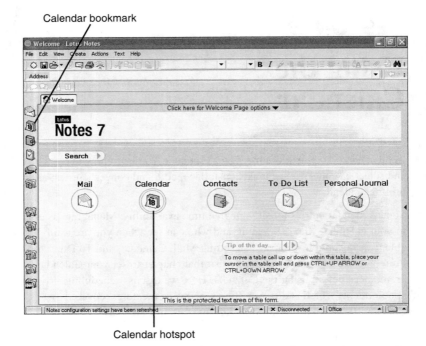

Calendar hotspot

FIGURE 9.1   You can access your Calendar by clicking the hotspot on the Welcome page or by clicking the icon on the Bookmark bar.

The default views for the Calendar are Day, Week, Month, and All Calendar Entries. These views are available by clicking on the tabs at the top of your Calendar (see Figure 9.2). Click the triangle next to the Day, Week, Month, or All Calendar Entries to see more choices. For example, available views for Day include one day or two days, and views for Week include a week, a work week, two weeks, and two work weeks.

Click triangle for more view options   All Calendar Entries view

Date Picker   Day view   Week view   Month view

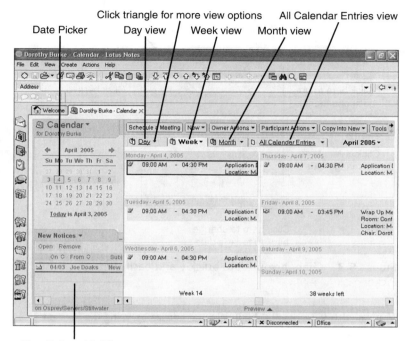

New Notices MiniView

FIGURE 9.2   The Calendar tabbed pages contain additional view options. This Calendar also contains the New Notices MiniView.

You can quickly go to a different date or change the month or year by using the Date Picker (see Figure 9.3).

Click here to select
from a list of months

Click here to select
from a list of years

Click here to go
back one month

Click here to go
forward one month

Click a date here
to change dates

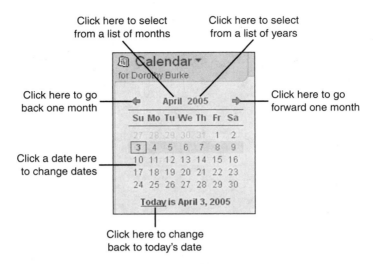

Click here to change
back to today's date

FIGURE 9.3   Change your date quickly and easily with the Date Picker.

You can also view details about calendar entries by using the Preview pane as shown in Figure 9.4.

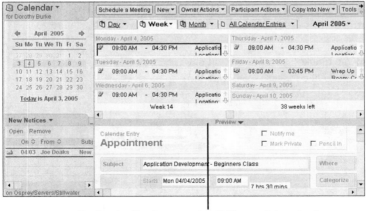

Resize the Preview pane by clicking and dragging here

FIGURE 9.4   Click the Preview pane triangle to open or close the Preview pane or click and drag it to resize it.

Understanding Calendar Entry Types

When you create calendar entries, they must fall into one of five categories:

- An **Appointment** is an entry in your calendar that does not include the process of inviting others in Notes. Appointments can have a start and end time, can be set to repeat, and can be marked private so that even those with access to your calendar cannot read the particulars about private appointments.

- An **Anniversary** is an occasion that has no time value, such as a birthday, working holiday, or payday. Anniversaries do not affect your free time. Anniversaries appear on your calendar only and can be set to repeat.

- **All Day Events** have a duration of at least one full day. Unlike appointments and invitations, you cannot specify a start time or end time. Events are typically used to schedule vacations, seminars, conventions, and the like.

- **Reminders** are notes to yourself that display on your Calendar on the time and date you assign to them. Reminders have a beginning time but no time value (that is, no ending time). They display on your Calendar only and can be set to repeat. One common use is a reminder to make a phone call. Do not confuse Reminders with Alarms or To Do's.

- **Meeting Invitations** are appointments in which you invite others. Meeting Invitations are distributed to the participants' Inboxes. Meetings also appear on the Calendars of invited participants when the participants are in a Notes organization/domain and have accepted the invitation. Like appointments, meetings have time values, have a beginning time and ending time within one calendar day, and can be set to repeat. You can send meeting invitations to people over the Internet and they will receive a text message, but not all of the formatting and graphics you see in the Notes form.

Creating Calendar Entries

The steps for creating an appointment, anniversary, reminder, or event are similar. Here, we discuss creating those kinds of calendar entries. The steps for scheduling a meeting are found in Chapter 10, under "Scheduling Meetings."

You can create a calendar entry at any time while in Lotus Notes. To create a calendar entry, do one of the following:

- **From your Calendar View**—To create an **Appointment**, **Anniversary**, **Reminder**, or **All Day Event**, click the **New** button on the Action bar. To create a meeting, click the **Schedule a Meeting** button on the Action bar.

- **From within a specific day**—Double-click a date or time slot in the Calendar displayed in the Calendar View. The type of entry usually defaults to Meeting (but this default can be changed in your Calendar preferences, as explained in Chapter 8). Click the down arrow next to Meeting and choose the calendar entry type from the dialog box that appears.

- **From outside of the Calendar (but within another view/folder in your mail database)**—Choose **Create, Calendar Entry** from the menu.

- **If your mail database isn't selected or open**—Choose **Create, Mail, Calendar Entry** from the menu.

Depending on the type of calendar entry you create, the entry fields vary slightly. Figure 9.5 shows the calendar event form for an appointment.

Use your mouse cursor or the **Tab** key to move from field to field when creating a calendar entry. Remember the fields available to you depend upon the type of calendar entry you're making, so you may not see all these fields in an All Day Event or a Reminder.

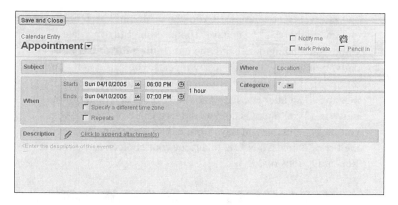

FIGURE 9.5 Appointments have an option field that allows you to add an attachment.

- **Subject**—Type in several words that describe the calendar entry. These words will appear in the Calendar view, and if sent to anyone else, in the Subject column in the Inbox.

- **When (Starts and Ends)**—Enter the starting and ending dates, or use the date picker if you don't want to accept the ones Notes entered automatically. Type in the start and end times for the calendar entry, or use the time picker to select them.

- **Specify a Different Time Zone**—If you specify a different time zone, new fields appear to help you select the time zone. You will also see a Local box that shows what time this will be locally.

- **Repeats**—Place an × in the **Repeats** check box to set parameters for calendar entries that occur more than once, such as a weekly status meeting. The Repeat Options dialog box appears (see Figure 9.6). Under Specify When the Meeting Repeats (it always calls it a meeting; this does not change to match the type of event), select the repeat interval from the drop-down list—Daily, Weekly, Monthly by Date, Monthly by Day, Yearly, or Custom. Based on that choice, set the specifics of the frequency and intervals (for example, if you chose Monthly by Day the frequency might be 2nd Sunday). Then, set the **Starting** date. Choose an ending date using the **continuing for** or **to** fields. For daily, monthly by date, or yearly repeats, you can specify an exception if the meeting falls on a weekend to either move the meeting to an alternate day that you specify, delete it, or not move it. If you pick Custom as the frequency of the meeting, you pick the individual days from a date picker and add them to the list of dates. Click **OK** to accept your choices and close the Repeat Options dialog box.

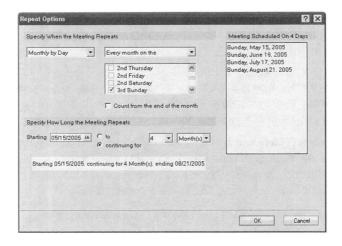

FIGURE 9.6 Fields in the Repeat Options dialog box change, depending on the type of repeat you select (monthly by date, weekly, and so forth).

- **Description**—Use this area to provide a more detailed description of the calendar entry. For example, you might want to supply an agenda for a proposed meeting. The Details field is a rich-text field, allowing you to apply text and paragraph formatting, as well as to add graphic images and embed objects such as files created in other programs. If you want to add an attachment, click the paper clip icon or the **Click to Append Attachments** link.

Date Picker—When entering dates, you can click the date picker icon at the right of the field and select the date. The date picker displays a miniature calendar. Use the left and right arrows at the top to move backward or forward in months. Click the month to see a list of months you can choose from. Clicking the year displays a list of years for selection. When you click on the date you want, the date picker closes and the date is entered in the field.

Time Picker—If you click the clock icon at the right of the time field, you will see a time scale. Drag the indicator up or down the scale to set the time of the appointment. Use the up and down triangles to see different parts of the scale. Click the green check mark to accept the time setting.

Using the date and time pickers eliminates the possibility of entering the date or time in a format Notes won't understand.

- **Pencil In**—Place an × in the check box to have the calendar entry appear on your Calendar, but have others still see this time as available if they check your schedule.

- **Mark Private**—This option is important if you have given other individuals access to *read* your Calendar. Placing an × in the check box prevents the other calendar readers from seeing this appointment. Use this if you want to enter a confidential calendar entry such as a doctor's visit. Others will see that your time is blocked but will not have access to the appointment information.

- **Notify Me**—Place an × in the **Notify Me** check box or click the alarm clock icon to set the parameters for seeing and hearing a reminder for this calendar entry. In the Alarm Notification Options dialog box, specify when you want the alarm to go off, the on-screen message, the sound to play, and whether you want an email notification to go to yourself or others.

Imagine yourself at home, snuggled up sleeping in your bed. The ringing of your phone shatters the still of the night. "Hello?" A digitized voice rasps, "This is your Lotus Notes notification. You have a meeting at 10:00 a.m. with the Production Team." *NOT!* Your computer must be on and you must have Lotus Notes open (even if minimized), or you must have Notes Minder running, to see or hear calendar entry notifications.

- **Where**—Enter the Location for the entry, such as the address of the person you are meeting.

- **Categorize**—Select the category for this calendar entry document from the pull-down list. Personal Categories are defined in your Calendar Preferences (**Tools, Preferences**). Review Chapter 8 for more information about setting Calendar preferences.

Customizing Calendar Entries

You can change the way that calendar entries appear in your Calendar. Notes allows you to color-code your entries and to change which fields appear in the views.

Color Coding Calendar Entries

You can select the background and text colors for the different types of calendar entries. To set colors from the Calendar view, choose **Tools, Preferences** from the menu. On the **Calendar & To Do** tab, click the **Colors** tab. For each color you want to change, click the arrow in the **Background Color** or **Text Color** fields. Choose your colors from the palette using the sliders or eyedropper as shown in Figure 9.7. When you are finished selecting your colors, click **OK** to save your choices and close the dialog box.

Move sliders

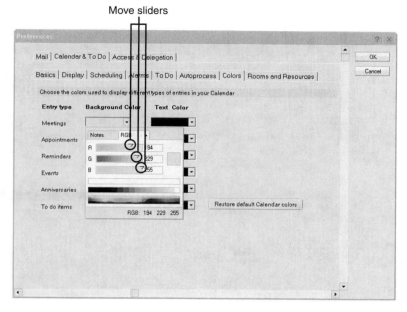

FIGURE 9.7 Move the sliders to select your color (R=Red, G=Green, B=Blue). If you want to return to the default Notes Calendar colors, click the **Restore Default Calendar Colors** button.

Changing the Data Displayed

In your Calendar views, each entry displays a standard set of fields. Figure 9.8 shows the default calendar entry display.

The customized entry shown in Figure 9.9 displays an icon, start time, and description.

To customize your Calendar view

1. Open the Calendar and choose **View, Customize This View** from the menu.

2. (Optional) Select or deselect the items you want to display in the Customize View dialog box (see Figure 9.10).

Start time   End time
Icon   Dash   Description

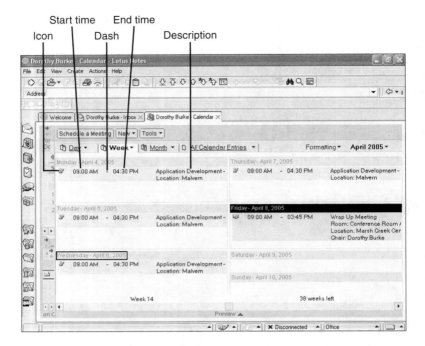

FIGURE 9.8   The standard calendar entry displays an icon, start and end time, and description.

3. (Optional) Use the **Move Up** and **Move Down** buttons to change the order in which items appear in your calendar entry. To return to the default settings, click the **Defaults** button.

4. (Optional) Choose **Hide in This Calendar Format Only** to have your new selections apply to the current view (week, month, and so forth) of your calendar, but not in other views.

5. (Optional) Change the format for field width, row spacing, and lines per row in the **Entire View** section.

6. Click **OK** to save your changes and close the dialog box.

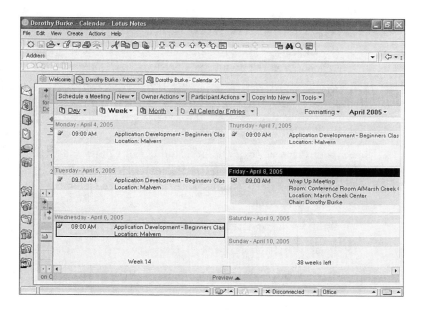

FIGURE 9.9   In this customized view, we've removed the dash and end time for calendar entries.

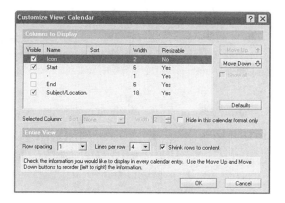

FIGURE 9.10   To customize the entries as shown in FIGURE 9.9, we deselected the dash and end.

Printing the Calendar

Notes has many choices for printing Calendars. You can choose to include or exclude weekends, you can print banner headings, and you can select from a large list of formats such as Day-Timer and DayRunner formats.

To print a Calendar view, do the following:

1. Choose **File**, **Print** from the menu.

2. Select your **Printer**, **Print Quality**, **Number of Copies** and **Print Range** on the Printer tab (see Figure 9.11). Under **What to Print**, choose **Print Calendar** and then select the **Calendar style** you want to print:

   - **Daily Style** prints one day per page.

   - **Weekly Style** prints one week per page.

   - **Work Week Style** prints one work week per page. By default that is a five-day work week, from Monday through Friday. If you selected different work week settings in Calendar preferences (**Tools, Preferences** on the Calendar & To Do tab under Display), those days print.

   - **Monthly Style** prints one month per page.

   - **Rolling Style** prints the time period you entered as the print range. It starts with the week in which the **From** date occurs and ends with the week in which the **To** day occurs.

   - **Calendar List** prints the calendar entries in a list.

   - **To Do List** prints the To Do entries in a list.

   - **Trifold Style** prints daily, weekly, and monthly in three panels on one sheet. Trifold Style works best when printed in Landscape (set on Page Setup tab).

Want to forward a calendar page to someone? Under What to Print, select **Print Calendar to a Document**. Make your other print settings and then click **Preview**. Click **Forward** and a mail memo opens with the document in the body of the memo. Address and send as usual.

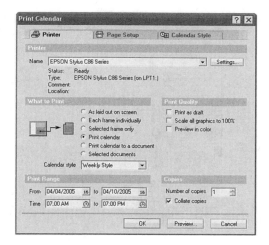

FIGURE 9.11 Your Print Range includes both a date range and, for each date, a time range for printing your calendar.

3. Click on the Calendar Style tab. Under **What to Print in Every Calendar Entry**, choose the fields you want to print in your Calendar (you can change the order of fields using the Up or Down buttons).

4. Under **Style Options**, place a check mark next to those options you wish to select for your calendar print job.

5. Under **Page Types** choose the type of page you wish to print. A Full Page is 8.5×11 paper.

6. To preview your Calendar before printing (we highly recommend this) click the **Preview** button (see Figure 9.12).

7. If you need to change the page setup, click the **Page Setup** tab. Here you can change the size of paper, margins, and so forth. Page setup is beyond the scope of this book; however, you can find directions and information in the Notes Help Database by searching for "page setup."

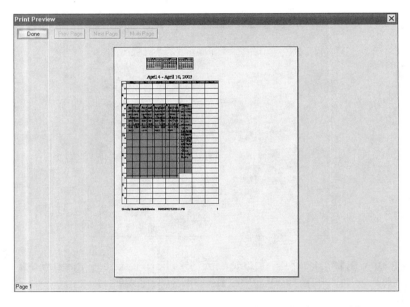

FIGURE 9.12   This preview shows a Calendar with the Franklin Day Planner Classic page type selected. Note that the calendar is off center. This is because Notes assumes I'm using a perforated form, which I can tear and fit into my Franklin Day Planner.

To print a single Calendar entry, open the entry and select **File, Print** from the menu. Set your Print Quality and Copies options, and then click **OK**.

If you want to print more than one entry, hold down the Shift key and click on each entry you want to print. A checkmark appears by each entry to show that it is selected. Then choose **File, Print** from the menu. Select **Selected Documents** under What to Print, set your Print Quality and Copies options, and then click **OK**.

Editing Calendar Entries

Our calendars aren't carved in stone—appointments are rescheduled, events are postponed, and meetings are called off. Notes supports your needs to modify calendar entries, move them to different dates, or delete them.

To modify a calendar entry, double-click the entry in Calendar view to open the document. You can alter any of the fields in the document, including Entry Type, to change the type of Calendar entry for the document. Save and close the document to have your changes take effect.

If you have a repeating entry, such as a weekly appointment, any changes you make to any of the entries will affect the related repeats. For example, say you try to change the start time for the appointment. When you try to save the entry change, the Change Repeating Entry dialog box appears and presents choices for how you want your changes to affect the related entries. You can choose to affect only the entry you have open, all the repeated entries related to this entry, only this and previous repeated entries, or only this and future repeated entries. Make your selection, and then choose **OK**.

You cannot change the frequency settings for the repeat entries, but you can delete future dates and re-enter the entry.

You can only set repeating entries when you create a calendar entry. You can't add repeating entries to an existing entry.

Although you can edit a calendar entry and change the dates and times, it's often quicker to drag and drop the appointment to the new date or time. When you drop the appointment in a new slot or day, the Reschedule Options dialog box appears. The new date or time you dragged to appears as the Start and End; click OK to confirm. However, if you drag a meeting entry for which you are not the owner, the Propose Options dialog box appears so you can suggest a different date or time for the meeting; an email is sent to the owner requesting the proposed change of time.

To drag an entry to a time you can't see on a date, hold the entry over one of the scroll arrows on the date and the Reschedule Options dialog box will appear. Needless to say, when you want to drag an entry to a new time, be sure the times show on the screen by right-clicking on the date and choosing **Show Time Slots** from the submenu.

If Notes asks whether you're sure you want to move the entry, click **Yes**.

Copying Mail into Calendar Entries

Mail messages you receive might contain information about appointments you need to make, events you need to attend, upcoming dates about which you want to remind yourself, or other date-related information. You can take that information directly from your mail message and convert it into a calendar entry.

Select or open the mail message, and click the **Copy into New** button on the Action bar. Select **New Calendar Entry**. A new entry document opens (see Figure 9.13). The **Subject** of the new entry matches the Subject line of the mail message. The body of the mail memo is added to the **Description** of the entry, but a horizontal line appears above it along with space for you to add any comments relating to the entry you're creating. From that point, make any changes you need to the entry, and then save it.

Calendar entries can likewise be used to generate mail memos. Select the entry in the Calendar view and then click **Copy into New** on the Action bar. Choose **New Memo**. A new mail memo opens, and the Subject of the Calendar entry becomes the subject of the mail memo. You complete the memo and send it to the recipients you specify.

You can also create To Do tasks from selected calendar entries. Click the **Copy into New** button and choose **New To Do**.

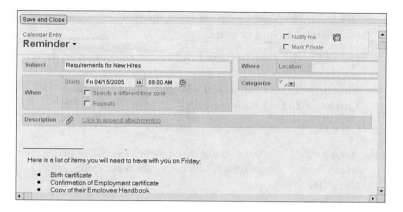

FIGURE 9.13 This reminder entry was based on an email that Joe Doaks sent to all new hires about orientation day.

Cleaning Up Your Calendar

You only want to see current entries when you look at your Calendar. You need to remove any entries that have been cancelled by deleting them.

When you need to delete a single calendar entry, open your Calendar, click the entry to select it (hold down **Shift** and click additional entries to select more than one), and then press **Delete**. Be very sure you want to delete the entry, because you won't be able to get it back.

For clearing past entries from your Calendar, you can use the Calendar Cleanup Tool.

1. Open your Calendar.

2. Click the **Tools** button on the Action bar. Select **Calendar Cleanup**.

3. In the Calendar Cleanup dialog box (see Figure 9.14), select which type of entries you want to delete:

Delete Entries That Occurred Over and specify the number of days, weeks, months or years.

Delete Entries That Occurred Before and enter or select the date.

4. Choose the type of entries you want to remove: **Calendar Entries** or **To Do Entries** or both.

5. Click **OK**.

6. A warning will appear to make sure you want to delete the entries because you won't be able to get them back once you do. Click **OK** to proceed.

FIGURE 9.14 If a set of repeating entries starts in the period specified for deletion but finishes after the period, none of the entries in the set will be deleted. Cleanup also won't delete any entries that are modified after the specified time period.

In this chapter, you learned how to switch Calendar views, create and edit Calendar entries, and print Calendars. In the next chapter, you learn how to create meetings and work with Group Calendaring.

LESSON 10

Working with Meetings and Group Calendaring

In this chapter you learn how to create and respond to meeting invitations and to create and use group calendars.

Scheduling Meetings

Lotus Notes is an ideal product for organizing group activities. Notes helps you schedule meetings and invite participants, as well as reserve rooms and resources for those meetings.

When you identify a need for a meeting, you must inform all the people involved of the meeting time and place—and, of course, that their attendance is requested. Do this by creating a meeting invitation. The first time you create a meeting invitation, it will take you some time to learn to use all the meeting invitation features, including how to view the free time of others. After you create one or two meeting invitations, you'll find that this task is easy and quick. Follow these steps to create an invitation:

- Create the invitation.

- Identify the invitees and others whom you want to inform about this meeting.

- Check the time of the invitees and (optionally) schedule your meeting time according to their availability.

- Determine how you want your invitees to respond to your meeting.

- Mail the meeting invitation.

To begin, open your Calendar and follow these steps:

1. With your Calendar open, click the **Schedule a Meeting** button on the Action bar.

2. In the Meeting document (see Figure 10.1), enter a brief description for the meeting in the **Subject** field.

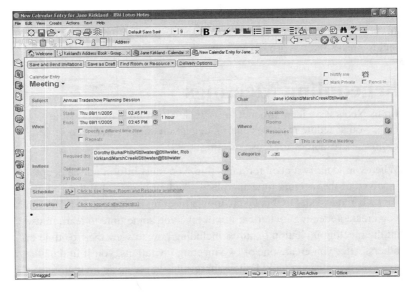

FIGURE 10.1   Enter the general meeting information first such as the names of the invitees in the Required (To), Optional (CC), and FYI (BCC) fields.

3. Enter or select the **Starts** and **Ends** dates and times (click the button at the right end of the field to use a date or time picker, as you learned in Chapter 9, "Using the Calendar").

4. For a meeting that will fall within a different time zone, choose **Specify a different time zone**. Click the button to the right of the time zone fields to select the time zone. The **Local** time for the meeting displays below.

5. For a meeting that will occur at regular intervals (such as a monthly meeting), select **Repeats** and enter your repeat options. For specific information on creating repeated meetings, see Chapter 9.

6. In the **Invitees Required (to)** field, enter the names of people you want to invite to the meeting (click the button at the right end of the field to select names from an address book).

7. (Optional) To provide a copy of the invitation to someone that informs him and keeps him updated about the meeting but doesn't *invite* him to the meeting, enter the person's name in the **cc** or **bcc** field. Use the **bcc** field only if you don't want other recipients to see the name of the person receiving an information-only copy of the invitation.

8. In the **Description** field (see Figure 10.2), enter important facts about your meeting, such as its purpose, directions to the location of the meeting, and so forth. You can embed files in this rich text field, such as supporting data for your meeting, and you can also attach a file by clicking the **Click to append attachment(s)** link (or the paper clip icon).

9. To check the availability of your invitees, click the **Click to see Invitee, Room and Resource availability** link (or expand the Scheduler button to the left of the link) in the **Scheduler** section of the form.

10. Be sure the **Details** radio button is selected in the **Show** section for this exercise. The Free Time section appears (see Figure 10.3). You can see the free time of each invitee (shown in white) sorted by the names of the invitees, by the week, by who can attend, by who cannot attend, or by whose time wasn't found. If the schedule is okay for everyone—that is, if a green bar appears for all names—go to step 12.

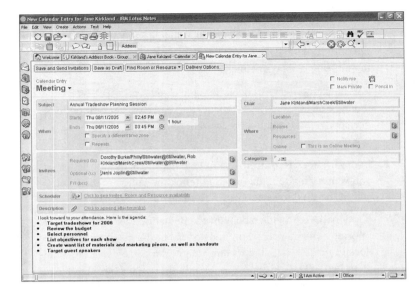

FIGURE 10.2   It's always a good idea to use the description field to provide further explanation about the meeting. This helps the invitees determine how best to prepare for the discussion.

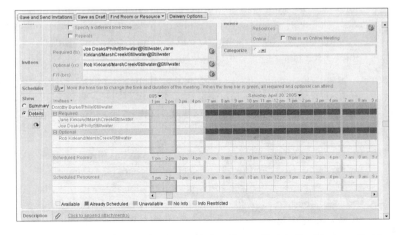

FIGURE 10.3   The details view of the Show field displays available times. A green bar indicates that everyone is available; a red bar indicates there is a conflict.

11. If you see a conflict (time shows in red) in the schedule, do one of the following:

- Point to the meeting time bar and drag it to a more appropriate time. When everyone is available for the meeting, the bar will turn green and you can release the mouse button.

- Select a time from a list of recommended times by clicking on the **Summary** radio button (see Figure 10.4). Double-click a suggested time in the summary, or select it and click the **Use Selected Time** button.

- Set a new date or time in the **Starts** or **Ends** fields.

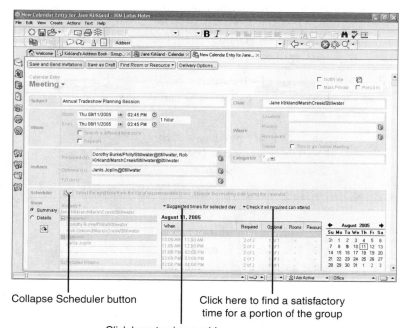

Collapse Scheduler button

Click here to find a satisfactory
time for a portion of the group

Click here to view a wider range
of possible dates and times

FIGURE 10.4 Summary view of the Show field displays suggested available times for all invitees.

12. When the meeting time is okay (green) for everyone, click the **Collapse Scheduler** button to close the section and continue with your meeting invitation. To schedule a resource, continue with step 13; otherwise, go to step 14.

13. (Optional) Click the helper button at the right end of the **Rooms** box to book a room for the meeting. Click the **Resources** helper button to reserve resources, such as audio-visual equipment, for the meeting. Handling these reservations is covered more fully later in this chapter.

14. (Optional) Check **Pencil In** if you want to keep the time of this meeting available in your free time schedule. Select **Mark Private** if you want to prevent people who have access to your Calendar from reading the invitation. If you want to set up a notification for the upcoming meeting, click **Notify Me** and pick the appropriate Alarm Options. From the **Categorize** field, select an appropriate category for the meeting.

15. Click the **Delivery Options** button on the Action bar to set any of the following options, and then click **OK** to close the dialog box:

- Set the **Delivery Report** and **Delivery Priority** as you would set them for email delivery. (Refer to Chapter 3, "Email Basics," for more information.)

- Check the **Return Receipt** box if you want notification that your meeting invitation has been received by the recipient(s).

- **I Do Not Want to Receive Replies from Participants** sends the invitation as a broadcast message that doesn't require a reply. Use this for large, general meetings where attendance is always required or there is such a large number of people invited that individual responses would be overwhelming.

- **Prevent Counter-Proposing** stops the recipient from proposing a different time schedule for the meeting.

- **Prevent Delegating** keeps the recipient from delegating attendance to another individual.

- **Sign** adds a digital signature to the invitation to guarantee that you are the person who sent it.

- **Encrypt** encrypts the invitation so only intended recipients can read it.

16. Save the invitation and send it to the invitees by clicking the **Save and Send Invitations** button on the Action bar. Alternately, click **Save as Draft** on the Action bar to save the invitation as a draft and send it at a later time.

Meetings can be held online, too, if your group uses IBM Lotus Instant Messaging and Web Conferencing (formerly known as Lotus Sametime). In such a meeting, each attendee remains at his or her computer and connects to an online meeting in which, optionally, there may be a whiteboard and one attendee or another can share the content of his or her screen with the other attendees. The attendees typically talk with each other by telephone.

If you check **This is an Online Meeting** in the Where section of the Meeting form, new fields appear. Choose a **Type**—Collaboration, Moderated presentation/demo, or Broadcast meeting—and enter the location (or click the button on the right to select one from the Directory) for the meeting in **Place**. You can also add meeting attachments, such as presentations, and assign a password to the meeting.

Managing Meetings

After you have scheduled a meeting, you will want to manage the meeting by checking on the status of responses to your meeting, rescheduling meetings when necessary, and possibly sending mail memos that relate to the meeting. All this management of the meeting can be done with the Notes Calendar and Notes Mail.

By default, the All Calendar Entries view of your Calendar displays a list of all your Calendar entries by date and time. When you click on the

down arrow on the All Calendar Entries tab, you can choose to view all
your entries in one of three ways:

- **On My Calendar** displays all the entries in your Calendar—
appointments, all-day events, anniversaries, meetings, reminders,
and penciled-in and draft meetings. Each instance of a repeating
meeting appears individually (if you open the instance, you will
see all the dates for the other instances).

- **All By Date** shows all the entries you see when you select On
My Calendar plus meeting workflow documents and any meetings to which you have been invited but haven't replied.

- **Meeting Threads** displays all meeting documents (see Figure
10.5), including meeting invitations to which you haven't
responded. Repeating meetings and workflow documents are
indented beneath the meeting to which they are related.

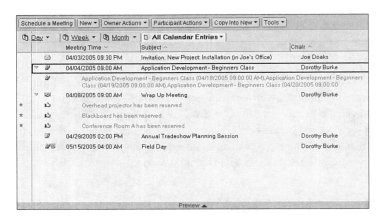

FIGURE 10.5   The Meetings Threads variation of the All Calendar
Entries view lists the meetings in date order, oldest to newest, and
also shows the responses from the invitees. Click on the Meeting
Time heading and you can change the order of appearance.

Using Action buttons in this view, you can create new meetings, take owner actions on selected meetings, or take participant actions on selected meetings. You can also copy meeting information into new memos, calendar entries, and To Do's.

To reschedule a meeting, follow these steps:

1. Open your Calendar and click the **All Calendar Entries** view tab. Select the meeting you want to change.

2. Click the **Owner Actions** button on the Action bar (because you created the meeting invitation you are considered the Chair or Owner), and select **Reschedule**.

3. The Reschedule Options dialog box opens (see Figure 10.6).

4. Modify the **Start** and **End** dates or times (click **Check Schedules** to use the free time schedule to see when your invitees are available).

5. Click **OK**. Notices will be sent to the invitees, informing them of the change of date or time. By checking **Include additional comments on notice** in the dialog box, you can add a short explanation along with the notice.

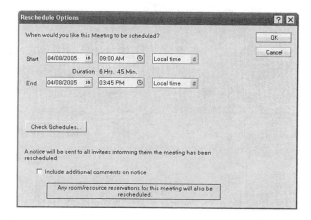

FIGURE 10.6   Room and Resources are automatically rescheduled when you reschedule the meeting.

When you cancel a meeting, you need to notify all the participants that the meeting has been cancelled. The steps for canceling a meeting are as follows:

1. Select the meeting document in the All Calendar Entries View of the Calendar.

2. Click the **Owner Actions** button on the Action bar, and select **Cancel**.

3. The Cancel Options dialog box appears (see Figure 10.7).

4. If you select **Permanently delete the Meeting and all notices and documents related to the Meeting**, Notes removes any documents related to the meeting. Or, you can remove the meeting from your Calendar but leave it in your All Calendar Entries view. Again, you have the option to include a message along with the notice. Click **OK** to close the dialog box. Notes automatically sends a cancellation notice to all the invitees for that meeting and removes any room or resource reservations related to the meeting.

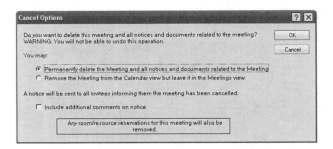

FIGURE 10.7   Notes automatically notifies all invitees of the cancellation and can clean up all related documents.

After you have received the responses to your meeting invitation, you should remove from the meeting document the names of invitees who won't be attending. You should then send a confirmation notice to the remaining invitees to let them know the meeting is indeed at the time and date specified. The notice will include the new list of participants for the meeting. To confirm a meeting, follow these steps:

1. Select the document from the All Calendar Entries view of the Calendar.

2. Click the **Owner Actions** button on the Action bar, and select **Confirm**.

3. (Optional) Select **Include additional comments on notice** in the dialog box to give yourself the chance to add your own text to the notice.

4. Click **OK** to close the dialog box.

Although the All Calendar Entries view displays response documents to meeting invitations, it's not easy to determine whether all the invitees have responded and accepted. To quickly review the status of the responses to your invitation, follow these steps:

1. Select the meeting in the All Calendar Entries view.

2. Click the **Owner Actions** button on the Action bar and select **View Invitee Status**.

3. The Invitee Status dialog box opens (see Figure 10.8), displaying the list of invitees, including optional or FYI invitees who were copied on the invitation. The dialog box displays the role of each person and the status of the invitation.

4. Click **Print** to print the list or **Close** to close the dialog box.

If you want to send a memo to all meeting participants to update the agenda or to provide more details about the upcoming meeting, follow these steps:

1. Select the meeting in the All Calendar Entries view.

2. Click the **Owner Actions** button on the Action bar, and choose **Send Memo to All invitees**, **Send Memo to Invitees Who Have Responded**, or **Send Memo To Invitees Who Have Not Responded**.

3. A new mail memo opens. The list of invitees appears in the **To** field, and optional invitees are in the **cc** or **bcc** field (depending on where you listed them in the meeting invitation).

4. The **Subject** field contains only the name of the meeting. The message area is blank, and you can create a message there as you would in any mail memo.

5. Click **Send** to send the memo to the invitees.

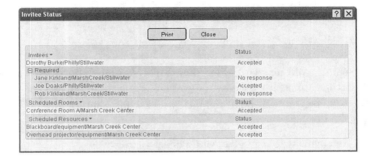

FIGURE 10.8   You can expand or collapse the Invitee status information by clicking the plus or minus signs next to the Required or Optional lists.

Making Room and Resource Reservations

Part of creating the meeting invitation is to specify and reserve a room and any equipment to be used for the meeting. As you learned earlier in this chapter, you can reserve a room or resource from the meeting invitation while you are creating an invitation, or even after the meeting has been scheduled (re-open the meeting entry and click the Add Reservation button).

To reserve rooms and resources, your organization must have rooms or resources in its Directory (Address Book). Check with your Notes administrator if you don't see such resources in your Directory.

Rooms and resources can be reserved using one of two methods: Reserve them by their names (overhead projector or Ellis Room), or search for them by criteria (conference room that seats 10 people) or categories (conference rooms, audiovisual equipment).

If you have difficulty or questions regarding room or resource reservations, consult with your help desk or your Notes administrator. Our instructions assume that resources are included in your Directory and that sites and categories have been assigned.

To reserve a room or resource by name, follow these steps:

1. Open a meeting invitation.

2. (To reserve a room) In the **Where** section, enter the name of the room you want to use in the **Rooms** field, or click the button at the right end of the field to select from a list of rooms.

3. (To reserve a resource) In the **Where** section, enter the name of the resource in the **Resources** field or select the name from the list that appears when you click the button for that field.

To search for a room by criteria (site and/or seating capacity), follow these steps:

1. Open the meeting invitation and click the **Find Room or Resource** button on the Action bar. Choose **Find Room(s)**.

2. The meeting dates and times appear automatically in the Scheduler dialog box (see Figure 10.9), as does the name of the

organization directory (you can change to another address book if you want). Click the helper button to the right of the **Site** field to select a site other than the one listed by default (the default site is set in Calendar Preferences, as explained in Chapter 8, "Setting Mail, Calendar, and To Do Preferences"). Sites are a service set up by the Notes administrator. If no sites are available, this field can be left blank.

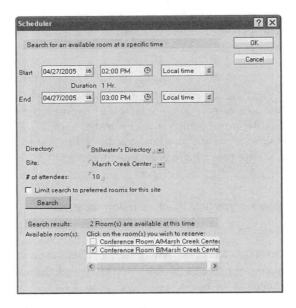

FIGURE 10.9   After you click Search, the list of available rooms at that site appear under Search Results.

3. Enter the **# of attendees** in that field. The number of attendees helps Notes find a room based on its seating capacity. Don't leave this field blank. If you pick a room that isn't large enough for the people specified, Notes will book the room but notify you that it is not the correct size for the number of people attending.

4. If you have set preferred rooms for the site in your Calendar Preferences (see Chapter 8), check **Limit search to preferred rooms for this site** to display only those rooms as choices.

5. Click the **Search** button.

6. Under **Search Results**, select the room you want to reserve, and click **OK**.

7. When you save the meeting entry, Notes sends a reservation request to your Resource Reservations database. This room is now "booked" and will not appear as an available resource during the time and date you have booked it. It is possible that some rooms and resources have been set by your administrator so they can they only be booked by their "owner". If you are not the "owner" all you can do is request a reservation and wait for confirmation from the owner.

To search for a resource, follow the preceding steps but choose **Find Resource(s)** instead of Find Room(s) in step 1. You also will have to specify a resource category before searching by clicking the **Category** button and then selecting the appropriate one from the dialog list.

If you need to cancel a room or reservation (if you don't cancel the entire meeting), open the meeting invitation and click the **Remove Room** or **Remove Resource** buttons below the Rooms or Resources fields. Save the invitation.

Responding to Meeting Invitations

You can accept or decline an invitation to a meeting. Unless prevented by the sender of the invitation, you can also propose a different meeting time that is more suitable for you, or delegate the meeting to someone else.

When you receive the invitation in your mail, you open the document (you can also open an invitation from the New Notices MiniView in your Calendar). Use the buttons on the Action bar to respond to the invitation (see Figure 10.10). Click **Request Information** to send a Meeting Update Request to the meeting owner with questions or comments. Click **Check Calendar** to see whether you are available at the meeting time.

Don't assume that the owner of the invitation checked your free time before inviting you to the meeting. To be sure you have the time available, click the **Check Calendar** button on the Action bar to see what you have scheduled for the day of the meeting before you respond to the invitation.

FIGURE 10.10   You can check your Calendar before responding to a meeting invitation by clicking the Check Calendar button.

 No respond button? The sender does not expect an answer to the meeting invitation because the memo is a broadcast invitation. Click **Add to Calendar** to add the meeting to your Calendar. Click **Request Information** if you want to know more about the meeting.

To respond to the invitation, click the **Respond** or **Respond with Comments** button and choose one of the following:

- **Accept** accepts the invitation. A memo of acceptance is sent, and an entry for the meeting appears on your Calendar.

- **Decline** rejects the invitation. A memo is sent noting that you decline the invitation.

- **Delegate** declines the invitation for you but enables you to specify the person to whom you want the invitation sent. Notes then forwards the invitation to that person. This option might not be available if the owner of the invitation chose to prevent delegation. You should also be aware that the person you delegated has the option to decline the invitation. You might want to check **Keep me informed of updates** so you continue to receive information about the meeting.

- **Propose New Time** gives you the opportunity to propose an alternative meeting time that is more convenient for your schedule. You specify the new date or time and click **OK**. A counterproposal memo goes to the invitation sender, but it displays the changes in schedule you propose. That proposal can also be accepted or declined. The Propose New Time option might not be available if the owner of the invitation chose to prevent new time proposals.

- **Tentatively Accept** accepts the meeting invitation and adds the meeting as an entry to your Calendar, but enables the **Pencil in** option on the Options page of the entry so the time still appears as free in your free time schedule.

If the meeting invitation is for a repeating meeting, your answer applies to each instance of the meeting. Check your schedule before you reply. Also, be aware you can't counter-propose for repeat meetings. You must first accept the invitation, then double-click the first instance in your Calendar of the meetings, click **Respond**, and choose **Propose New Time**.

If you choose **Respond with Comments**, add your comments to your answer and click **Send** to send your response. No response will be sent if you exit the form and don't save it.

Rather than responding individually to each meeting invitation, Notes can automatically answer them for you. Click the **Tools** button on the Action bar in the Calendar. Select **Preferences**. Click the **Calendar & To Do** tab and then the **Autoprocess** tab. Select **Enable automatic responses to meeting invitations**, and then complete the following fields:

- **When a meeting invitation is received from**—Use the drop-down list to select those people whose meeting invitations you would like to send automatic responses.

- **Perform the following action**—Use the drop-down menu to select **Automatically accept if time is available**. If you make this selection, you must then choose **and automatically decline if time is not available** or **and let me decide if time is not available**. If you select **Automatically accept even if time is not available**, Notes will double book the time and you will be able to resolve the conflict at a later time.

- Alternately, you can select **Delegate invitation to the following person instead of me**. Then, add the person's name to the **Delegee** field.

- **Automatic Inbox Management**—From the drop-down menu, choose an action for Notes to take when you delete a calendar notice from your Inbox or Mail folder. The choices are **Prompt to confirm deletion** or **Remove from this view/folder without prompting**. If you choose not to be prompted, then when you delete a calendar or to-do message from a view or folder, it will be permanently deleted from the database. If you choose to be prompted, then when you delete a calendar or to-do message from a view or folder, you will be prompted whether to remove the message from the folder or delete it entirely from the database. If you choose to delete the message, it will be permanently deleted from the database. If you are in a folder when you choose to remove the message, it will be removed from the folder but not deleted from the database (it will still appear in the All Documents view). But if you are in a view when you choose to remove the message, it will in fact be deleted permanently from the database (because users can't remove documents from views except by deleting them from the database).

Creating Group Calendars

A Group Calendar displays the free time schedules of a specified group of people. You quickly see who in the group is available or busy at a particular time. If you have access to their individual Calendars, you can display them below the Group Calendar.

To open a Group Calendar, open your Calendar and click **Tools**, **View and Create Group Calendars** from the Action bar. The Group Calendars View opens. If you want to create a new Group Calendar, click the **New Group Calendar** button on the Action bar. Enter a name for the Group Calendar, select the names of those you would like included, and then click **OK**. The Group Calendar opens, as shown in Figure 10.11.

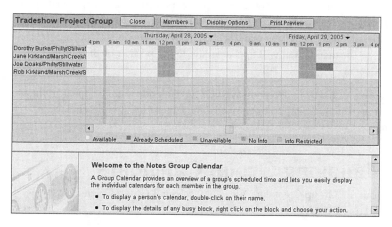

FIGURE 10.11 The Group Calendar displays the free time of all the members of the group. To display the details of any busy block, click it. If you have access to that Calendar, the event will appear at the bottom of the screen; otherwise, you see instructions on how to use the Group Calendar.

Group Calendars only display current and future dates. Older dates are marked as "No Info."

You determine the starting time of the Group Calendar and the total number of hours shown for each day. Click the **Display Options** button on the Action bar. In the Options dialog box (see Figure 10.12), select a **Starting Time** and **Duration**. Then, click **OK**.

FIGURE 10.12   In this dialog box, set the total number of hours showing for every day on the Calendar and the time the days begin.

In the Group Calendar you can see what times the members already have scheduled and when they are unavailable. If you have permission to view a person's calendar, you can double-click that person's name and the calendar for that person will appear in the lower portion of the Group Calendar.

Once you have created and saved Group Calendars, they appear in the group Calendar list. To open one of the Calendars, double-click on its name.

Managing Group Calendars

From the Group Calendars View, any selected Group Calendar can be edited or deleted.

Editing a Group Calendar involves changing the members or the title. You select the Group Calendar and click the **Edit** Action button. The New Group Calendar dialog box appears, so you can add or remove members or modify the title of the Group Calendar. Make your changes, and click **OK**.

To delete a Group Calendar, select it in the Group Calendars folder and then click the **Delete** button on the Action bar. The Group Calendar document disappears but can be seen in the Trash folder in Mail. Permanently remove the Group Calendar when you refresh your view, exit the mail database, or click **Empty Trash** on the Action bar of the Trash folder. Confirm the deletion.

In this chapter you learned how to work with group calendaring and how to schedule, manage, and accept or decline meeting invitations. In the next chapter you learn how to work with To Do items.

LESSON 11

Working with To Do Items

In this lesson, you learn how to manage your To Do list. You learn how to create and respond to To Do items, convert Mail Messages to To Do items, and view To Do status.

Creating To Do Items

To help keep track of all the things you have to do, create a personal To Do item. The difference between a To Do item in Notes and a Follow Up item (see Chapter 4, "Managing Mail") is that a Follow Up item flags an email as a reminder and a To Do item allows you to fill in detailed information about the item.

Once created, you can view To Do items in your To Do view or optionally display them in your calendar. To access the To Do view, click the To Do bookmark as shown in Figure 11.1.

You can also switch to your To Do view by clicking on the word **Mail** in the Navigator pane of your mail database and choosing **Switch to To Do** from the drop-down list as shown in Figure 11.2.

Lastly, you can see the "MiniView" of your To Do view by clicking on the tab at the bottom of your Mail Views and Folders pane and selecting To Do as shown in Figure 11.3.

To Do Bookmark

FIGURE 11.1 The To Do view is accessed by clicking the To Do bookmark.

In previous versions of Lotus Notes, To Do items were called *tasks*, and we tend to use these two words interchangeably throughout this book. To create a personal To Do entry, do the following:

1. From anywhere in Notes, click the To Do bookmark on the left of your screen. The To Do view opens, as shown in Figure 11.4.

2. Click the **New To Do** item button on the Action bar. The To Do item form appears, as shown in Figure 11.5.

3. (Optional) Select **Mark Private** if you do not want to give access to this To Do item to others to whom you give access to your email.

FIGURE 11.2 You can switch to your To Do view from the drop-down menu in your mail database.

FIGURE 11.3 When you click on the MiniView tab you can choose to view the To Do, Follow Up, or New Notices MiniViews.

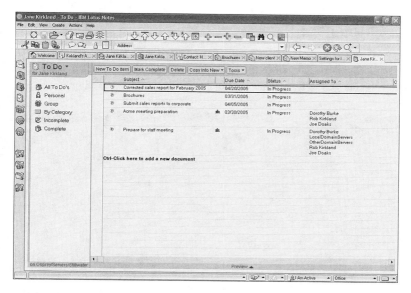

FIGURE 11.4 The To Do view enables you to see the status of To Do items, as well as their due date and to whom items are assigned.

4. Enter a description for this To Do item in the **Subject** field.

5. Choose to assign this task to yourself or to others. If you select others, the form changes so you can add a list of assignees, as shown in Figure 11.6.

6. To establish a start date for the task, enter the date in the **Starts by** box or click the Date icon next to the box to select a date from the drop-down calendar. Enter a date in the **Due by** box to set a due date for the task, or click the **Date** icon next to the box to select a date from the drop-down calendar.

7. (Optional) If you have a repetitive task, select **Repeats**. The Repeat Options dialog box appears (see Figure 11.7). Under When the To Do repeats, select the frequency of the repeat (such as **Monthly by Day**, then **Every other month on the**, and then the day). Under how long the To Do repeats, specify when the

repeating task ends by setting the number of days or an ending date. To prevent the due date of the task from falling on a weekend, select an option under **If the Date Occurs on a Weekend**. Choose OK to close the dialog box. If you need to go back and change the Recurrence options later, click the **Settings** button.

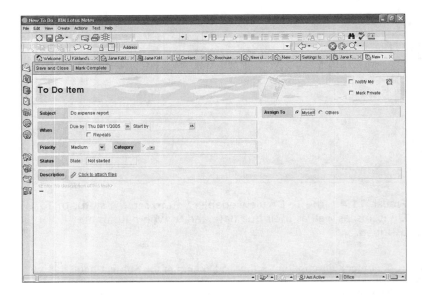

FIGURE 11.5   The To Do form in Lotus Notes 7 allows you to write a To Do list for others, create a repeating To Do item, and mark an item as Private.

Once a To Do item is saved as a non-repeating item, you cannot change it to a repeating item. You must recreate it from scratch.

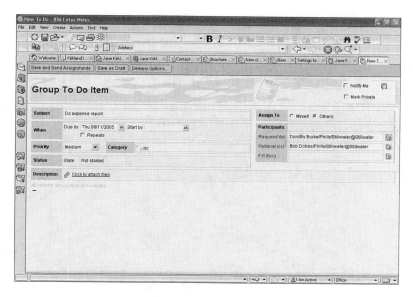

FIGURE 11.6 Complete the participant fields as you would complete the header of an email. The three fields here represent the to:, cc:, and bcc: fields of an email. Others will automatically be notified by email when you save this To Do item. By including others on your To Do item, it becomes a "group to do" item.

8. To set a priority for the task, click **High**, **Medium**, **Low**, or **None** (the default is **Medium**). Setting this priority affects the order that To Do items appear in your To Do list. Those with a high priority will appear with an icon labeled "1" and will appear before any 2s (medium priorities) and any 3s (low priorities). All no-priority tasks appear last on their respective dates in your To Do views.

9. (Optional) Choose an appropriate Category such as **Holiday** or **Vacation** from the drop-down list, or type your own category in the **Categorize** field.

10. To attach files to this To Do item, click the Attach Files field and choose a file or files to attach.

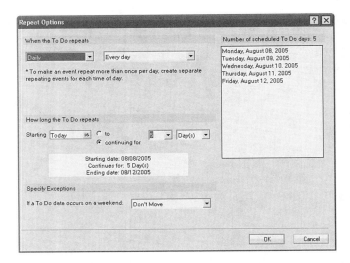

FIGURE 11.7   The Repeat Options dialog box is the same dialog box you see when you create a repeating calendar entry, such as a meeting.

11. (Optional) If you are assigning this to others, click the **Delivery Options** button on the Action bar to set the following options:

   • Choose your **Delivery Report**, **Delivery Priority**, and **Return Receipt** options. These options are the same as the options you find when you send a Mail Memo.

   • Check **I do not want to review replies from participants** if you do not require the participants to respond to your assignment.

   • Check **Prevent counter-proposing** to prevent the recipient from sending the task back to you with a counter proposal.

   • Check **Prevent delegating if you do not want the recipient to assign this task to someone else.**

   • Check **Sign and/or Encrypt to encrypt or attach an electronic signature to the memo.**

12. Click the **Save and Close** button (available if you're making a personal To Do) or the **Save and Send Assignments** button (available if you're assigning to others). The task appears in your To Do view.

Once you've saved a To Do item, you can view it by opening it from your To Do view. A new button appears on the Action bar of saved or saved and sent To Do items. That button, **Chat**, allows you to chat with members of the To Do item (see figure 11.8). To learn more about instant messaging, see Chapter 18, "Instant Messaging."

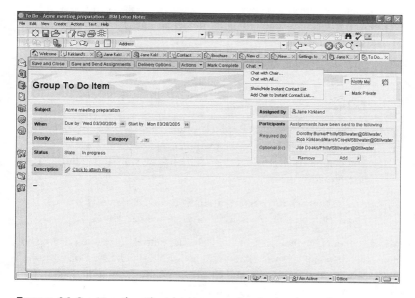

FIGURE 11.8 Use the Chat button on the Action bar of saved To Do items to instant message anyone listed in the Assign To fields.

In addition to displaying in your To Do view, To Do items also appear in your calendar. You can change the default settings of Notes if you do not want To Do items to appear in your calendar. See Chapter 19, "Customizing Notes," for more information.

To edit a To Do item, simply click once in the Subject field and you can edit it while in your To Do view. You can also double-click a To Do item to edit it.

Converting Mail Messages to To Do Items

You can convert mail messages to To Do items so that they appear in your To Do list. For example, you can convert a mail message from your manager that asks you to prepare your department's budget for next year to a task, which adds that message to your To Do list so that you won't forget to follow up. To convert a mail message to a task, do the following:

1. Select the document in your Inbox view pane or open the message.

2. Click the **Copy Into New** button on the Action bar. Select **New To Do**.

3. A new To Do opens. The subject of the mail message appears as the Subject. The body of the mail message becomes the Details. You can make any changes or additions you want to the information provided there.

4. Assign the task to yourself or others and click the **Save and Close** button on the Action bar or press the **Esc** key.

You also can create new tasks from Calendar entries. If you're creating an entry that also happens to be the deadline for a task, choose **Copy Into New, New To Do** from the menu. Change any information in the new To Do document and then save and close it.

Existing tasks often generate new tasks, and you can create new tasks from an existing task document. With the existing task selected or open, choose **Actions, Copy Into, New To Do** from the menu. Complete the new To Do document, save it, and close it.

Viewing To Do Status

To keep track of the tasks you assign to yourself, tasks others assign to you, and tasks you assign to others, open the To Do view in the Mail database.

Several views are available for the To Do list: **All To Do's**, **Personal**, **Group**, **By Category**, **Incomplete**, and **Complete**. You can change the status of an item by completing it and clicking the **Mark Complete** button on the Action bar. You can also cancel or reschedule a group To Do by choosing **Actions**, **Reschedule**, or **Cancel** from the Action bar.

Responding to a To Do Item

When you are named as a participant on a To Do document, you receive a mail message in your Inbox. When you open the message, you find choices for responding to this To Do assignment on the Action bar. Click the appropriate button on the Action bar:

- **Respond**—Click here to **Accept** or **Decline** the task, **Delegate** the task to another person, or **Propose New Time**, which allows you to change the due date. If you delegate the task, you must name a person to handle the task. However, you can request updates from the owner of the task (the person who created the To Do document). You can also receive updates if you decline the task. The last choice in this menu is **Completed**, which marks the task as completed and notifies the sender that you have completed the task.

- **Respond with Comments**—Contains the same choices as found in the Respond menu, but the return form includes a field for you to add comments when accepting, declining, delegating, proposing a new time, or completing the item.

- **Request Information**—Click here to ask for further information before or after accepting the task. When you select this, you also have the opportunity to **Include comments on the reply message**.

When you select a response option, a mail message is generated and sent to the owner of the task. When the owner receives your response, he too has options, which are available under the Actions button on the Action bar in the To Do view. These actions are also available for To Do items you have saved, not just those to which you are responding. These include the following:

- Reschedule

- Cancel

- Confirm

- View Invitee Status

- Send Memo to Invitees who have Responded

- Send Memo to Invitees who have not Responded

In this chapter, you learned how to assign To Do items to yourself and to others, how to mark the To Do items as completed, and how to view the items. In the next chapter, you will learn how to use the Address Books.

LESSON 12

Using the Address Books

In this chapter, you learn about the two address books found in Lotus Notes—the Public Address Book and the Personal Address Book—and how to use your Personal Address Book for creating Business Cards and Groups.

Defining the Address Books

Like Notes Mail, Notes Address Books are databases. Information such as email addresses and phone numbers are stored in your Address Book. At least two address books are available to you: your Personal Address Book and your Company Address Book (sometimes referred to as the Domino Directory or the Public Address Book; see Figure 12.1). Your system administrator might make other address books available to you, too.

Using Your Personal Address Book

As is the case with your Mail database, the contents of the Personal Address Book are controlled completely by you. You are the *Manager* (see Appendix A, "Understanding Security and Access Rights," for a complete explanation of security and access rights) of this database. You're the only one who can read, modify, or delete contact entries. You don't need to add your fellow employees because everyone in your company is already in the Domino Directory, so avoid duplicating entries that might already be found there. If you are a remote or mobile user, your system administrator might have installed a mobile directly catalog on your workstation so you have access to all entries in the Domino Directory. If not, remote users should add people from the Public Address Book to their Personal Address Book because they may need to access the Domino

Directory when they're not connected to the Domino server. For more information on remote users, see Chapter 17, "Using Notes Remotely."

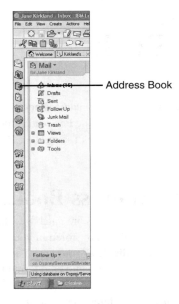

Address Book

FIGURE 12.1   Click the Address Book icon to access your personal database. For quick access to a Domino Directory, open the directory on the server by choosing File, Database, Open, and bookmark the directory in your Favorites or Database bookmarks.

After you click the Address Book bookmark, the Personal Address Book Navigation pane displays the following views:

- **Contacts**—Displays the people in your Address Book alphabetically. (If you are new to Lotus Notes Mail, your Address Book is probably empty.)

- **Contacts By Category**—The same people that are listed in your Contacts view, but now they are sorted by categories that you create. (If you are new to Notes Mail, you don't yet have categories created.)

- **Groups**—Lists the groups of people you created as mailing distribution lists.

- **Birthdays and Anniversaries**—Lists the dates of birthdays and anniversaries of contacts. Of course, if you don't include a birthday or anniversary date of a contact in his contact information, it won't show in this view. Don't confuse this with anniversary dates you create in your calendar.

- **Advanced**—The Advanced views are ones which you would not need to access or make changes to unless directed to do so by your system administrator.

Creating Contacts

The information you store about a person—name, title, company, address, phone, fax, email address, and so on—is kept in a Contact document, such as the one shown in Figure 12.2.

To create a Contact document for a new person, click the **New Contact** hotspot (if one exists) on your **Welcome page**, or open your Address Book and click the **New** button on the Action bar and choose **Contact**. The following describes the fields for adding a new contact:

- At the top level of this form are fields for names, title, suffix, and email. Either the last name field or the company field (in the Business section) is required. All other fields are optional.

- When you fill in the **Email** address field, be sure to click the icon on the left of the field. Here, you'll tell Notes what kind of email client you're adding. This information helps Notes to format the contacts email address correctly. If you don't know the details then don't make a selection, but if, at the very least, you know enough about the contact to choose Notes or Internet, choose one of those two. If you have more than one email address for a contact, type the email address you use most for them in the email field and put the remaining email addresses in the Other Email fields on the bottom left of the Business tab section.

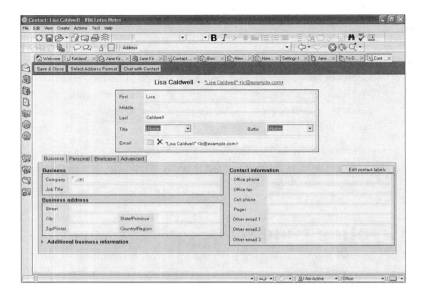

FIGURE 12.2 Tabs separate the Business, Personal, Briefcase, and Advanced sections of a Contact document where you can keep business as well as personal contact information.

- The **Business** section of the contact contains, appropriately, business information about that contact such as her company name, job title, and so forth. Start typing the business name and autofill will complete it for you if it is a company that exists in your Address Book. Alternately, click the drop-down arrow button and choose the company from the drop-down list. Click the triangle next to Additional Business Information to include such items as the company website address. There are no required fields here, so if you only know part of the business information such as the city, but not the street address, you can fill in the information you know (see Figure 12.3).

- On the **Personal** tabbed page add personal information about this contact, such as his home address, birthday, or anniversary (see Figure 12.4).

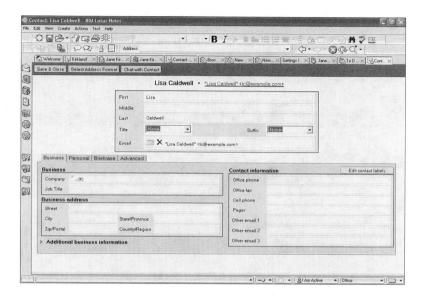

FIGURE 12.3   It is not required that you fill in every field in your contact information document. These phone number labels can be customized by clicking the Edit Contact Labels button discussed later in this chapter.

- The **Briefcase** tabbed page provides space to save photos, attach files, or add comments to your contact. For example, you could store a resume, a map to a client's office, or a copy of an employee's review.

- The **Advanced** tabbed page allows you to categorize your contact so that it will show in the appropriate category when using the view **Contacts by Category**. Autofill will complete any category entry you begin to type. If you want a contact to display under more than one category, separate the categories with commas. Be consistent and watch your spelling, or you'll end up with several similar categories—Friends, Friend, Fiend—which makes it harder to find people. You can also choose which information, business or personal, you want displayed in your Preview pane when previewing the contact information.

- When you add a new contact, click the **Save and Close** button on the Action bar to save this information in your address book.

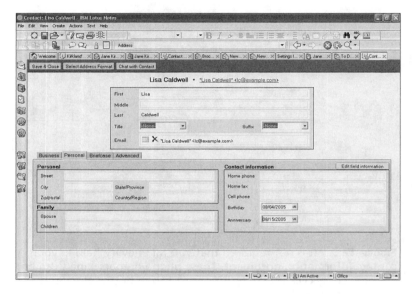

FIGURE 12.4 When you include a birthday or an anniversary on the Personal tab of a contact, that contact will be included in the Birthdays and Anniversaries view of your Address Book.

Creating Mailing Lists

To send a mail message to more than one person, you can type each person's name, separated by a comma, or you can create a *mailing list*. To create a mailing list, follow these steps:

1. Select **Groups** from the Personal Address Book Navigation pane.

2. Click the **New** button on the Action bar and choose **Group**.

3. The Basics section of the Group document is displayed, as in Figure 12.5. Type a short, descriptive name for your group in the **Group Name field**.

The form and information found for contacts in your Personal Address Book differs from the information you find on an individual in the Company Address Book. For example, the Company Address Book does not have a field for a web page or birthday. You might want to record this information about a fellow co-worker because lots of people have personal web pages these days. In this case, instead of creating a new contact in your Address Book, copy that person from the Company Address Book into your Personal Address Book. Once added to your Personal Address Book, complete the information you want to keep. Remember, you don't need to copy the Company Address Book into your Personal Address Book for the mere purpose of being able to send email to a fellow employee. However, if a person's name or address changes in the Company Address Book, you will have erroneous information in your Personal Address Book. If you are a mobile Notes user, please be certain to read Chapters 18, "Instant Messaging," and 19, "Customizing Notes," so you have a full understanding of Address Books and replication.

 When you receive a mail message from a person who is not listed in your Personal Address Book, you can add that person to your address book. Open or select the mail message and then click the **Tools** button on the Action bar and select **Add Sender to Address Book**.

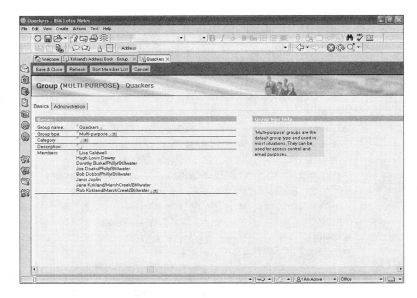

Figure 12.5   Mailing Lists can save time when you are addressing mail.

4. You can ignore the **Group Type** field entirely and leave it as Multipurpose, or you can click the small triangle to the right of the **Group Type field** and select **Mail Only** for your group. The other options, **Multipurpose** (the default), **Access Control List Only**, and **Servers only**, are for use by your system administrator.

5. Type a short description of the group in the Description field. Although this is not a mandatory field, it might remind you why you created this group.

6. Click the down arrow next to the field and select the names from your Personal Address Book.

Lotus Notes saves a copy of your mail by default. Including yourself in a group results in your having two copies of a mail message, the one you saved and the one you sent to yourself as a member of the group.

7. When you're done, click the **Save and Close** button.

If you have a mail message open that includes a list of recipients, you can create a group for that list. Open the message and choose **Actions, Add Recipients,** to **new Group in Address Book** from the menu. A dialog box opens with a list of recipients checked. Click **OK** and a new Group document is created. Another way to create a Group document is to check multiple people in your Contacts view of your Address Book and choose **Tools, Copy into New Group** on the Action bar.

After you create the group, you can use it when you address memos. Simply type the name of the group in the To field (Quick address completes the name as you type), and Notes sends your email to all the people in the group. If a person drops out of the group or a new person is added, you can edit the group document by selecting it from the **Groups** view and clicking the **Edit Group** button on the Action bar. By using the group name when addressing your mail, you can save a lot of typing.

To quickly address a memo to a group, open the group view, highlight the group, and click **Write Memo.**

Some groups need to exist only for the length of a project on which you're working. When you need to remove a group from your Personal Address Book, select it from the **Groups** view and click the **Delete Group** button on the Action bar.

Customizing the Address Book

By default, Notes sorts contacts in views by their first name. To change this default so you view contacts by last name, follow these steps:

1. Choose **Actions, Edit Address Book Preferences** from the menu or **Tools, Preferences** from the Action bar.

2. Select **Display names by default in Contact form/views(s):Lastname Firstname**.

3. Click **Update All Entries** to change existing entries as well as new entries.

4. Click **Save** and **Close**.

For any contact, you can customize field names (Lotus calls them *labels*) on the Business and Personal tabs. Perhaps you want the *Other email 1* label to say *Home email*. To do this, click the **Edit Contact Labels** button near the top of the Contact Information section and rename the labels (see Figure 12.6).

You can also customize a contact's address format. Notes provides six different internationally accepted formats for addressing mail. These formats are applied when you print labels from your address book. To apply an address format, open a contact and click the **Select Address Format** button on the Action bar. Choose the address format you prefer and **Save and Close** the contact.

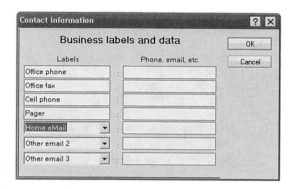

FIGURE 12.6 When you click Edit Contact Labels, a dialog box appears. There, you can use field name suggestions provided by Notes in a drop-down menu, or you can type in your own names for fields.

Printing from Your Address Book

You can print an alphabetical list of your contacts with their phone numbers and email addresses, and you can also print address or shipping labels in various sizes. Printing lists and labels for Address Books is available for local Address Books only, so if you need to print from your Domino Directory, you must replicate the directory to your hard drive or copy the Domino Directory into your Address Book. For more information on replication, see Appendix B, "Understanding Replication." To print from your Address Book, follow these steps:

1. Open your Address Book and select the contact names you want to print by placing a checkmark in the margin. If you want to select your entire Address Book, choose **Edit, Select All** from the menu.

2. With your contacts selected, choose **File, Print** from the menu. The Print dialog box appears as shown in Figure 12.7.

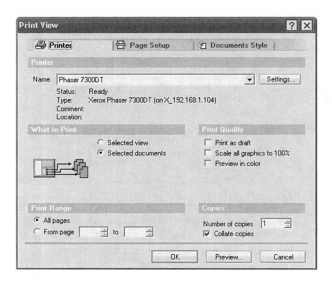

FIGURE 12.7   You can print documents, selected documents, or a selected view from the Print menu.

3. Click the **Documents Style** tab. To print a list, under the How to Print Each Document option, choose how many contacts to print on each page. You can click the **Preview** button to preview your options.

4. To print labels or a list other than the standard default list of contacts, go to the **Format Each Document Using** section and click the **Alternate Form** radio button.

5. A drop-down menu appears in which you can select the labels or lists you want (see Figure 12.8). There are choices here for both address labels and shipping labels.

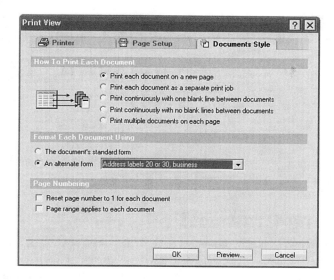

FIGURE 12.8 Various formats are available for shipping and address labels. Be sure to select the correct printer tray when you are printing labels.

6. (Optional) Specify page-numbering options.

7. (Optional) Click the **Page Setup** tab and specify additional page formatting as well as paper source (important when you are creating labels). Click **OK** when you are finished with your selections, and Notes will print your list or labels.

In this chapter, you learned about the Address Books and how to use your Personal Address Book for creating contacts and groups, as well as lists and labels. In the next chapter, you learn how to navigate the Web using Lotus Notes.

LESSON 13
Navigating the Web

In this chapter, you learn how to browse web pages with Notes, bookmark the web pages you visit frequently, and set browser options.

Setting Browser Preferences

You can browse Internet or intranet pages with Notes, or you can use other browser applications, such as Netscape Navigator, Firefox, or Microsoft Internet Explorer. A major advantage to using Notes as your browser is that Notes automatically stores copies of web pages as documents in a local Notes database called Personal Web Navigator. Then you can view them at any time, even if you are no longer connected to the Web.

 When you retrieve web pages and store them locally for offline use, Notes as a web browser may seem slower than other browsers. This is because of the extra time it takes to store each page you visit.

An offsetting disadvantage of using Notes to browse the Web is that Notes's built-in browser may not be able to display all retrieved pages correctly. So, as an alternative, you can set up Notes to use an embedded copy of Internet Explorer to browse the Web. When you do this, you are actually using Internet Explorer as your browser, but it displays all content inside your Notes window. When you browse this way, you can set up Notes either to store retrieved web pages automatically or to store them manually, on demand.

Yet another way to browse the Web from within Notes is to have Notes open your favorite web browser in a separate window. When you browse this way, you don't have the ability to store web pages in the Personal Web Navigator database. (You can, however, save pages to disk for later review.)

Configure your web browser options in your Location documents. Location documents are stored in your Personal Address Book. They tell Notes how to function from any particular location. For example, if your computer is located in your office at work, where you have a high-speed connection to your home server, an "Office" location document tells Notes to connect to the server over the network. But if your computer is traveling with you and you are in a hotel room with no high-speed Internet access, your "Travel" location document might tell Notes to use a particular telephone dialing sequence to connect to the Internet, then to your passthru server, and finally to your mail server.

In addition, many of the settings in your Location documents have little or nothing to do with where your computer is located. For example, one setting tells Notes which browser you want to use when you tell it to display a web page. You might prefer to use, say, Firefox as your everyday browser. But you may occasionally want to switch to Notes or the embedded version of Internet Explorer in order to store a web page in the Personal Web Navigator database. You could accomplish this switch by defining separate Location documents for each web browser you might want to use, then switching among them as needed.

Here are some useful techniques for changing your Location documents:

- To edit your current Location document, you can click the Location box in the Status Bar (lower right corner of your Notes window) and choose Edit Current (the last item in the list).

- To edit a non-current Location document, you can open your Personal Directory and navigate to the Advanced\Locations view. Or, in the Notes menu, you can choose File, Mobile, Locations.

- To set which web browser to use, open a Location document in Edit mode, navigate to the Internet Browser tab, and select a browser in the Internet Browser field (see Figure 13.1).

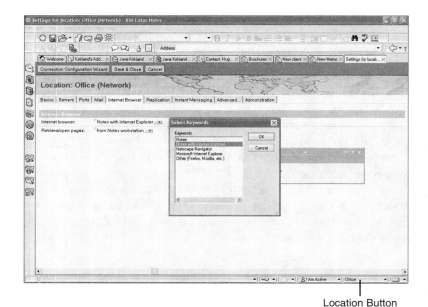

Location Button

FIGURE 13.1   Choose the web browser you want from this list in the keyword dialog box which appears when you click the arrow key in the Internet browser field of a Location Document.

- To make Notes your default browser for all locations, choose File, Preferences, User Preferences from the menu. From the Additional Options list, select Make Notes the Default Web Browser on My System. Then, click OK.

Another good use of Location documents is to easily change your Internet return address. Say you usually want your mail to be from Joe.Doaks@acme.com, but occasionally you want your mail to be from sales@acme.com or Joe.Doaks@beta.com. You can set up different Location documents, each with a different address in the Internet Mail Address field. Then you can switch between the Location documents whenever you want to switch your return address. If you want to do this, have your administrator set up your Person document with each address you want to use; else replies may not be deliverable to you.

Opening Web Pages

There are several ways to open web pages from within Notes, but the easiest is to enter the URL (Uniform Resource Locator) into the **Address** box on the toolbar (see Figure 13.2). Press Enter, and Notes retrieves the page. It isn't necessary to enter the complete address, because Notes assumes the http:// part of the URL. Just start the address with the www (when applicable) when you enter it, such as www.takeawalk.com. If you have visited that page previously, you can click the down arrow at the right end of the Address field and select the URL from the list.

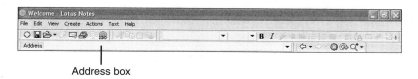

Address box

FIGURE 13.2 Open web pages by entering the URL in the Address box, just as you do in many browsers.

Use Bookmarks to mark your most frequently visited web pages. This will save you time in opening those websites in the future. To create a Bookmark, drag a page's tab to the bookmark bar or right-click on the Window tab for the web page and select **Create Bookmark** from the context menu to open the Add Bookmark dialog box. Give the bookmark a name and select a folder in which to store it (or put it on the Bookmark bar). Click **OK**.

URL addresses you see in emails or other Notes documents are *hotspots*. When you click on one of these hotspots, the web page opens.

 To have Notes automatically create hotspots from URLs that appear in rich text fields of Notes documents like the body of a mail memo, choose **File, Preferences, User Preferences** from the menu. On the Basics page, select **Make Internet URLs (http:// ...) into Hotspots** from the Additional Options list. For Notes to detect text as a URL in the rich text field, however, it must begin with http://. Documents in edit mode must be closed and reopened for the URL to become a hotspot. When the hotspots appear in the documents you open, click them to open the URL.

Like any browser, Notes has tools to help you navigate the Web. These same tools work when navigating Notes—databases, documents, views, or web pages. These tools are on the Navigation toolbar (see Figure 13.3). Table 13.1 explains their uses.

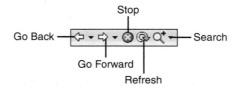

FIGURE 13.3   Navigate though web pages using these buttons.

TABLE 13.1   Navigation Buttons for Web Pages

Name	Description
Go Back	Takes you to the previous page you had open when you click once. Click the down arrow next to the button to see a list of where you have been and select one to revisit.
Go Forward	After you have gone backward, clicking Go Forward takes you to the next page after the one you're on. Click the down arrow next to the button to see a list of where you have been and select one to revisit.
Stop	Stops loading the page you requested from the Web.
Refresh	Reloads a web page directly from the Web.
Search	Click to search for text in a view or a web page. Click the down arrow next to the button to search for people or databases, or to start an Internet search engine such as Lycos.

Storing Retrieved Pages

When you use Notes to retrieve web pages, the pages are stored in the Personal Web Navigator database located on your local drive. When you use "Notes with Internet Explorer" to retrieve web pages, the pages may automatically be stored in the Personal Web Navigator database, or you may opt to store pages manually. You can make this choice as follows:

1. Open the Personal Web Navigator database.

2. Choose **Actions, Internet Options** from the menu.

3. Select the **Size Options** tab.

4. Select **Automatically store pages for disconnected use** or **Manually store pages for disconnected use**.

5. Click **Save and Close**.

If you opt to manually store pages, you can store them by displaying the desired page in the Notes menu, then choosing **Keep Page** in the **Actions** menu.

If you are storing web pages in the Personal Web Navigator database, you should manage the stored pages. For example, you need to specify how often stored pages should be updated. From the menu, choose **File, Preferences, Location Preferences**. When the current Location document opens, select the **Advanced** tab, and then click the **Web Retriever** tab (see Figure 13.4).

Select an option from Update cache:

- **Never**—Select this option if you never want to update your stored web pages.

- **Once Per Session**—This is the default setting. This option updates stored web pages once per Notes session.

- **Every Time**—Select to update stored web pages each time you open one. This is especially important when you need up-to-date information every time you open a page (such as with stock prices).

Click the **Save & Close** button on the Action bar to save your choices.

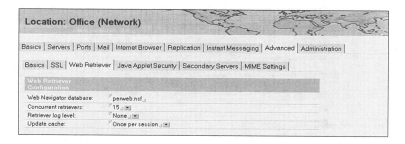

FIGURE 13.4   Messages about web retrieval are stored in your Notes log, along with the daily activities Notes performs. For Retriever log level, select None (the default) to have no messages sent about web retrieval, Terse to send minimal messages, or Verbose to send all messages.

How many parts of a web page do you want to retrieve at once? Do you want to retrieve the text, images, and video all at the same time? You can set Notes to retrieve more than one at a time by choosing **File, Preferences, Location Preferences** from the menu, clicking the **Advanced** tab, selecting the **Web Retriever** tab, and then selecting a number in the **Concurrent Retrievers** field (15 is the default). However, the more retrievals you have working at the same time, the more computer memory you use, and the slower your computer will be in downloading pages.

Viewing Pages Offline

To browse when you are disconnected from the Internet, change your Location document (or switch to a location that is disconnected, such as Island). Choose **File, Preferences, Location Preferences** from the menu to open the current Location document. Select the **Internet Browser** tab. From the Retrieve/open pages field, choose **work offline** and click **OK**. Then, click the **Save & Close** button on the Action bar.

Quickly edit a location document by clicking the location in the status bar and choosing **Edit Current** from the pop-up menu. To switch locations, select a different location from the pop-up menu.

With **work offline** selected, Notes will only retrieve pages from the Personal Web Navigator or Server Web Navigator databases. Notes won't retrieve pages from the Web. You will have to reconnect and change the setting in the Location document before you can retrieve new or updated pages.

If you switch to the Island (disconnected) location, you should use this setup so you can continue viewing web pages you've stored.

Forwarding and Mailing Pages

Forwarding a web page sends the body of the web page to the recipient (be sure you also include the URL). That way, the recipient can immediately see why the page caught your attention, making it more likely that the person will visit the page. However, to ensure that the person can access all the features of the page, you should forward the *URL* instead of the page.

To forward a page, open the web page and choose **Actions, Forward** from the menu. Then select **Forward copy of this page**. In the new mail memo that opens, enter or select the names of the recipients in the To field. Type any necessary comments, and then click **Send**.

 The page you forward might not look to the recipient exactly as you saw it on the Web. That's because browsers control how pages are displayed, and the recipient may use a different browser than you use, or it may be differently configured than yours.

To forward a URL, start from the open web page and choose **Actions, Forward** from the menu. You then select **Forward bookmark to this page** and click **OK**. You enter the names of the recipients in the To field of the new memo (see Figure 13.5) or select them from the Address Book. Type any comments you want to accompany the URL, and then click **Send**.

FIGURE 13.5 This Mail Memo forwards the URL of a web page to two recipients. When the memo is received, the recipient can click the URL to open the web page.

Using Page Minder

When you need to check a web page frequently to see if there are any new updates, the Page Minder agent can do that for you. Whenever a change to the specific page occurs, the agent either sends you an email with a summary or the actual page.

Before you can run an agent such as Page Minder or Housekeeping, you must enable scheduled local agents first. If you've done this once, you need not do it again. If you've not enabled scheduled agents, choose **File, Preferences, User Preferences,** and place a check mark next to **Enable scheduled local agents.** Click **OK**. Remember that agents will only run when Notes is running.

To set up the Page Minder agent, do the following:

1. Open a web page and choose **Actions, Internet Options** from the menu.

2. Select the **Page Minder** tab (see Figure 13.6).

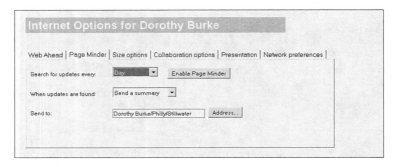

FIGURE 13.6 Save yourself time by setting Page Minder to check for updates on important web pages.

3. From the "Search for Updates Every" drop-down list, choose how often you want the agent to run—every hour, 4 hours, day, or week.

4. Determine whether you want Page Minder to Send a Summary or Mail the Actual Page when updates are found.

5. Enter the names of the users who should receive the updates. Your name is automatically entered; click **Address** to select additional users.

6. Click **Enable Page Minder** to turn on the agent.

7. Click **Save and Close**.

When you are ready to specify a page that you want to be monitored, open the web page and choose **Actions, Move to Folder**. Under the Web Bots folder, select the Page Minder folder and click **Add**.

You stop monitoring a web page from the Personal Web Navigator database. Open the database by choosing **File, Database, Open** from the menu. Then select **Personal Web Navigator** from the list of local databases and click **Open**. Click the **Page Minder** folder, select the page, and click the **Delete** button on the Action bar.

When you want to disable the Page Minder agent, open a web page and choose **Actions, Internet Options** from the menu. Open the **Page Minder** tab and click **Disable Page Minder**. Then click **Save and Close**.

Performing Housekeeping

Storing all the web pages you visit could result in a very large database file. At some time, you'll have to remove some of those files. One way to do this is to use the Housekeeping agent to automatically delete stored web pages. When enabled, this agent runs daily at 1:00 a.m. To enable Housekeeping, follow these steps:

1. Open a the Personal Web Navigator database.

2. Choose **Actions, Internet Options** from the menu.

3. Click the **Size Options** tab (see Figure 13.7), and select one of these options:

   • **Reduce Full Pages to Links If Not Read Within**—Select this option to have Notes delete the contents of the web page but save the URL so you can still open the page on the Web. Then specify the number of days that the web page should be in the database before deletion.

   • **Remove Pages from Database If Not Read In**—Choose this option to have Notes delete the entire web page. Then specify the number of days that the web page should be in the database before deletion.

   • **Disable**—Select this option to disable the agent so it won't automatically delete stored web pages.

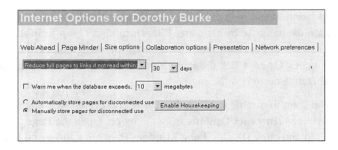

FIGURE 13.7   Set your housekeeping options to reduce the size of web pages that haven't been read recently or to delete those pages.

4. (Optional) If you want to be warned when the database gets to a certain size, select **Warn Me When the Database Exceeds** and then specify a size in megabytes.

5. Click **Enable Housekeeping**.

6. Click **Save and Close**.

You must enable scheduled local agents first in order to use the Housekeeping agent.

If you prefer, you can delete web pages manually. Open the Personal Web Navigator and do one of the following:

- Select **Other, House Cleaning** in the Navigation pane to display a list of documents sorted in descending order by document size (these include web pages and files associated with them, such as cookies and stylesheets). Select the documents you want to remove then click **Delete** on the Action bar. Notes deletes the selected documents.

- Select **Other, File Archive** if you want to delete files based on file name. Notes displays a list of files, sorted alphabetically by file name (although you can click the sorting arrows in the File Size column heading to sort the view by file size). Select the files you want to remove, and then click **Delete** on the Action bar. Notes deletes the selected files.

In this chapter you learned how to use Notes to browse web pages, how pages are saved, and how to perform housekeeping. You also learned how to forward a web page or its URL in a mail memo. In the next chapter you learn to edit and format documents.

LESSON 14

Editing and Enhancing Documents

In this chapter, you learn how to complete forms, create links, use the permanent pen and highlighter, and how to work with tables. You also learn several text formatting techniques.

Completing Form Fields

Notes forms contain several types of fields. Some are automatically filled in and others are fields in which you enter information. Notes fields in which you enter data are easily identified because they are the white boxes—usually to the right or below the text that describes the field—where you type in information, as you have seen in the subject of a Mail Memo form.

The following list describes the common field types you find in Notes database forms. Not all forms contain all of these elements.

- **Text Fields**—Fields in which you can enter words and sentences, usually titles or topics. You cannot format text in a text field. The Subject in a Mail Memo is a text field.

- **Rich Text Fields**—Fields in which you can enter text, import text, import graphics such as GIF or JPEG files, and attach files. The body of the Mail Memo is a rich text field. You can apply both text and paragraph formatting in rich text fields.

- **List Fields**—Fields in which you select choices from a list. The Title field on the New Contact form in your address book is a list field. Depending on the database design, you might be able to enter or even add your own list items.

- **Date/Time Fields**—Very often, these fields are automatically filled by Notes, using your computer's clock. Most time fields display hour and minute, while most date fields display month, date, and year. In the Calendar Appointment Entry form there is a date field and a time field for Starts and Ends.

- **Number Fields**—Fields that can contain only numbers, such as currency or quantities. You will get an error if you enter text in a number field. A number field might be the quantity you enter in an order form.

To enter information into a field, click inside of the field and begin typing. To move from field to field on a form, press the **Tab** key.

Most fields within the mail database are not fixed-length fields; they grow in size as you type information into them. In some cases, a database designer can make a field fixed-length to keep the integrity of the data consistent. For example, he might design the area code field to accept only three characters.

For the most part, information that you place in Notes fields can be copied, moved, or deleted as you would in any word processor. However, as stated above, the ability to format text and paragraphs in a field is reserved for rich text fields.

Formatting Text

You can change character formatting in any rich text field to make your documents more interesting or attractive, or to emphasize important text. As pictured in Figure 14.1, character formatting includes working with the following characteristics:

- **Font**—Apply a typeface to text in the document. For example, you can make a title stand out by applying a different typeface to it. You are limited to the fonts available in your operating system.

- **Size**—Apply a size to the text to increase or decrease the size of the printed or displayed text. Typically, larger text (say, 24-point size) commands more attention, and smaller text (10-point, for example) is reserved for details.

- **Style**—Apply special text formatting—plain, bold, italic, underline, strikethrough, subscript, superscript, shadow, emboss, or extrude—to add emphasis and clarity to your document.

- **Color**—Apply color to text to further define the text in your document.

 Try these keyboard hotkeys:—**Ctrl+B** for Bold, **Ctrl+I** for Italic, **Ctrl+U** for Underlining, **F2** to increase the font size, **Shift+F2** to decrease the font size. More hotkeys are listed in the Text pull-down menu.

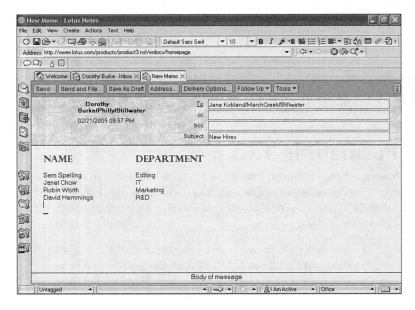

FIGURE 14.1 Character formatting makes your documents more attractive and easier to read if you don't overdo the number of fonts and types of formatting.

Select your text before you apply formatting. There are several methods of applying text formatting after you have selected it:

- **Status bar**—If you customized your Status bar to show font and font size, you click directly on the font name and font size and select your new choices from the pop-up lists.

- **Menu**—Press **Alt+T** on your keyboard to open the **Text** menu or click on **Text**. Select your character formatting from the pull-down menu.

- **Text Properties box**—Press **Ctrl+K** or select **Text, Text Properties** from the menu bar. Font properties are changed in the first tab as seen in Figure 14.2.

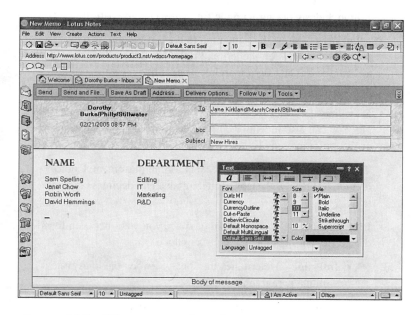

FIGURE 14.2   When you are done formatting your text, close the Properties Box by clicking on the X in the upper-right corner.

- **Tools**—Bold and Italic **Icons** and Font and Font Size drop-downs are available on the Text Formatting toolbar by default.

- **Right-click**—Choose the most common types of text formatting from the shortcut menu.

Formatting Paragraphs

You apply paragraph formatting for the same reasons as you apply character formatting—that is, to add emphasis and clarity to your documents. It is helpful to view the ruler in Notes as you work. To display the ruler, place your cursor in a rich text field (such as the body of a memo) and choose **View, Ruler** from the menu. As pictured in Figure 14.3, paragraph formatting includes working with the following characteristics:

- **Alignment**—Move the paragraph to the left margin or right margin, center it between the left and right margins, fully justify it to both the left and right margins, or continue it past the right margin without word wrapping.

- **Margins**—Set ruler measurements for your left and right margin. You can also indent or outdent the first line of a paragraph or the entire paragraph.

- **Tab Stops**—Set ruler measurements for tab placement. Choices include left tabs, right tabs, centered tabs, and decimal place tabs.

- **Line Spacing**—Set the amount of space you want between lines of text in your document. Choices include

  - **Interline**—Determines the space between the lines of text within a paragraph.

  - **Above**—Determines extra space added above a paragraph.

  - **Below**—Determines extra space added below a paragraph.

  - **Single, 1$\frac{1}{2}$, or Double**—Sets the spacing for the selected paragraph.

- **Lists**—Extremely helpful for adding emphasis to documents, each item on the list is preceded by sequential numbers, bullets, check boxes, square boxes, or circles.

Ruler

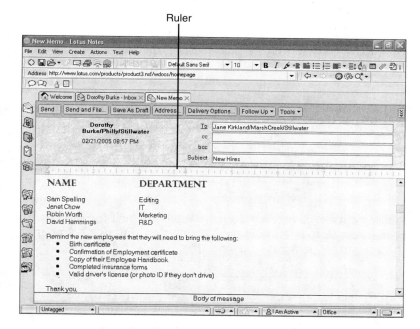

FIGURE 14.3   Very effective documents are created when you combine both character and paragraph formatting.

Like formatting text, you can change formatting options before you begin typing or you can select your typed paragraph and then apply formatting. There are several methods of applying paragraph formatting after you have selected your paragraph:

- **Menu**—Press **Alt+T** on your keyboard to open the **Text** menu. Select your individual paragraph formatting from the pull-down menu.

- **Keyboard Hotkeys**—**F8** for Indent, **Shift+F8** for Outdent. *Hint: Hotkeys are listed in the Text pull-down menu.*

- **Text Properties box**—Press **Ctrl+K** or select **Text, Text Properties** from the menu bar. Paragraph properties are changed in the second and third tab, as seen in Figure 14.4.

- **Icons**—Alignment, Indent, Outdent, and List icons are available by default on the toolbar.

- **Right-click**—Choose the most common types of paragraph formatting from the shortcut menu.

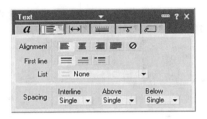

Figure 14.4   Click on the Paragraph tab of the text formatting properties box to select paragraph formatting options. Click on the third tab to set paragraph margins.

 In Notes, a paragraph is defined as text contained between hard paragraph returns (which you create by pressing **Enter**). To see your paragraphs as you type, choose **View, Show, Hidden Characters**. To maintain formatting options but put a return within a paragraph (called a soft return) press **Shift + Enter**.

If you find yourself frequently reformatting paragraphs to look a certain way, you should use styles for this purpose. After formatting your paragraph the way you want it to look, and while the text cursor is still in the paragraph, open the Text properties box, click the last (Paragraph Styles) tab, and click the Create Style button. Give your style a name, select any of the other options you like, and choose OK. Later, whenever you want a paragraph to look as defined by the style, you can place the text cursor in the paragraph and select your defined style from the Paragraph Style list in the Status bar.

Using the Permanent Pen and Highlighter

The permanent pen enables you to add text in a different color, typeface and type style, or font than the default font settings so that it stands out from the rest of the document. This is especially useful for collaborative projects because each user can work in a different color permanent pen; everyone can see who contributed to the document by the color of the text. This feature is easier to use when you want to apply the same text formatting to noncontiguous text that you've already typed, or when you are inserting new text into existing text such as comments. Permanent pen only works in a rich text field such as the body of a message. The default permanent pen is bold red text.

When a message or document is forwarded to you from another person, you can edit your copy of the original message. However, because it is not appropriate to modify the sender's text without her knowledge, use permanent pen to add your own comments before forwarding it on to anyone else.

To turn on the permanent pen, choose **Text, Permanent Pen, Use Permanent Pen** or click the **Permanent Pen** icon. "Permanent Pen enabled" displays in the status bar at the bottom of your screen. Then, type the text you want to appear in the permanent pen style. To stop using the permanent pen and begin using normal text again, click the **Permanent Pen** Icon again, or remove the check mark next to **Use Permanent Pen** in the menu.

Strikethrough text is used to mark text that you want to edit out (for example: ~~Outlook~~ Notes). To accomplish this with the permanent pen, first select the words you want to strike through. Then use the hotkey combination **Shift+Backspace** to mark the text.

To change the look of the permanent pen from the default bold red text, type some text and apply the formatting to that text. Then, select the text and choose **Text, Permanent Pen, Set Permanent Pen Style**. In setting the permanent pen formatting, you can set the font, the font color, and the size and style.

Another useful tool for collaborating or bringing someone's attention to text is the *highlighter*. It looks just like you used a highlighting marker on your text. Choose **Text, Highlighter** from the menu and then select your color: yellow, blue, or pink. As you drag your mouse cursor over text, the background color of the text changes.

You can also highlight selected text. After you select the text, turn on the highlighter and Notes will apply the highlighting to the selected text.

Don't forget to turn the highlighter off when you are done by choosing **Text, Highlighter** and deselecting the highlighter color.

Creating Links

Links are pointers to other documents, views, or Lotus Notes databases. If you want to send a mail message and refer to a page in the Help database, you can create a document link in your mail message. When the recipient receives your mail, he can click the **Document Link** icon and see the page to which you are referring.

There are four types of Lotus Notes links that you can create and include in your mail messages or Lotus Notes documents (see Table 14.1).

It's important to understand that links only work when they are linked to documents, views, and databases to which others have access. If you link to a document that has been deleted or to a database not available to or accessible by the person to whom you are sending the link (such as your Mail database), it simply won't work.

TABLE 14.1 Types of Links

This Icon	Named	Does This
	Document Link	Connects to another Lotus Notes document. It can be a document in the same database or within an entirely different database. Double-clicking a document link results in the linked document appearing on the screen.
	Anchor Link	Connects to a *specific location* in the same document, or in a different document.
	Database Link	Connects to another database opened at its default view.
	View Link	Connects to a specific view in the current or different database.

Document Links

The examples in this chapter create links from a Mail Memo to a document located in the Help database. We use the example of the help database because we can't be certain of other databases your company has made available to you. If you create a link to your local copy of the Help database, the link won't work so if you're following our example, be certain to create a link to the server copy of the Help database. If you have access to discussion databases or other types of Lotus Notes databases, try these exercises using those databases instead of the Help and mail databases.

To create a document link, follow these steps:

1. Begin a mail message by filling in the header (address, subject line, and so on) information.

2. In the body field of your message, type a sentence telling the recipient what information is in the document that's linked to your Mail Memo (this is a courtesy, not a requirement). You might type something such as **I'm learning how to create a document link. If you want to learn too, click here**.

3. Press the **Spacebar** (or to create an arrow **-->** press spacebar, dash, dash, greater than sign) at the end of your sentence.

4. Choose **Help, Help Topics** from the menu to open the Help database. Click on the **Working with Documents** twistie to expand the topic, and then expand **Linking to other data**. Click the **Creating Links to Documents, Views, Folders or Databases** topic to open it.

5. With the Help document open, choose **Edit, Copy as Link, Document Link** from the menu.

6. You created your document link. The next step is to paste it into your mail message. Return to your Inbox and click on the New Memo task button.

7. Place your cursor at the end of your sentence, remembering to leave the blank space. Choose **Edit, Paste** to insert the Document Link icon into your mail message (see Figure 14.5).

8. Send your mail message. Press **Esc** to close the Help database if you haven't already.

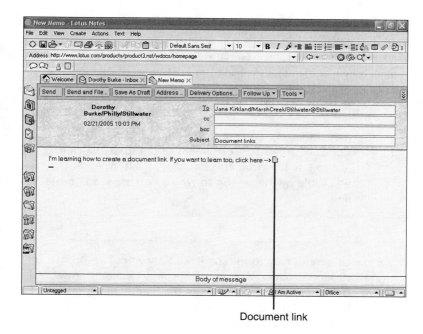

Document link

FIGURE 14.5   A document link is inserted at the position of your cursor when you create the link.

You can see the results of your document link by looking at the copy of the mail message you just sent. Open the Sent view of your mailbox and double-click the copy of the mail message you just created. If you want to display the name of the linked document, point at the document link icon and hold your mouse pointer there without clicking. A small hand appears, pointing at the link icon.

If you want to see the linked document, click the **Document Link** icon.

Lotus Notes automatically creates document links when you use the reply option of Mail. Look in your Inbox and locate a mail message you've received as a reply. It's easy to identify replies when you use the Discussion Thread view because the replies are indented. You can generally find them in your Inbox, too, because the subject line usually starts with **Re:**. Double-click to open a reply. You see a document link located at the end of the subject line. Lotus Notes automatically placed that document link; it points to the message to which this message is replying. Click the document link, and you can see the original message. This is an extremely helpful Mail tool, enabling you to easily work your way back through the path of mail messages.

 Remember, the success of links depends on the proper rights, or access to a document or database. Be careful not to link to documents or databases that are not accessible by the person to whom you are sending the link.

 One quick way to see the linked document without clicking on the document link icon is to choose **View, Document Link Preview** from the menu. The name of the linked document appears in a Preview pane at the bottom of the screen.

Anchor Links

To link to a particular location in a document, you should use an *anchor link*. Anchor links consist of an anchor and a link. You can use anchor links entirely within a single document or split between two documents. A table of contents is an example of using anchor links entirely within one document; you create the anchor in the content paragraph and the link in the table of contents. When the reader clicks the link, the document scrolls to the anchor paragraph. If the anchor and link are split between two documents, clicking the link in one document would cause the second document to open, then scroll to the anchor paragraph.

1. Open the document you want to link to and put it in **Edit** mode (try using **Ctrl+E** to do so). If the document you want to link to is the same one you are working in, you will have to save the document (**Ctrl+S**) before you can create an anchor link in it.

2. Place your cursor anywhere in the content paragraph that you want to link to.

3. Choose **Edit, Copy as Link, Anchor Link** from the menu. A dialog will open, showing the first few words of the paragraph. Edit or accept the words, then click **anchor**. A small anchor link icon appears next to the paragraph (it can only be seen in Edit mode).

4. If you want to place the link in the same document, place the text cursor at the point in the document where you want the link to appear. If you want to open the document where you want to place the link, making sure that it is in Edit mode.

5. Click where you want the link to appear, and then choose **Edit, Paste** from the menu.

 Mail has a special **Link Message** mail memo you can use to send document links. When Mail is open, choose **Create, Special, Link Message**. A mail memo opens with **Link Message** as the subject (you can add to this) and a place in the body for you to paste the link. Instructions are already in the memo that tell the recipient to open the document by clicking on the link icon. You only need to enter the recipient information and send it.

Database Links

A database link connects to the default view of another database. To create a database link, choose **Edit, Copy as Link, Database Link** from the menu while the database is opened.

View Links

A view link works similarly to document links and database links. To create a view link, follow the previous steps, but open the view to which you want to link when you copy your view link. Choose **Edit, Copy as Link, View Link** as your menu commands.

Creating Hotspots

Hotspots are areas, usually text or pictures, where you click and then a new website opens, or a new document appears, or you see a small balloon pop up with additional text. You can only create hotspots in a rich text field, such as the body of a mail memo.

Text Pop-up Hotspots

When you point to a highlighted or boxed-in word or phrase and see a rectangle appear above or below the word with more text, that is a *text pop-up hotspot*. This type of hotspot is handy to further clarify a sentence or word. Recipients can mouse over the hotspot and the additional information appears. Point to the text and the additional text appears with the explanation of the term, as seen in Figure 14.6.

To create a text pop-up hotspot in a mail memo, follow these steps:

1. Begin a mail message by filling in the header information.

2. In the body of the mail message, type your message. Determine which word(s) you want to become the text hotspot word or phrase (Figure 14.5 uses *TAW site*).

3. Highlight that word or phrase by selecting it with your mouse. Choose **Create, Hotspot, Text Pop-Up** from the menu.

4. The **HotSpot Pop-up Properties** box appears, as shown in Figure 14.7.

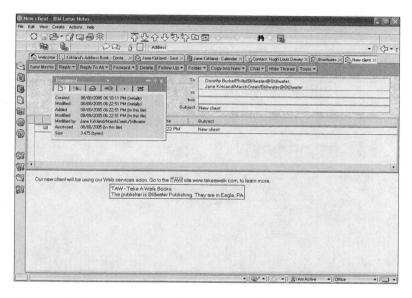

FIGURE 14.6 A text pop-up hotspot usually contains instructions, additional information, or directions.

5. In the Popup Text box, fill in the text you want to pop up when this hotspot is clicked. When you have finished typing the text, click the check mark.

6. Choose whether you want the pop-up to appear when the user holds the mouse over your text (**On mouse over**) or clicks on the pop-up (**On Click**).

7. Determine your hotspot appearance by selecting one of the Hotspot styles.

8. Close the Properties box. Finish and send your message.

You can see the effects of your pop-up by looking at the copy of your message in Sent mail.

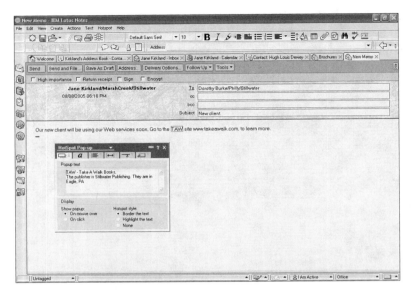

FIGURE 14.7   Additional help is available by clicking on the question mark in the upper-right corner of the HotSpot Pop-up Properties box.

Link Hotspots

A *link hotspot* is usually text or a picture that the user clicks to open a document, view, database, or URL. To add one to your mail message, follow these steps:

1. In the body of the mail message, type the text you want to serve as the link and then select it.

2. Choose **Create, Hotspot, Link Hotspot** from the menu.

3. In the HotSpot Resource Link properties box (see Figure 14.8), select the Type of hotspot you want to create:

FIGURE 14.8 When the user clicks on the text you turned into the hotspot link, he will go to the item specified in the Value field.

- **URL**—Use this type to link to a website. Enter the URL for the website in the Value field, such as **http://www.ibm.com**. Make sure to use the full address, including the "http://" at the beginning of the URL.

- **Link**—This type links to a document, anchor, view, or database. For this type of link to work, you must first go to the document, view, or database to which you want to link. Then choose **Edit, Copy As Link** from the menu and select the type of item you want. After you create the hotspot, **Link** will automatically be selected as the type and the Value will be the name of the item which you copied as the link.

- **Named Element**—To link to a view, a form, or a folder, use this type to specify the element. After you select **Named Element** from the Type field, a list field appears to the right with selections of the elements to which you can link. Select **View**, **Form**, or **Folder**. Below the field, click on the small folder icon to browse for the specific element you want. In the dialog box that appears (see Figure 14.9), select the **Database** where the element is and then select the element by name. Click **OK** to put that information into the Value field of the hotspot.

4. Close the properties box.

If you just want to put a URL link in a rich text field and you don't mind if the URL shows, you don't need to make a URL link hotspot. Just type the full address, such as **http://takeawalk.com**, or copy it from the address area of your browser and Notes will automatically make the hotspot for you.

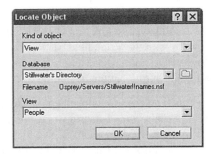

FIGURE 14.9   Make sure that the database and the element you select are ones to which the recipient has access, or he won't be able to open it from your link.

Inserting Tables

Tables offer an excellent way to organize data, and you can easily add tables to your mail messages. Figure 14.10 shows a mail message with a table inserted.

To insert a table in your mail message, follow these steps:

1. Create a new memo.

2. Position your cursor in the body field where you want the table to appear.

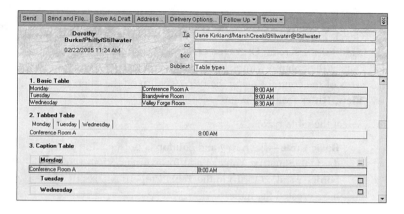

FIGURE 14.10 Here's a table created in three table types: 1. A Basic table, 2. A Tabbed table, and 3. A Caption table.

3. Choose **Create, Table** or click the **Insert Table** Icon. The Create Table dialog box appears (see Figure 14.11).

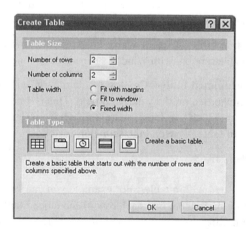

FIGURE 14.11 When you create a table, you must indicate the Table Type in the Create Table dialog box.The various types of tables available in Notes give you a lot of flexibility for saving space, drawing attention to rows, and displaying data in different formats.

4. Enter the number of Rows and Columns you want in your table. Check **Fixed Width** if you do not want the table to adjust to the width of the screen. Once you create a fixed-width table, you can set the column widths in the Table Properties box or drag the sizes of the columns using the ruler. To turn on the ruler, choose **View, Ruler** from the menu.

5. Select the table type:

- **Basic table**—Each row and column is presented in a standard table matrix. You can add formatting options (colors, borders, and so forth) in the Table Properties box after you have created the table.

- **Tabbed table**—Each row is presented as a different tabbed page. To move from row to row, click the tabs. Add labels for the tabs in the Table Properties box after you have created the table.

- **Animated table**—Creates a table which displays a different row every two seconds. Intervals can be set in the Table Properties box after you have created the table.

- **Caption table**—Creates a table in which each row shows as a clickable caption, with Windows expand and reduce buttons.

- **Programmed table**—Creates a table that presents a different row based on the value of a field. This is an advanced table in which you must create a field and so forth, and this type of table is beyond the scope of this book.

6. Click **OK**.

Tables can be created within tables. For example you can create a tabbed table then insert a basic table into each row of the tabbed table. Experiment with different table types and by inserting tables within tables to better understand the flexibility and power of tables in Lotus Notes.

You can also edit; insert columns and rows; and add borders, colors, and shading to tables. If you right-click an element of the table, the properties box appears, from which you can select properties for tables, rows, columns, or text (see Figure 14.12).

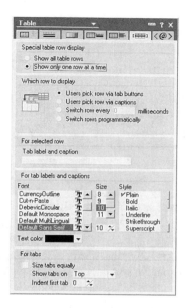

FIGURE 14.12   The Table Properties box contains options for table formatting such as the option for displaying tabs on any side of a table.

To help you determine which type of table is best for your use and to learn more about editing and formatting tables, search the Help database for *table*.

Creating Sections

Sections are helpful in making large documents more manageable. You can gather all the information on one topic into a section. Sections collapse into one-line paragraphs or expand to display all the text in the section, so a reader doesn't have to read sections that aren't of any interest. Figure 14.13 shows a document with both expanded and collapsed sections.

Twistie

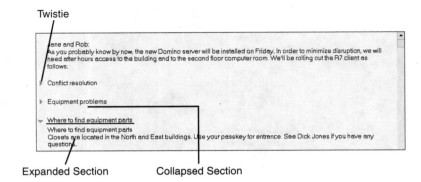

Expanded Section   Collapsed Section

FIGURE 14.13   Twisties are indicators that the document contains collapsed sections.

When you gather text into a section, a small triangle appears to the left of the section head. To expand a section, click this triangle (called a *twistie*). Clicking again on the twistie collapses the section. To expand all the sections in a document, choose **View, Expand All Sections** from the menu. To collapse all sections, choose **View, Collapse All Sections** from the menu.

To create a section in your message, follow these steps:

1. Create a new mail message. Type several paragraphs in the body field.

2. Select the paragraphs you want to make into a section. If you are creating a section from a single paragraph, you don't need to select the paragraph, simply place your cursor anywhere in the paragraph before you proceed to step 3.

3. Choose **Create, Section** from the menu.

The first 128 characters of the paragraph become the section title. If you want to change it, follow these steps:

1. Click the section title.

2. Choose **Section, Section Properties** from the menu (see Figure 14.14).

FIGURE 14.14   In the Section properties box, set the option to create a section title, visible even when the section is collapsed.

3. Click the **Title** tab.

4. Select Text, and then replace the text in the Title box with the section title you want. Don't use carriage returns, hotspots, or buttons in section titles.

5. Under Section Border, choose a **Border Style** from the list box and a **Border Color** from the list box.

6. If you want to hide the title of the section when it expands, click the **Expand/Collapse** tab, and check **Hide Title When Expanded** (see Figure 14.15).

7. If you want to format the section title, select it and choose **Section, Section Properties**. Click the **Font** tab; select the font, size, style, and color you want for the section title.

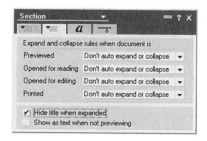

FIGURE 14.15   The Expand/Collapse tab of the Section Properties box is where you set expand and collapse options for each section.

You can copy and move sections as you would any other text or paragraphs with Cut, Copy, and Paste commands. When you want to remove a section but still want to keep all the text in the section, select the section and choose **Section, Remove Section** from the menu. If you want to remove the section and all its text, however, choose **Edit, Clear** or press the **Delete** key.

When sending documents containing sections over the Internet, the title of the section is lost but the text in the section remains. In that case you might want the title repeated in the section text.

In this chapter, you learned about enhancing your documents by applying character and paragraph formatting, using the permanent pen and the highlighter, and adding links, tables, and sections. In the next chapter, you learn how to create attachments.

LESSON 15
Working with Attachments

In this chapter, you learn how to create, manage, detach, and launch file attachments.

Understanding Attachments

There might be times when you want to send a file to someone through email. That file might be a Domino database, a spreadsheet, a word processing document, a compressed file, a graphics file, or a scanned photograph of your grandchildren—almost any type of file. In Lotus Notes, you can attach an entire file within the body of your mail message and send it. The file you attach is a copy, so your original remains intact on your computer.

The user who receives your mail can detach your file and save it. If the recipient has the same application program in which the file was created, she can launch the application, opening the file in its native application.

Be careful about opening an attachment. It could be a virus! If you have virus protection software running on your email, you should be notified if the attachment is a potential virus. But if you don't have virus software, you should not open any attachment unless you are expecting the file or know the person sending you the file.

Attachments can be placed only in rich text fields, and the body of the mail message (where you type your message) is the only rich text field in the Mail Message form.

 Although you tend to use attachments most often when working with your mail database, you can attach a file to any database document that has a rich text, or body, field. For example, in a personnel database there might be an attachment in a person's document that is a scanned picture—the person's portrait.

Creating Attachments

To attach a file to a Lotus Notes mail message, do the following:

1. Create the mail message. Make sure your insertion point (cursor) is in the message body at the exact point at which you want the attachment to appear.

2. Choose **File**, **Attach** or click the **Attach** icon on the toolbar. The Create Attachments dialog box appears, as shown in Figure 15.1.

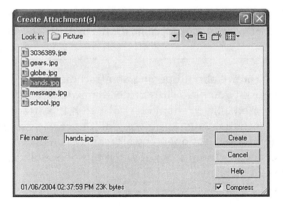

FIGURE 15.1 The Create Attachment(s) dialog box allows you to search for the file or files you wish to attach.

3. In the Create Attachments dialog box, select the location of the file from the Look In drop-down field and navigate to the location of the file in your file system.

4. The **Compress** box is enabled by default. Leave this box checked.

 Compressed files use less space on a disk and take less time to transfer from one place to another than uncompressed files. But don't have Notes compress a file that you intend to send to a non-Notes user; the mail router will just have to decompress the file again before transferring it because Notes uses proprietary compression techniques and other mail programs probably won't be able to decompress the file. If you want to compress a file for sending to a non-Notes mail recipient, use a compression program such as WinZip.

5. Click the **Create** button. The attached file appears as an icon within the body of your mail message (see Figure 15.2).

The appearance of the icon depends on the type of file it represents and whether you have the original software that this file was created in installed on your PC. If you are attaching an Adobe Acrobat PDF file, you see an Adobe Acrobat icon in your mail message. If the file is a Microsoft Word file, you see a Microsoft Word icon in your mail message. If you don't have native software installed for that file, you see a generic document icon.

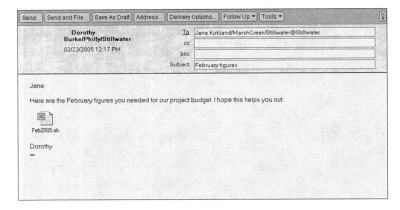

FIGURE 15.2 The attachment icon in this mail memo shows that the file is a Microsoft Excel spreadsheet.

When you receive mail that has an attachment, a paper clip icon appears next to the mail message in your Inbox (see Figure 15.3).

You can add attachments to Notes documents by dragging and dropping them from your file system. To do this, resize your Lotus Notes program window and open and resize your My Documents folder (or the Windows Explorer window that displays the file you want to drag). Place the windows side-by-side and drag the file from My Documents to a rich text field in your Lotus Notes document or mail memo.

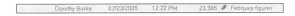

FIGURE 15.3 A paper clip icon in the Inbox indicates that the document has an attachment.

Viewing Attachments

When you receive an attached file, you can view, open, edit, save, or delete the file. Viewing a file means that you can see the file contents, even if you don't have the application in which the file was created. To view a file, open the mail message, double-click the attachment icon, and click the **View** button in the Properties box (see Figure 15.4). You might not be able to see the file exactly as it was originally formatted because the Notes Viewer doesn't read all formatting from all software programs, but the Viewer provides a menu that lets you see the file in different ways depending on the type of file. For example, you can display a spreadsheet file with or without gridlines. After you finish looking at the file, press **Esc** to leave the view.

FIGURE 15.4   The Attachment Properties box provides details about the file and enables you to view, open, edit, save, or delete the attachment.

Deleting Attachments

To delete the attached file, do the following:

1. Double-click the attached file icon.

2. Click the **Delete** button on the Properties box.

3. This removes the file from your email but first gives you a warning, as shown in Figure 15.5.

4. Click **Yes** to proceed and delete the attachment. A notation appears in the memo stating the attachment file name and who deleted it.

There are three possible reasons for failing to view or open an attachment. First, the Attachment Viewer must be installed on your PC in order to view the attachment. If it is not, consult with your Notes administrator. Second, the file you are trying to view must be one supported by Lotus Notes. Many types of files are supported by Lotus Notes; for a complete list, consult the **Help** database and from the **Index** view, do a quick search for **attachments**. Then click **supported file formats**, select **Opening, saving or deleting attachments** and click on **To view file attachments**. Lastly, if you're trying to *launch* the attachment, you must have access to the application that can display the file format.

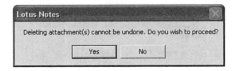

FIGURE 15.5 The Delete Attachment dialog box warns you that deleting a file cannot be undone. Deleting a file from an email does not save the file to your hard drive. Instead, it deletes the file completely.

When you reply with history to a mail message that has an attached file, or forward the message, you might not want to send the attachment on to the next recipient. You don't have to delete it from the reply; Notes will do that for you if you choose **Reply without Attachment(s)** or **Forward without Attachment(s)**.

Saving Attached Files

When you want to save a copy of the attached file to your own file system, you click **Save** on the Attachment properties box. The Save Attachment dialog box appears, as shown in Figure 15.6. Specify the drive and directory, or folder, in which you want to save the file. You can also rename the file in this dialog box by typing a new name in the File name field. Be sure to keep the same file extension when you rename a file. Click **OK**.

When you right-click an attachment you can see options for the attachment not shown in the Attachment dialog box, such as **Save and Delete** which saves the attachments and also deletes them from your email, saving valuable disk space, and **Save All** which allows you to save all attachments at once. Try right-clicking an attachment to explore the options.

You can watch the progress of the save on the Status bar. After the save is finished, a message appears on the Status bar telling you that the save is completed and in what drive and folder the file is saved.

To save, delete, or save and delete more than one attachment, right-click one of the attachments and choose **Save All**, **Save and Delete All**, or **Delete All** from the pop-up menu.

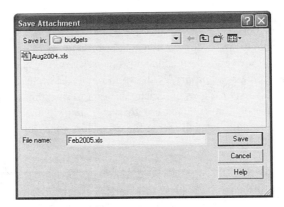

FIGURE 15.6   The Save Attachment dialog box. When you choose Save All, the title of this dialog box says "Save Attachments To:" and it will save all the attachments in your email to the folder you indicate.

Opening Files

If you want to look at an attached file in the application in which it was created, opening the file launches the application from within Notes mail. To open an attachment, double-click the attachment icon and then click the **Open** button on the Properties box. You can then view the document and make changes. You can save it or print it from the application. You can close the application when you finish with the file. Lotus Notes and your mail message remain open the entire time you are working in the other application.

If you can't launch the attachment, you probably don't have that application installed on your computer. You can still use the View option, as described in the beginning of this chapter, to view the formatted contents of the attachment.

Editing the Attachment

Editing an attachment allows you to open the attachment in its originating software, and when you save your changes, Notes automatically saves your changes in the attachment. You simply choose **Edit** in the attachment properties box, edit the document in Word, or whichever application the file was created in, click **Save**, and close Word, and you are automatically returned to the email in Lotus Notes. Press the **Esc** key and Notes will ask you if you want to save your changes. Click **Save**. Now you can reply with attachments to that email, and your edited attachment will be returned to the recipient.

If you edit documents and return the edited copy to the sender, it's a good idea to save the document with a different file name. For example, if you receive PressRelease1.doc for your review and you open and edit the document, save it as PressRelease1R.doc so everyone knows that the document has been edited and is different than the document you originally received.

If you decide to make changes to a file you launched and you want to save two versions, the one you received and the one you made changes to, use the Save As command to give it a name you will remember. At the same time, specify a location on your computer where you want to store the file. Saving changes this way does not affect the original attachment sent to you.

Printing an Attachment

The easiest way to print an attachment is to open it in its originating software. If, however, you don't have the originating software installed, complete the following steps:

1. Double-click the attachment icon to open the File Properties box.

2. Click the **View** button on the Properties box.

3. Choose **File**, **Print**. The File Print dialog box appears. The default setting in the File Print dialog box is to print all of the document. If you want to print only a portion of the attachment, highlight that segment before you choose **File**, **Print**. Then, after you open the File Print dialog box, choose **Selection** under Print

Range. For more information on printing, see Chapter 4,
"Managing Mail."

4. Click **OK** to print the document.

Unexpected results, such as code lines or unusual characters, might occur
when you print from the viewer. Whenever possible, therefore, it is better
to print from the native application.

 Although sending attachments seems faster and easier
than embedding files, Notes does have the capability
to embed files. By embedding instead of attaching
files, recipients do not need additional software to
read the contents of your file. We suggest you learn
more about embedding files in the Notes Help
Database to see if embedding is a better option for
you.

In this chapter, you learned how to create, launch, edit, detach, and print
attachments. In the next chapter, you learn how to access your mail from
the Web when you don't have Notes available.

LESSON 16

WebMail and Domino Web Access

In this chapter, you will learn how to access your Mail, Calendar, and To Do list when you away from the office and don't have a computer with you that has Lotus Notes installed on it.

Accessing Mail from a Web Browser

What do you do when you are not in the office and the only computer available to you does not have Lotus Notes on it? Don't panic. As long as your Domino administrator has set up the mail server to allow you access to your mail via the Web, all you need is a computer with an Internet connection. Just make sure before you leave town that you ask your administrator for the following information:

- Your user name. This may be the same user name as you use in Lotus Notes, or it could be a shortened version of your name.

- Your *Internet password*. This is only used when you need web access to a Notes database.

- The URL you must enter to access your mail file. This is usually in this format: http://server.organization.com/mail/yourname.nsf.

Your *Internet password* is automatically assigned to you by your Domino administrator. Depending on policy settings established by your system administrator, you will initially have either no Internet password or your password will be the same as your Notes password. To change your Internet password, enter the URL for your Mail with **?changepassword** added to the end, such as http://server.organiztion.com/mail/ yourname.nsf?changepassword. When the Change Password dialog box appears, enter you old password and then your new password, and then confirm your new password by typing it again. Click **Submit**. Your old and your new passwords are both usable for the next two days. Keep in mind that if you are changing your Lotus Notes password you might also be changing your Internet password, depending upon the choices your system administrator made when setting up Lotus Notes.

When you need to access your mail, open the web browser (such as Microsoft Internet Explorer or Netscape Navigator) for the computer you are using and enter the URL in the address field. A login dialog box appears where you enter your user name and password. That will authenticate you with the server and identify you as having access to your mail file.

How your mail looks and works after you open it depends on whether you are set up to use WebMail or Domino Web Access.

Using WebMail

After you log in, your mail opens in your web browser. *WebMail* looks similar to the way Mail appears in Lotus Notes (see Figure 16.1), but there are some differences.

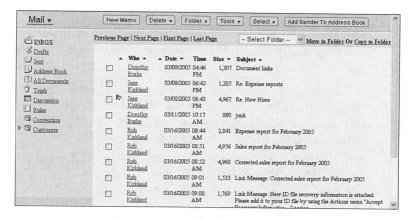

FIGURE 16.1 To open a document in a view or folder in WebMail, you click the link for the name of the sender (or recipient for sent mail).

- The Navigation pane shows all the folders and views as links. When you click on one, such as Inbox, it changes to the same word all in uppercase (INBOX). The navigation links change to a different color after you open one to show you have already visited that view or folder.

- The toolbars you see belong to your browser software. The only buttons available in WebMail are the Action bar buttons, and there are fewer buttons available than in Notes. For example, you don't see **Reply To** or **Follow Up** in the Inbox view.

- To see another screen of mail messages in the View pane, use the **Previous Page**, **Next Page**, **First Page**, and **Last Page** links.

- When you want to select messages, you click the checkbox to the left of the message or click the **Select** Action button and choose **Select all** or **Deselect all**.

- To move or add a message to a folder, choose the name of the folder from the **Select Folder** list and then click the **Move to Folder** or **Copy to Folder** link.

- Your Personal Address Book is not available from WebMail. WebMail has its own address book. See the section on "Working with the WebMail Address Book" later in this chapter to learn how to set up contacts.

- When you want to delete a mail message, you must select it and then click the **Delete** button on the Action bar. Select **Delete**. That marks the message for deletion, adds it to the Trash folder, and displays a small trash can to the left of the document. To completely remove the message from your database, click **Delete, Empty Trash** on the Action bar.

Creating and Replying to Messages

To create a new message in WebMail, click the **New Memo** button on the Action bar. The memo form is similar to the one you see in Notes (see Figure 16.2).

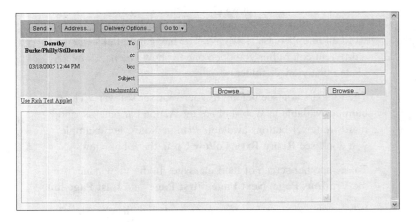

FIGURE 16.2 From any document, you can return to the Inbox, Calendar, or To Do by making the appropriate choice under the Go To button.

You can enter the full email addresses of the recipients or click the Address button to open a dialog box that lets you select names from the organization directory or your address book.

You can only attach two files to the memo. Click the **Browse** button for each file and select a file on your computer (or a CD, DVD, or floppy disk inserted in the PC's drives).

The body field is just one big empty box where you can type your message. If the web browser is set up to use Java applets, click the Use Rich Text Applet link (you will lose anything you have put into the memo up to that time). The memo will refresh and display a new toolbar above the body field (see Figure 16.3) that allows you to format the body text, add and edit tables, and cut, copy, and paste.

FIGURE 16.3   If you want to send a message with formatted text, you have to enable the Rich Text Applet. Then this toolbar appears.

> Don't know if your browser is set up for Java applets? Search the browser Help for Java applet to find out how to turn the setting on, if it isn't already set. In Microsoft Internet Explorer 6.0, for example, you check the setting by going to **Tools, Internet Options** on the menu. Select the **Advanced** tab and scroll down to **Java (Sun)** or **Microsoft VM** to see if the options are enabled.

To reply to a mail message, you have to open the message first. You click on the name of the sender to open it. In the open memo, click on the **Reply** button on the Action bar and choose one of the reply options: **Reply, Reply with History, Reply without Attachment(s), Reply to All, Reply to All with History,** or **Reply to All without Attachments.** If you just reply or reply to all, the recipient(s) names appear in the To field (you can't go back and choose Reply to All afterwards; you have to use the Address button to add recipients) and the Subject is filled in. The body field displays without the Java applet toolbar, unless you reply with history.

Delivery options are limited in WebMail. You can set the importance, request a delivery report, set delivery priority, or get a return receipt.

After you complete the mail message, click the **Send** button on the Action bar and choose **Send**, **Send and Save**, or **Save as Draft**.

Your Calendar and To Do list are also available with WebMail. To see either of these from one of the views, click on **Mail** at the top of the Navigation pane and select **Switch to Calendar** or **Switch to To Do**. From an open mail memo, click the **Go To** button and select **Calendar** or **To Do**.

Working with the WebMail Address Book

Your *WebMail address book* doesn't automatically synchronize with your Personal Address Book in Lotus Notes. To add new contacts, you can do one of these:

- Click the **Address Book** link to open up the Contacts view. Then click the **New, Contact** button on the Action bar. Fill out the information in the Contact document (see Figure 16.4). Click **Save and Close** to save it.

- From the **Contacts** view, click the **Import from Directories** button on the Action bar. In the Import Contacts and Groups dialog box (see Figure 16.5), select the directory and then the names of the people you want to add as contacts. Click **OK** to add them to your Contacts list.

- From the Inbox, select a document sent by the person and then click the **Add Sender to Address Book** button on the Action bar.

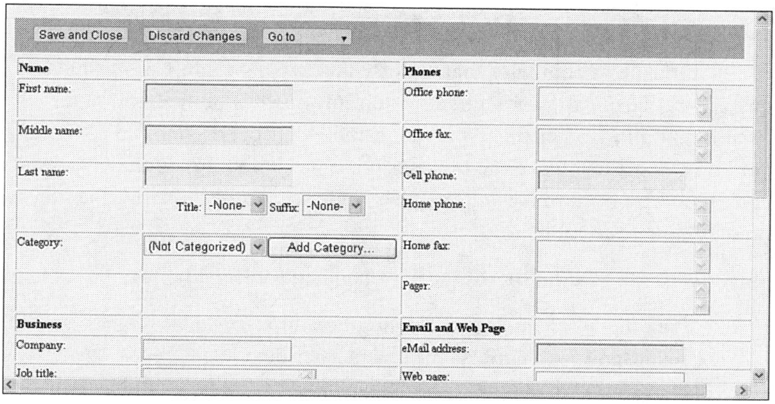

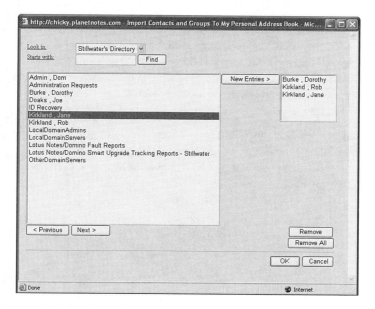

FIGURE 16.4   Fill out the Contact form to add someone to your Address Book. Make sure you put in an email address if you want to send mail to the person.

FIGURE 16.5   Select the name of the person and click New Entries to put them into the New Entries list. Then click OK to add them to your contacts.

Logging Out of WebMail

If you are using a computer that is not your own, you don't want to leave
any traces of your files or authentication information on that computer.
That might allow other people on the same PC to open your mail. To prevent this, don't just leave the browser open when you are done with the
computer. You need to *log out* properly and have WebMail close the window by doing the following:

1. Click on **Mail** in the Navigation pane and select **Logout**.

2. When the WebMail Logout dialog box appears, click **Logout &
Close Browser Window** to protect your data.

Using Domino Web Access

Domino Web Access is a more robust product than WebMail, giving you
access to Mail, Calendar and Scheduling, To Do, Contacts, and more.

Your Domino administrator must set up your mail database to use the
Domino Web Access mail template before you can use the product. You
access your mail the same way you do with WebMail, using the URL,
user name, and password supplied to you by your Domino administrator,
but because your mail is using the Domino Web Access template, you see
a different user interface.

When you open Domino Web Access for the first time, you will need to
download the Domino Web Access Control from IBM Corporation.
Answer **Yes**, so you will have all the components you need to run the
software properly.

Domino Web Access works with these web browsers: Microsoft Internet Explorer 5.5 or later, and Mozilla 1.4.1 and 1.7.1 browsers for Linux clients. Optimally, the screen resolution of your PC monitor should be 1024x768 pixels, but 800x600 pixels is acceptable. Font size settings are controlled by the browser. You'll also need to have Adobe Acrobat Reader 4.0 or later loaded on the PC if you want to print Calendar entries.

The Domino Web Access screen displays several tabs for the different tasks available to you while using the software (see Figure 16.6):

FIGURE 16.6 Click Edit Layout to customize your Welcome page. Select a layout of up to four panes and then choose the contents you want in each pane of your new layout, such as the Inbox, Schedule, To Do list, a web page, or Quick Links (a list of web page links).

- **Welcome**—This is the opening screen, and you may be able to customize it to fit your needs, depending on the settings made by the Domino administrator.

- **Mail**—Click on the tab to see your Mail or click on the down arrow on the tab to select a particular view to open or choose to create a new mail memo.

- **Calendar**—Click on the tab to see your Calendar or click on the down arrow to select a Calendar view (one-day, one-week, two-week, month and so on) or to look at views of your Meeting Notices or your Group Calendars. You can also choose to create a new Calendar entry from the menu.

- **To Do**—Click on the tab to see your To Do list or click on the down arrow to see one-day, one-week, one-month or one-year versions of your To Do list. You can also choose to create a new To Do.

- **Contacts**—Click on the tab to see your list of contacts or click on the down arrow to choose to create a new contact or a new e-mail group. Contacts that you create here are stored in your mail database. Contacts that you create when using Lotus Notes are stored in your Personal Directory. You can synchronize the two contact lists by opening your mail database in Lotus Notes and choosing Actions, Synchronize Address Book.

- **Notebook**—The Notebook allows you to create documents where you can keep important information or write notes to yourself about what you are doing, like you can do with the Personal Journal in Lotus Notes. Click on the tab to see your Notebook or to create a new Notebook page. Pages that you create here are stored in your mail database. You can synchronize your Notebook documents with your Personal Journal by opening your mail database in Lotus Notes and choosing Actions, Synchronize Journal.

Depending on whether or not Instant Messaging has been set up by your administrator, you may also be able to use Chat when using Domino Web Access. Check with your administrator to see what you have to do to use this feature.

 Domino Web Access can also be set up to work with Microsoft Outlook. See your Domino administrator if you need this configuration.

Creating and Replying to Mail

To create a new mail memo in Domino Web Access, do the following:

1. Click the down arrow on the **Mail** tab.

2. Choose **New Message** from the drop-down menu.

3. A mail memo form opens in a new window (see Figure 16.7).

4. Enter the email addresses of the recipients. Click the **To:, cc:,** or **bcc:** buttons to select names from your Contacts list or the organization directory.

5. Enter a Subject and then type your message in the Body field. Notice that you have a full toolbar above the field that has tools for text formatting, inserting and editing tables, creating page breaks, inserting images, inserting links, spell checking, and selecting your dictionary language. The toolbar disappears if you choose **Plain Text from the Format** button on the Action bar at the top of the memo window.

6. (Optional) If you want to add attachments to the message, click on the small down arrow next to Attachments to expand the Add Attachments area of the memo form. Click the folder icon to browse your file system for the attachment(s) you want to make (click the trash can when you want to delete a selected

attachment). The remaining tools above the attachment field control how the list of files is displayed.

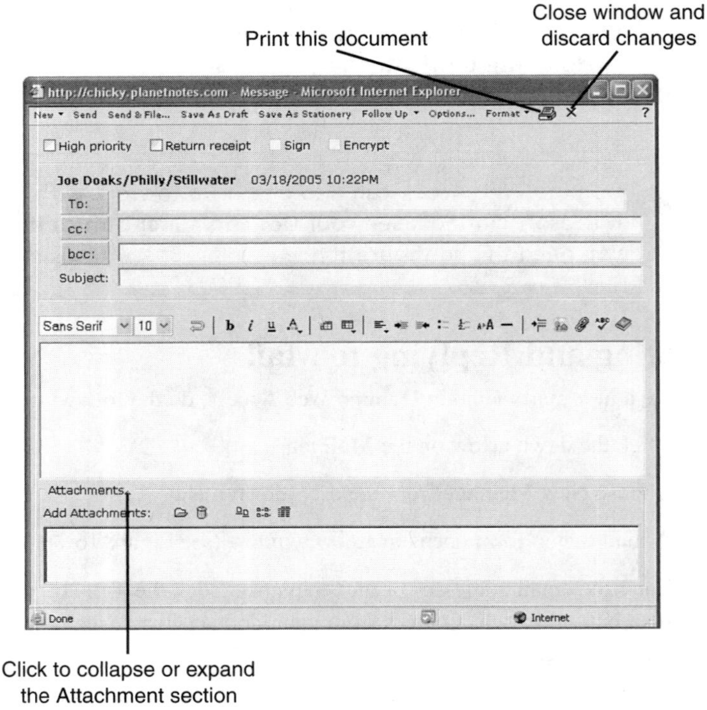

FIGURE 16.7   The Domino Web Access mail memo offers most of the same options as Lotus Notes Mail.

7. (Optional) Set your delivery options by selecting the checkboxes at the top of the memo: **High Priority**, **Return Receipt**, **Sign**, or **Encrypt** (for more information on these options, see Chapter 3, "Email Basics"). For more delivery option choices, click the **Options** button on the Action bar. In the Delivery Options dialog box, you can set Delivery Report options, select a priority other than High Priority, choose your security options, and ask for a return receipt.

8. (Optional) Click the **Follow Up** button on the Action bar if you need to flag this message for further action later. Select **Quick Follow Up** to flag the message automatically with normal priority; select **Add/Edit Flag** to open a dialog box where you can choose the priority (urgent, normal or low), enter text about the follow up action, set a follow up date and time, and set a reminder alarm. The **Remove Flag** option removes any existing flags (for more information on using the Follow Up feature, see Chapter 4, "Managing Mail").

9. (Optional) Click the **Print This Document** icon on the Action bar to print the memo.

10. Click one of the following Action bar buttons:

   • **Send** to simply send the message without saving it.

   • **Send & File** to send the message and select a folder where you want to store a copy.

   • **Save As Draft** to save the memo so you can complete it later and send it then.

   • **Save As Stationery** to save the memo as a form memo that you can use later. This is a good way to handle repetitive mail messages you must send.

11. The memo window closes.

When you receive an email, it displays in red in the Inbox until you open and read it. In the Inbox view, press **Enter** to open the selected memo or double-click on the document. The message opens in a separate window (see Figure 16.8).

The Action buttons give you the same options as you would have with an email you receive in Notes: Reply (to just the sender or all, with or without history, with or without attachments, or with internet-style history), Forward (with or without attachments or in Internet-style), Move (to a folder or copy to a folder), and Follow Up (add or edit flags, remove them, or just do a Quick flag). From the Tools button you can add the sender to your Contacts list or copy the memo into a new Calendar entry or To Do. There are also buttons to Show Mail Threads, edit the document, print the document, delete the document, or close the window. If you choose to show mail threads, a section appears at the bottom of the memo window that shows a view of the current memo and all the related memos in the full conversation.

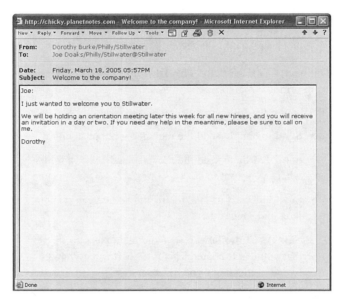

FIGURE 16.8 Click the up and down arrows on the Action bar of the memo to go to the next or previous memo in the Inbox view.

 To get assistance on the tasks you need to perform, click the **Help** button (the question mark) in the upper right corner of the Domino Web Access window and choose either **Help Topics** or **Help on this page**. You will also find a ? (question mark) on most windows. Click it and open a Help window on what to do within that window.

Using the Calendar

The Calendar in Domino Web Access has most of the features of your Lotus Notes Calendar. You can view it in One Day, Two Day, Five Day, One Week, Two Week, One Month or One Year formats (see Figure 16.9). You can also view a list of meeting notices or your group calendars. Select the one you want to view from either the Calendar Navigation pane or by clicking the down arrow next to the Calendar tab.

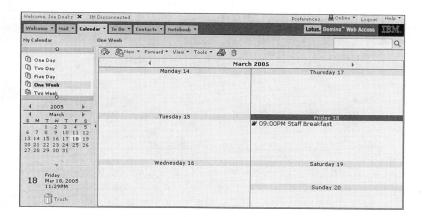

FIGURE 16.9   You click on New to create a Calendar Entry.

In the Calendar Entry window (see Figure 16.10), click the down arrow on the **Appointment** tab to choose the type of entry you want to create: Meeting, Appointment, All Day Event, Anniversary, or Reminder.

For an appointment you enter the Subject and set the **Starting Date** and **Time** and **Duration**. You can enter a **Location** or set a **Category**. You can even set an **Alarm** to alert you prior to the appointment. Click the down arrow next to **Details** to see a body field where you can enter more information. If you want to add an attachment, click the down arrow next to **Attachments** to expand that section. For an appointment that has regularly set times, you can click the **Repeat** tab to set up the subsequent dates and times.

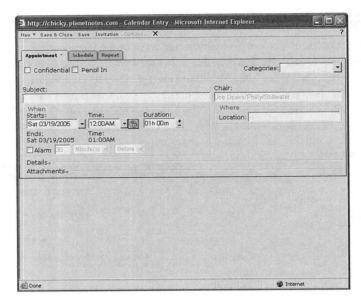

FIGURE 16.10   This Calendar Entry window is set up to create an appointment. Select another type of entry from the Appointment tab to schedule meetings, all day events, anniversaries, or reminders.

Both all day events and anniversaries show the starting date, but not the time or duration. A reminder is similar but also has a time setting. Repeats can be set for all.

Meetings are more elaborate because they also include Invitees, Optional, and FYI recipients, as well as showing Rooms and Resources. You can even set up Online Meetings and send invitations. Use the Schedule tab to see the free times of all invitees (if they have allowed their free time to be seen) and pick a mutually acceptable meeting time. Click the Repeat tab to set up repeat meetings.

For more information on creating Calendar entries, see Chapter 9, "Using the Calendar." Learn more about setting up meetings in Chapter 10, "Working with Meetings and Group Calendaring."

Using the Contacts List

If you already had contacts listed in your Personal Address Book when you first opened Domino Web Access, those contacts will not appear in the Domino Web Access Contacts list. To add them, open your mail database in Lotus Notes and choose Actions, Synchronize Address Book.

You can add new contacts by doing one of the following:

- Click the arrow on the **Contacts** tab and select **New Contact** or **New E-mail Group.** The Contact Information dialog box opens (see Figure 16.11).

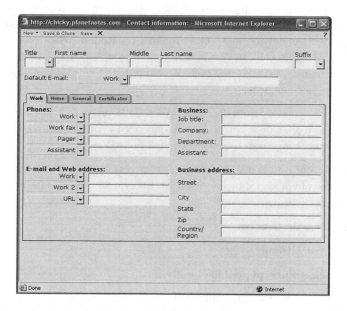

Figure 16.11 In the Contact Information form, you can click the down arrows next to the field labels to choose the appropriate label for the data you are entering. For example, when you click the arrow next to Work (under Phones) you can select Work, Work 2, Work 3, Home, and so on.

- With the Contacts list open, click the arrow on the **New** button on the Action bar and select **Contact** or **E-mail Group**. The Contact Information dialog box opens.

- With a mail memo open, click the **Tools** button on the Action bar and select **Add Sender to Contacts**.

Using Domino Web Access Offline

Being away from the office may also mean that you can't maintain a connection at all times with the server. Provided your Domino administrator has set your mail file up to work offline, you can create mail, make new contacts, schedule appointments, add To Do items, and make Notebook entries without having a network or Internet connection. When you are connected again, you can *synchronize* your copy of the Mail database with the one on the server to bring both copies up to date with additions, modifications, and deletions.

Before you go away from the office, you need to set up Domino Web Access to work with *offline* mail. You only need to do this setup once, unless you change your user name or your user ID expires.

Because your offline mail is vulnerable to access by other parties, your first step is to protect it by encrypting it. Encrypt your local mail file by following these steps:

1. Click **Preferences**.

2. Click **Offline**.

3. Select **Encrypt mail file locally**.

4. Choose **Simple Encryption** (protects against casual snooping), **Medium Encryption** (a balance between security, strength, and fast database access), or **Strong Encryption** (slows database access but is the best choice when security is all important).

5. Click **OK**.

Some of the other offline preferences may also be important for you to select:

- **Include server's Domino Directory**—This option won't appear unless your Domino administrator has made a condensed or extended directory catalog on your mail or directory server for you to take offline. You want to select this item so you can do address lookups offline; however, it will lengthen the synchronization process.

- **Compact mail file after sync**—You want to compact the mail file to reduce the amount of disk space it uses, but it will slow down the synchronization process.

- **Update full text index after sync**—This automatically updates the full text index for searching purposes, but enabling it will slow down the synchronization process.

- **Limit document attachments during sync**—If you enable this option, any attachments over 100K will be omitted during synchronization. It will minimize the size of your local mail file.

- **Only sync documents modified in last [specify] days**—This option limits the size of your local mail file and the amount of synchronization time by only synchronizing files created or modified in the specified time period.

You then need to install a synchronization manager to manage your offline subscriptions and work with your mail file offline. You will need your Notes ID to do this. This file is usually stored in your \notes\data directory and has an **.id** extension (such as user.id).

Follow these steps to install a synchronization manager:

1. Click the **Online** button on the top right of the Domino Web Access window and select **Go Offline**.

2. If your web browser is Microsoft Internet Explorer, click **Yes** to install Lotus Domino Sync Manager. If you use Linux Mozilla, click **Yes** to install DWA Sync.

3. Accept the license agreement.

4. Select a folder where you want your offline mail installed.

5. If prompted for a Notes ID, browse to select your ID file.

6. Enter and confirm a web application password (this is the password for your Notes ID).

After you have set up Domino Web Access to work offline, click the **Online** button and choose **Go Offline**. When you choose **Go Online** after you are connected again, your local mail file will synchronize with your mail file on the server.

Protecting Your Data

Browsers store pages that you read in them in a cache, so that they can redisplay the pages quickly if you decide to look at them again later on. When you access your mail database from a browser, potentially sensitive information gets cached. When you close your browser, that information may be left behind for some other browser user to peruse. If your organization cares about the security of the information you retrieve into your browser, specifically into your Domino Web Access mail reader, your administrator may have enabled a feature called Browser Cache Management, which causes Notes mail data to be purged from the browser cache when you log out of Domino Web Access.

Depending on how your administrator configured Browser Cache Management, it may install itself in your browser automatically when you load Domino Web Access, or you may have the option of installing/uninstalling it manually. (If your administrator hasn't enabled it, it won't be installable in your browser at all.) If you have the option of installing it manually, a category called "Logout" will appear in the Domino Web Access preferences page.

To install Browser Cache Management, do the following:

1. Click on **Preferences**.

2. Click on **Logout**.

3. Under Browser Cache Management, click the **Install** button.

4. Click **OK** to close the alert box that tells you Browser Cache Management is installed. Then click **OK** to close the Preferences dialog box.

Now, whenever you are ready to leave Domino Web Access, click **Logout** at the top right of the Domino Web Access window. You will see a message saying that you are logged out and that all mail-related files have been deleted from your Temporary Internet Files folder. Click the **Close Window** button.

In this chapter you learned about using WebMail and Domino Web Access to access your mail from a web browser. In the next chapter you will learn how to use Lotus Notes when you are away from the office.

LESSON 17
Using Notes Remotely

In this chapter, you'll learn how to work with Notes when you aren't in the office—by replicating mail, creating replicas of databases, and encrypting local databases.

Understanding Mobile Users

A *mobile* user is one who works from multiple locations and sometimes works in Notes while disconnected from the Notes network. Non-mobile Notes users typically just turn on Notes and start working; they never have to think about how to connect to their servers.

As a mobile user, you have to decide as you move from place to place or from computer to computer how you will connect from that place or computer to the Domino servers where your data resides. Luckily, you will probably connect in only one of two ways—either to the local area network in your office or to the Internet. But you may have to decide whether to make that connection using your computer's wired Ethernet adapter, its wireless Ethernet adapter, or its modem adapter. And you may have to figure out how to dial a long distance call from a hotel room. And you may have to decide whether to work with databases residing on the server or locally.

If you use one computer at work and a second computer at home, you have to think about how you'll keep the Personal Address Books and personal journals on those two computers in sync with each other. Luckily, Notes takes much of the pain out of all of these decisions. And hopefully your administrator did the basic setup for you.

If you are a mobile user who has a high-speed connection to the Internet, such as a DSL line or cable modem, you might not have to set up replication of your databases and mail. After you set up your connection, you can work almost as if you were in the office. Even when we are traveling, we always try to find a hotel that has high-speed connections. However, they aren't always available or working properly, so it is good to be prepared to connect via a phone connection.

As a mobile user you may have to make sure of the following (especially if you will be traveling):

- Your location and connection documents are set up.

- You have local replicas of any databases you'll be using and you've added any necessary entries to the Replicator page.

- You have telephone and Ethernet cables.

- You have the phone number for your Domino administrator. (Please don't tell him we suggested you travel with his cell phone number, home phone number, and beeper number!)

- You have a copy of the Help database on your computer.

Depending on how your organization sets up its web access, it's possible to access your mail or other databases with a web browser with no need to install the Notes client on your laptop. Check with your Domino administrator to find out whether you can do this.

Connecting

Aside from connecting cables, getting connected to your servers is entirely an exercise in configuring location and connection documents, then choosing the right ones for your situation. Location and connection documents reside in your Personal Directory. Between them (and information stored in your operating system) they provide all the information Notes needs to establish connections to your servers. The location document tells Notes where it is currently located, what servers it should rely on from that location, whether to use local or server-resident databases, and, if local, how often to replicate with the servers. The connection document tells Notes *how* to connect to the server. The easiest way to configure location and connection documents is, okay, to have your administrator do it. But if you have to do it yourself, you want to set up your location document first, then your connection document.

The Location Document

Notes includes several predefined location documents. Unless your administrator has deleted them you should be able to adapt them to your use. The ones that you will find most useful are those labeled Office, Internet, Home (Network Dialup), and Island (Disconnected). Their characteristics are set forth in Table 17.1.

TABLE 17.1   Location Documents and their Characteristics

Location Name	Mode of Connection	Location of Mail Database
Office	Local Area Network	On Server
Internet	Local Area Network	Local
Home (Network Connection	Modem Connection to Internet Service Provider or Remote Access Server	Local
Island (Disconnected)	No connection available	Local

The other predefined connection documents—Home (Notes Direct Dialup) and Travel (Notes Direct Dialup) assume you will connect by modem directly to a Domino server. Now that the Internet offers universal connectivity, organizations rarely bother to set up direct modem server connections for their users, so we won't discuss them further.

You can often use these location documents as is. Their best uses are as follows:

- **Office**—Wherever 1) you can connect to your office network or the Internet by Ethernet, Cable Modem, or DSL adapter and 2) you want to work directly in your mail server's copy of your mail database.

- **Internet**—Wherever 1) you can connect to your office network or the Internet by Ethernet, Cable Modem, or DSL adapter and 2) you want to work in your workstation's copy of your mail database.

- **Home** (Network Connection)—Wherever you must use a modem to connect to the Internet.

- **Island** (Disconnected)—Wherever you cannot establish a connection to a Domino server, such as in an airplane.

The above location documents will generally work as is in every situation except when you are away from home and have to use a modem to connect to other computers. For that situation, you may need to create a new location document from scratch or, better yet, adapt the Home (Network Connection) location document.

To adapt the Home (Network Connection) or any other location document, we recommend that you make a copy of it, then edit the copy. To make a copy of a location document, select it in the Locations view of your Personal Directory, then in the menu choose Edit, Copy, then Edit, Paste. The new document will appear just below the original. To edit it, select it, then press Ctrl+E. Edit the **Location name** field (Basics tab) to give it a new name. Other fields that you as a mobile user may want to edit are listed below:

- **Prompt for time/date/phone** (Basics tab)—Set to **Yes** for any location document that you plan to use while traveling. Each time you start Notes, you will be prompted for the time, date, and phone number where you are located.

- **Server fields** (Servers tab)—Enter the full name of your home/mail server (e.g., Osprey/Servers/Stillwater) in the Home/Mail server field. The other server fields are optional. If you are working in a copy of an existing location document, these fields may be correctly populated already. But if, say, you intend to use a location document at a branch office of your company thousands of miles from your own office, you may want to repopulate some of these fields with the names of servers local to where you will use this document, rather than those back home. Ask your administrator about this.

- **Replication fields** (Replication tab)—You may want to enable scheduled replication. See Appendix B, "Understanding Replication," for details about this.

- **Use operating system's time zone settings** (Advanced, Basics tab)—You may want to set this to **No**. If you do, other fields will appear where you can specify the time zone settings that Notes should use when this location document is selected. You may prefer to do this instead of changing the time zone settings in your operating system at travel time.

- **Load images** (Advanced, Basics tab)—You may want to change this to **On request** to improve download performance when using a modem.

- **Network dialup idle time** (Advanced, Basics tab)—Insert a number of minutes in this field to ensure that you don't rack up huge long distance charges because you forgot to disconnect from the server.

- **Secondary TCP/IP Notes name server** (Advanced, Secondary Servers tab)—You can enter the name of a Domino server will act as a backup name, home, and mail server should your primary home server become unavailable. This might be especially useful if you travel internationally. Ask your administrator about setting this field.

- **Secondary TCP/IP host name or address** (Advanced, Secondary Servers tab)—If you set the previously listed field, you will want to enter that server's hostname or IP address in this field.

After you have saved your new location document, you can select it (or any other) at any time in either of two ways. In the menu you can choose File, Mobile, Choose Current Location, then choose it from the list. Or, with your mouse, you can choose it from the Location list in the bottom right corner of your Notes window.

The Connection Document

The connection document holds the information Notes needs to complete a connection to a particular Domino server. You won't always need a connection document to connect to a given server. On the other hand, for a given server you might find you need multiple connection documents, one for each location document.

The connection document is a companion document to the location document and a good way to create one is to use the **Connection Configuration Wizard**. Follow these steps:

1. Open your Personal Directory and navigate to the Advanced, Locations view.

2. Open the location document that needs the new connection document, then click the **Connection Configuration Wizard** action button.

3. Fill in the fields as prompted, then click Finish. The information you will be prompted for include things like the Domino name and hostname of the destination server, or the phone number that connects you to your ISP. When you click Finish, the wizard will create your connection document.

You can also create a connection document from scratch by clicking the **New** action button, visible from any view in your Personal Directory, and choosing **Server Connection**. You might prefer to do this if the connection document will be used with more than one location document. Most likely, you will only ever have to create two kinds of connection document: Local Area Network or Network Dialup. If you ever have to use one of the other kinds, your administrator will undoubtedly create it for you.

To create a connection document for use with a Local Area Network type of location document (for example, Office and Internet), follow these steps:

1. In your Personal Directory, click the New Action button and choose Server Connection.

2. On the Basics tab, set the fields as follows:

   - **Connection type**—Select Local Area Network.

   - **Use LAN port**—Select TCP/IP. (Your TCP/IP port might have a different name, but it should be obvious that it is a TCP/IP port. Don't choose a port that isn't obviously a TCP/IP port.)

   - **Server name**—Enter the full name of the server to which you want to connect.

3. On the Comments tab, enter any text that will help you, years from now, to remember why you created this document.

4. On the Advanced tab, set the fields as follows:

   - **Only from Location(s)**—Select one or more location documents that this connection will be used with. The default is all location documents.

   - **Only for user**—Select one or more users for which the location document will be available. The default is all users of the machine.

   - **Usage priority**—Select Normal.

   - **Destination server address**—Enter the server's hostname or IP address.

5. Save and close the document. It will appear in the Connections view of your Personal Directory.

To create a connection document for use with a Network Dialup type of location document (for example, Home [Network Dialup]), follow the same steps as above, but with three changes:

- Before you create this connection document, create a dialup network connection in your computer's operating system. If you have already created one that you can use with this connection, write down its name. To create a new dialup network connection record in Windows, open the Control Panel, choose Network Connections, and choose Create a new connection under Network Tasks or select New Connection in the File menu. The New Connection Wizard will appear. There you can choose **Connect to the Internet**, then choose **Set up my connection manually**, and finally choose **Connect using a dial-up modem**. From that point forward, you'll be prompted to enter your account name at your ISP, your password with the ISP, and a phone number provided by your ISP or your Domino administrator. Record the name of this connection; you will need it when setting up your Notes connection document.

- In the Notes connection document, under the Basics tab, in the Connection type field, select Network Dialup. When you do, another tab will appear, labeled Network Dialup.

- In the Notes connection document, on the Network Dialup tab, in the Choose a server type field, choose the server type for your operating system. For Windows, choose Microsoft Dial-Up Networking. Then click the Edit Configuration button. In the dialog box that appears, enter the name of the dialup connection you created in your computer's operating system. You can enter data in the other fields, too, but you don't have to re-enter any data that you entered in the dialup connection you created in the operating system. Click OK when finished.

Creating Replicas

When you need to work on databases that are stored on the server at the office, but you're working away from the office, you may want to make local copies of the databases. It's a good idea to create the replicas while you are still in the office with a fast network connection because it may take a long time, but not nearly as long as it would take with the slow connection you may have on the road.

The most important database to replicate locally is your mail database. See Figure 17.1 for the Open Database dialog box. Before you begin, verify that you need to make a new replica. There could be one on your laptop already that you don't know about. To find out if a replica is on your computer, right-click the bookmark for your mail file and choose **Open Replica**. If **local** appears in the list of replicas, you already have the replica on your laptop.

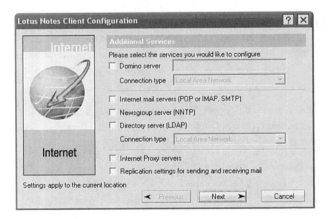

FIGURE 17.1   The Open Database dialog box. Some of the databases may be in folders at the bottom of the list, like Mail.

The following procedure will make a local replica of your mail database (or of any other database, for that matter):

1. Open your mail database, and then choose **File, Replication, New Replica** from the menu (or right-click the bookmark, and choose **Replication, New Replica** from the menu).

2. The **Create Replica for Database [database title]** dialog box appears (see Figure 17.2).

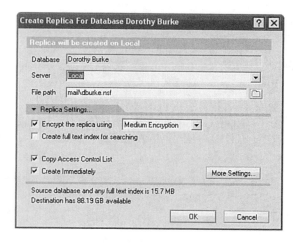

FIGURE 17.2 Click the twistie by Replica Settings to encrypt the replica, create a full text index for searching, or have the replica created immediately (versus the next time replication occurs). Encrypt the Replica Using is a default setting; deselect it if you don't need the security or choose a higher level of encryption if you do.

3. Make sure the Server displayed is **Local**. Notes automatically fills in the Database and the File path. You can change the path to put the file in a different location if you want, but for your mail database, you should not change the target location. If you do, your mail bookmarks won't work correctly.

4. Click the twistie by Replica Settings, and then select **Create Immediately**.

5. Click **OK**.

Replicating Databases

Having created local replicas of databases, periodically you have to sync them with the originals on your server(s). To do so, you can use the Replication page. The Replication page provides a central location to handle all your replication needs. By using the features available on the Replication page, you can set options to control replication of your mail and any other databases you might use. Access the Replication page by clicking the Replication bookmark.

When you create a local replica of any database, Notes adds an entry for that database to your Replication page. In addition there will be entries for sending outgoing mail and possibly for sending mail directly to the Internet. See Figure 17.3.

To replicate, click **Start Now**. To replicate only the mail database and transfer outgoing mail, click the arrow next to Start Now and select **Start Mail Only Now**.

 You can also send and/or receive mail without opening the Replication page by clicking the **Quickpick** button on the status bar. Choose **Receive Mail, Send Outgoing Mail,** or **Send & Receive Mail** from the pop-up menu.

At the bottom of the Replication page, you'll see the progress of the replication. After replication is complete, a note appears at the bottom of the page indicating when the last replication was completed. For information on how the Replication page works, see "Using the Replication Page" in Appendix B.

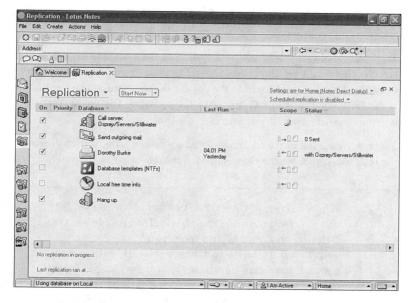

FIGURE 17.3   The Replication page lists all the databases for which you have replicas. Put a checkmark in front of the items that you want replicated.

Replicating and Sending Mail

Notes handles your local mail a little differently than it does other local databases. When you send messages, Notes deposits them into a database whose filename is mail.box. When you work with your server-based mail database, Notes deposits outgoing messages into your mail server's mail.box database, named [SERVERNAME] Mailbox. But when you work in your local mail database, Notes deposits your outgoing messages into a local mail.box, named Outgoing Mail. The local mail.box isn't a replica of the one on the server, so outgoing mail isn't replicated back to the server. Rather, when you tell Notes to send outgoing mail, it removes the outgoing messages from the local mail.box and redeposits them into the server's mailbox. Meanwhile, the router on your mail server delivers incoming messages into the server's copy of your mail database. Your server and local mail databases *are* replicas of each other, so incoming messages *do* replicate from the server to the local mail database.

To see the mail that is waiting to be sent, open the Outgoing Mail database by choosing **File**, **Database**, **Open** from the menu. You won't see the Outgoing Mail database listed in the databases. You need to enter *mail.box* in the Filename box. Click **Open** to see the database. You might want to bookmark the database if you intend to use it again.

You can view a list of the messages awaiting delivery, but you can't read the mail message from the Outgoing Mail database.

When you work directly with your server-based mail, you can't snatch your mail back after you've sent it. Deleting the Mail Memo from your mail database won't stop its delivery. When you work with a local copy of your mail database, however, you can stop the mail before it gets to the server. If you haven't sent outgoing mail to the server yet, the mail is still in the Outgoing Mail database. Open the database, select the mail message, and click the **Delete Message** button on the Action bar. You'll also want to delete any copy of it that you may have saved in your mail database.

Encrypting Local Databases

Security is an issue in every company, and if your laptop becomes lost or stolen, the information stored in your Notes databases is no longer secure. To help ensure that information on your laptop is available to only you, encrypt the local copies of databases on your laptop.

To encrypt a local database, follow these steps:

1. Right-click the database bookmark, and choose **Database**, **Properties**.

2. On the Database Basics tab, click the **Encryption Settings** button.

3. From the **Locally Encrypt This Database Using** drop-down list
   (see Figure 17.4), select **Medium Encryption**. Select **Strong
   Encryption** only if your system administrator instructs you to
   do so.

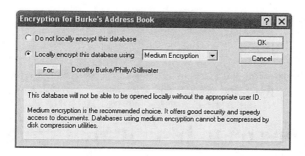

FIGURE 17.4   Choose to locally encrypt databases in the Encryption
dialog box.

4. Click **OK**.

Working Offline

There are times when you won't be able to connect to the server—via a
LAN, a WAN, or a modem. For example, you might be traveling by plane
or train or staying in an older hotel/motel with hard-wired phones. In
these cases, you can only work *offline*. Change your location to **Island
(Disconnected)** so your computer does not attempt to connect to the
server if you accidentally try to open one of the databases only found on
the server.

Remember to change your location again when you reach a site where
you can connect to the server.

In this chapter, you learned how to work remotely with Notes. In the next
chapter, you learn about instant messaging and web conferencing.

LESSON 18
Instant Messaging

In this chapter, you will learn how to participate in instant messaging, which is the IBM Lotus way to chat online with your co-workers.

Logging on to Instant Messaging

Instant messaging, or chat, enables you to find any co-workers who are currently online and to open a real-time text conversation with them in a chat window. It's a perfect way to get a quick answer, to reach someone who is on the phone, or to check whether the person can take a phone call. You can even save a transcript of the chat conversation.

You won't be able to use instant messaging in Lotus Notes unless your organization has an IBM Lotus Instant Messaging and Web Conferencing (IBM Lotus Sametime) server and you are using Lotus Notes with a Windows operating system. If instant messaging is not obviously available to you, check with your Domino administrator to see if this feature is an option.

When Lotus Notes was set up on your computer, one of the setup options determined how you would connect to instant messaging. If **At Notes Logon** was selected, connection will be established after you log on to Lotus Notes. If **Manually** was chosen, you will have to log on to instant messaging by choosing **File**, **Instant Messaging**, **Log On Instant Messaging** from the menu (or click the **Instant Messaging** button on the status bar and select **Log On To Instant Messaging** from the pop-up menu).

When you log on manually, the **Log On to Instant Messaging** dialog box may appear (see Figure 18.1). Enter your username and password (these might be different than the ones you use to log on to Lotus Notes, so check with your administrator to be sure). Select **Save your password**, so this dialog box won't appear next time, and then click **Log On**.

FIGURE 18.1   This dialog box appears only the first time you log on or if your PC loses its connection to the instant messaging server.

If you would like to log on to Lotus Notes using a single user name and password for both Notes and instant messaging, you need to enable single sign-on. To use single sign-on your instant messaging server must be set up for multi-server authentication so check with your administrator to see if this option is available to you. To enable single sign-on, choose **File, Preferences, User Preferences** from the menu. Click the **Instant Messaging, General** tab and select **Log onto IBM Lotus Instant Messaging using Single Sign-On (SSO)**. Click **OK**.

If you want to disconnect from instant messaging but continue to work in Lotus Notes, you need to log off. Choose **File**, **Instant Messaging**, **Log Off Instant Messaging** from the menu or click the **Instant Messaging** button on the status bar and choose **Log Off Instant Messaging** from the pop-up menu.

Setting Up Your Instant Contact List

Your Instant Contact List shows a list of people you want to regularly contact via instant messaging. To display the list, do one of the following:

- Choose **File**, **Instant Messaging**, **Show/Hide Instant Contact List** from the menu.

- Click the **Instant Messaging** button on the Status Bar and choose **Show/Hide Instant Contact List** from the pop-up menu (see Figure 18.2).

- Click the **Chat** button on the Action bar and select **Show/Hide Instant Contact List**.

- Click the **Show/Hide Instant Contact List** icon on the Instant Messaging toolbar.

- Press **Ctrl+Shift+C**.

- Click the **Sametime Connect** bookmark icon.

The Instant Contact List displays in a separate window (see Figure 18.3).

To add people to your Instant Contact List, do one of the following:

- Click the **Add to Instant Contact List** button at the top of the Instant Contact List window.

- Choose **File**, **Instant Messaging**, **Add to Instant Contact List** from the menu.

- Click the **Add to Instant Contact List** icon on the Instant Messaging toolbar.

The Add Person or Group dialog box opens (see Figure 18.4). Select **Add a person to the instant contact list**, and then enter the name of the person in the **Name** field (or click the button at the right of the field to select the name from the directory). From the **Add to private group** drop-down list, select the name of the private group under which you want the person's name to appear in your list (Work is the default group). Then click **Add** to add the person to your list and close the dialog box.

Show/Hide Instant Contact List icon — Chat

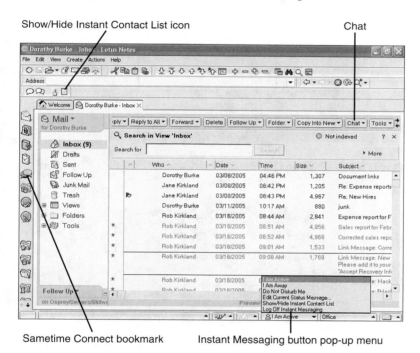

Sametime Connect bookmark — Instant Messaging button pop-up menu

FIGURE 18.2 There are several ways to display or hide your Instant Contact List.

Private groups in your instant contact list are there just to help you organize the list. You might want to organize people by departments or by project teams, so you can create a private group for that purpose. You then add names to that group.

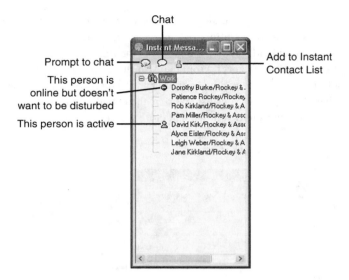

Chat

Prompt to chat

This person is online but doesn't want to be disturbed

This person is active

Add to Instant Contact List

FIGURE 18.3 The Instant Contact List shows your list of contacts and indicates their online statuses.

FIGURE 18.4 Although you can type the person's name to enter it, it is better to select the name from the directory to be sure you have the correct name and spelling.

If you want to create a private group, click the **New** button in the Add Person or Group dialog box, enter the group name in the dialog box that appears, and click **OK**. You can then assign people to that new group. A person can be in more than one group.

Your administrator adds the *public groups* (the list of everyone in your organization who uses instant messaging) to the instant messaging directory. You have no control over who belongs to these groups; however, you can add a public group to *your* instant messaging contacts list, which means you are adding all the individuals in the group at one time.

To add a public group, choose **Add a public group to the instant contact list** from the Add Person or Group dialog box and enter the name or select it from the directory by clicking the button at the right end of the Name field. Then click **Add**.

To remove a name from your instant contacts list, right-click the name and choose **Remove** from the submenu.

Do you want to add a new instant contact right from your Mail? When you have your Inbox open, select a message from the person you want to add to your instant contacts list. Then click the **Chat** button on the Action bar and select **Add to Instant Contact List**. Choose the name of the group under which you want the name to appear and click **OK**.

By default, the instant contacts list shows the full Notes hierarchical name of each person, such as Susan Kramer/Marsh Creek/Stillwater, or the full Internet style name (skramer@stillwater.com). It also shows you the complete list of your contacts, whether they are online or not. People also appear on the list in the order you added them. You can change your instant messaging preferences to modify any of these features:

1. Choose **File**, **Preferences**, **User Preferences** from the menu.

2. Click on **Instant Messaging**, **Options** (see Figure 18.5).

3. Select any of the following options, and then click **OK**:

- **Show online people only**—Select this to display only those people in your private groups who are currently online.

- **Show short names**—If you select this option, your list will display the short Notes names of your contacts (such as Sue Kramer).

- **Show list sorted**—Select this option to have your private groups appear in alphabetical order and the names within each private group also display in alphabetical order.

- **Bring the message window to the front**—Select this to notify you of messaging by displaying the chat window on top of your workspace when someone initiates a message. If this option is selected, any text you are typing in another program might appear in the instant messaging window. That text won't be sent, however, unless you click the **Send** button or press **Enter**.

- **Blink the message window**—If you select this option, your message window will blink when there is activity in the instant messaging window.

- **Play a sound**—Select this option to notify you of activity in the instant messaging window with a sound. Click the **Browse** button to select which sound file you want to hear as your notification signal.

You can set defaults for saving chat transcripts in this dialog box. Choose one option from the following three:

- **Do not save transcripts automatically.**—This is the default (and recommended by the authors) selection. Transcripts are not saved without intervention by you.

- **Prompt to save transcripts**—If you have a need to selectively save transcripts and are concerned that you will forget to do so, select this option. When you are finished with a chat, you'll be prompted to optionally save the chat.

- **Always save transcripts**—Select this option to always save every transcript. This is probably overkill and we suggest you probably don't need to choose this option.

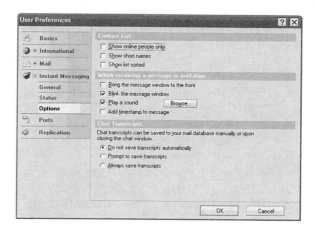

FIGURE 18.5 All your instant messaging preferences are set from the User Preferences dialog box.

Changing Your Online Status

Your current online status displays on the Instant Messaging button on the Status bar.

- **I Am Active**—This means you are online and able to receive chats.

- **I Am Away**—Your computer might be online, but you are not sitting in front of your computer. You might have stepped away for a break or to go to a meeting. People can still send you chats, but they can't expect you to answer them right away. The chat window, however, will appear on your screen until you return; you can answer it then.

- **Do Not Disturb Me**—You are online but you don't want anyone to send you a chat. You might be in a meeting or working on an important project and you don't want to be interrupted. People will not be able to send you chat messages.

- **Disconnected**—You are not online.

When others in your organization are connected to instant messaging they are able to tell what your status is, just as you can view theirs. This is called *presence awareness*. Presence awareness allows you to see the online status icons next to names in your Mail, Calendar, discussion databases, Teamrooms, document libraries, and Personal Address Book for anyone who is currently connected to instant messaging. These same icons display in your instant messaging contact list. Table 18.1 shows the status icons you will see.

TABLE 18.1   Instant Messaging Online Status

Icon	Status	Default Message
👤	Active	I am active.
📱	Active (mobile user)	I am active.
🔄	Away	I am away.
⊖	Do Not Disturb	Do not disturb.

To hide this presence awareness, choose **File, Preferences, User Preferences** from the menu. Click on **Instant Messaging, General** and deselect **Show instant messaging status for names**. Click **OK**.

When you point to the name of a person in your instant messaging contacts list (or where you see a status icon displayed), you will see a pop-up message that relates to the person's online status. The default messages appear in Table 18.1. You can change the messages that display for your name.

To change your status messages, choose **File, Preferences, User Preferences** and click on **Instant Messaging, Status** (see Figure 18.6). Enter the text you want people to see in the appropriate message field. You can see a list of previous messages by clicking the down arrow next to the field; select one if you want to use it again. If you want to change the message each time you select a different status, select the check box below the message field. Click **OK** to save your status messages.

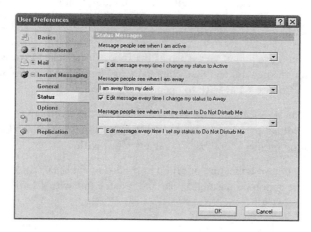

FIGURE 18.6 You can change your status messages here or click on the **Instant Messaging** button on the status bar and choose **Edit Current Status Message**.

Chatting

You can initiate a chat message from your instant messaging contact list or from a mail message, from a mail view or folder, from the Calendar view, from your Personal Address Book, from a meeting or group to-do document, or from the menu.

To open a chat window, do one of the following:

- With the instant messaging contact list open, select the name of a contact and click the **Chat** icon on the toolbar at the top of the list. You can also right-click the person's name and choose **Chat with** from the submenu.

- When you have a mail message open you can chat with the sender by clicking the **Chat** button on the Action bar and choosing **Chat with Sender**. Choose **Chat with All** to have all the recipients included in the chat.

- If you have a mail view such as the Inbox open, select a message from the person, and then click the **Chat** button on the Action bar. Choose **Chat with** to open the chat window.

- From the Calendar view you can chat with the chairman of a scheduled meeting. Select the meeting document, click the **Chat** button on the Action bar, and select **Chat with**.

- If you have a meeting or group to-do document open, click the **Chat** button on the Action bar and select **Chat with Chair** or **Chat with**.

- In your Personal Address Book, open a contact document and click on the **Chat with Contact** button.

- Choose **File**, **Instant Messaging**, **Chat** from the menu. Enter the name of the person you want to chat with in the **Choose Name to Start a Chat** dialog box (see Figure 18.7). If you aren't sure of the person's full name, enter either the first or last name and press Enter to see a list of possible matches, and then select the name of the person. Click **OK**.

FIGURE 18.7 This dialog box also appears if you click the **Chat** icon on the Instant Messaging toolbar or the **Chat With** button at the top of your instant messaging contact list.

 You can only chat with people who are active. If the recipient is away, the chat window will open on his screen but remains idle until he returns and responds. You cannot send chats to people who are disconnected or who have set their status to Do Not Disturb.

After you start the chat, the Send Message window opens (see Figure 18.8). Enter your message and click **Send** (or press Enter).

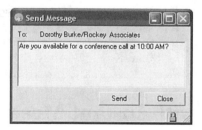

FIGURE 18.8 In addition to text, you can include document, view, and database links. If you type a URL, that also appears as a clickable link.

The Send Message window expands to allow space for the responding person to write an answer (see Figure 18.9). When that person clicks **Send**, the message appears in the top window so you can see it. You can then respond by entering text in the lower window, and it won't be seen by the recipient until you click **Send**.

Figure 18.9   Enter your answer in the Type Your Text box. Your message won't appear in the upper box until you click Send. Until you do, the status at the bottom of the window says "Waiting for response."

To end the conversation, click **Close**.

You can keep a transcript of your chat conversation. In the chat window, choose **Meeting, Save As File**. In the Save As dialog box, a default name is assigned to the file. The name includes the date and time, such as .3232005.904 PM.txt. You can replace that name before you click **Save**.

Working with Instant Meetings

Do you want to bring another person into the conversation? Do the following from the chat window:

1. Click the **Invite Others** button in the chat window (see Figure 18.9).

2. The Invite Others to a Meeting dialog box appears (see Figure 18.10). Click the **Add Invitees** button.

FIGURE 18.10   You can change the default "Please join this chat meeting" message.

3. In the Add to Invitation dialog box (see Figure 18.11), do one of the following:

- Enter the name of the person you want to join your instant meeting. Click **Add**. Repeat to add another person, or click **Close** when you are finished adding names.

- To select the name from the directory, click the button to the right of the User Name field to open the Browse Directory dialog box (see Figure 18.12). Select the name you want and click **Add**. Repeat for each name you want to invite. Click **Close** when you have added all the names you want.

FIGURE 18.11   You can enter either the first or last name and click **Add**. If the name is found in the directory it is added to the list of invitees. If not, a list of possible matches is presented and you can select the person you want.

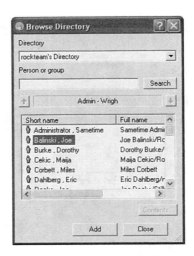

FIGURE 18.12   You can choose only one name at a time, clicking **Add** after each name.

4. Click **Send**.

If they are online, the invitees can respond in one of the following ways:

- Accept the invitation by clicking the **Join** button on the meeting invitation.

- Decline and close the invitation by clicking **Close**. The person who issued the invitation does not get any notice that the invitee declined.

- Chat privately with the sender of the invitation by clicking **Respond**. In this case, the invitation stays on the screen so the invitee can join later.

When the invitees join the meeting, they can contribute comments just as they would in a two-way chat. Comments are all identified by the name of the person.

There are other ways to start an instant meeting:

- In the instant messaging contact list, select the names of the people you want in the meeting (press **Ctrl** as you click to select more than one name; press **Shift** to select names that are next to each other). Click the **Chat** button at the top of the list.

- With a mail message open, click the **Chat** button on the Action bar and choose **Chat with All** to start a meeting with everyone in the To and cc fields.

- Click the **Chat** button on the Action bar and choose **Chat with All** when you have a meeting or group to do document open.

- Choose **File, Instant Messaging, Start Instant Chat Meeting** from the menu.

You can also start application-sharing instant meetings by choosing **File, Instant Messaging** from the menu and then selecting **Start Instant Audio Meeting, Start Instant Video Meeting, Start Instant Shared Meeting,** or **Start Instant Collaboration Meeting**.

When you use these methods the Start Instant Meeting dialog box appears (see Figure 18.13).

Follow these steps:

1. Enter a meeting title or subject in the Topic field, or leave the default topic.

2. In the Message field, enter a new invitation message, or leave the default message.

3. To add people to the Invitees list, click the **Add Invitees** button. Then do one of the following:

- Enter the name of the person you want to join your instant meeting. Click **Add**. Repeat to add another person, or click **Close** when you are finished adding names.

- To select the name from the directory, click the button to the right of the User Name field to open the Browse Directory dialog box. Select the name you want and click **Add**. Repeat for each name you want to invite. Click **Close** when you have added all the names you want.

FIGURE 18.13   Choose the tools you want for your meeting, but first be sure your invitees are able to use them.

4. Under Meeting Tools, select the tools you want to use in your meeting:

- **Chat** denotes a multi-person text message meeting.

- **Screen sharing** enables the other invitees to see what is happening on your computer screen.

- **Whiteboard** gives you an area on which to draw, type, or display files, such as presentations.

- **Audio** enables the participants to speak and listen via their own computers. It requires those speaking to have microphones and those listening to have speakers on their computers.

- **Video** enables the participants to see one another. It requires the participants who will be seen to have video cameras on their computers.

 Before beginning a meeting using audio and/or video, all participants should test their equipment to see whether it is compatible with Sametime. Go to the Sametime server meeting center (check with your administrator for the URL), choose **Attend a Meeting**, and click the **Test Meeting** link.

5. If you want to be sure that your meeting is confidential, check **Secure meeting** to encrypt your meeting and make sure that no one outside the meeting can read the messages you are sending or receiving.

6. Click **Send** to issue the invitations. Invitees will either join the meeting or decline.

If you use tools other than Chat, you will be starting a web conference.

Web Conferencing

Web conferencing is available if you have the proper Same liscensing. Check with your system administrator to determine if this option is available to you. If so, a web conference can be started as an instant meeting, but more often it is a scheduled event. You can schedule online meetings from the Calendar:

1. Open your Calendar and click the **Schedule a Meeting** button on the Action bar.

2. Fill out the Meeting document details as you would any other meeting (see Chapter 10, "Working with Meetings and Group Calendaring").

3. When you specify where the meeting is to be held, click **This is an Online Meeting** (see Figure 18.14).

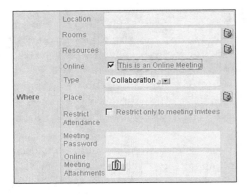

FIGURE 18.14   Be sure you have permission to create online meetings before you schedule your first meeting.

4. From the Type field, select the type of meeting:

    • **Collaboration**—Choose this for meetings with only a few participants or meetings where you have several presenters or you expect the participants to interact a great deal. The participants immediately have control of many of the tools.

    • **Moderated presentation/demo**—Use this for meetings with many participants where you want one or two people to control the tools, on the lines of a seminar.

    • **Broadcast meeting**—Reserve this type of meeting for a large group where the participants watch and listen and all activity comes from the moderator.

5. In Place, enter the name of the online resource or click the icon to open a dialog box and select the resource from a list. Invitees will see a link to the resource in their meeting invitations.

6. If you want to limit attendance to the meeting, select **Restrict only to meeting invitees**.

7. To truly restrict the attendance, you can enter a **Meeting Password**. Invitees will see the password in their meeting invitations and will be prompted for it when they click the link to the meeting resource.

8. Attach any files you need for the meeting, such as a presentation file to display on the whiteboard, by clicking the **Attachments** button and selecting the file(s) you want.

9. Click **Send and Save Invitations** to send the invitations.

When the users, or you, attend the meeting by clicking on the link in the meeting invitation, the web conference opens on a Sametime server. The Meeting room has several features, as seen in Figure 18.15.

If you are the moderator of the meeting, you have control of all the tools (in Collaboration meetings your participants have access to most of the tools, too). You can grant or revoke permissions for others to use the tools. Only the moderator can end the meeting (choose **Meeting, End Meeting** from the menu).

As a participant, you can communicate with the moderator by raising your hand (click the Hand Raise button) to attract the moderator's notice or by typing a chat message. Just remember, anyone in the meeting can see what you put in this chat, which is why it is called the public chat. To chat privately, right-click a participant's name and choose **Chat** from the submenu.

The moderator can also send web pages to the participants or ask polling questions. When the moderator clicks on Screen Sharing, there are several options for sharing screens, including allowing other participants to control the cursor or mouse.

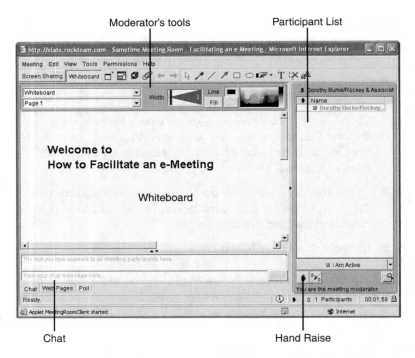

FIGURE 18.15   You can raise your hand for questions by clicking on the Hand Raise button at the bottom of the Participant List.

Web conferencing is a powerful feature for group collaboration, either for training, demonstrations, or sharing information. You can learn more about how this tool works from the *Lotus Instant Messaging and Web Conferencing User's Guide*. You can access this document by opening the Sametime meeting center in a browser (use the URL for your Sametime meetings) and clicking on **Documentation**.

In this chapter, you learned how to set up an instant messaging contacts list, how to start a chat, how to invite others to an instant meeting, and how to start a web conference (if it is an available option to you). In the next chapter, you will learn about customizing Notes.

LESSON 19
Customizing Notes

In this chapter, you learn how to customize the way you work in Notes by changing the user and toolbar preferences and by customizing your Welcome page.

Setting User Preferences

The options found in the User Preferences (shown in Figure 19.1) dialog box enable you to change settings that affect your workspace such as when Notes scans for unread documents, when your trash is emptied, and whether Notes saves a copy of the mail you send. To open the **User Preferences** dialog box, choose **File, Preferences, User Preferences**.

 More Information This chapter covers only the common, most basic options you can customize in User Preferences. If you need more information about customizing User Preferences, press the F1 key while viewing the User Preferences dialog box to access Lotus Notes Help.

The User Preferences dialog box gives you access to change your preferences in six areas: Basics, International, Mail, Instant Messaging, Ports, and Replication. The dialog box opens with the Basics section highlighted (refer to Figure 19.1). Table 19.1 describes areas where you might want to make changes. Before making changes in the dialog box in areas not covered here, please consult with your system administrator.

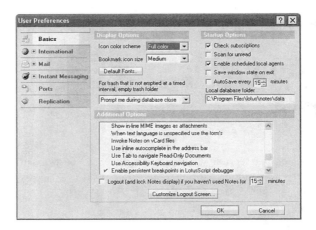

FIGURE 19.1 Keep in mind that some of the Preference settings won't take effect until the next time you start Notes. When the change requires that you restart Notes you'll see an alert to that effect after you click OK.

TABLE 19.1   User Preferences Basics Options

Option	Description
Display options	Choose your icon color scheme, bookmark size, and default font in this section. You can also decide when you want your Trash folder emptied—automatically during database close, when you are prompted at database close, or manually.
Startup options	Contains check boxes for commands that are performed automatically when you open Notes. If you are set up to use subscriptions, select the **Check Subscriptions** check box to display new additions when you open

TABLE 19.1 User Preferences Basics Options

Option	Description
	Notes. Place a check mark in the **Scan for unread** check box if you want Notes to look for unread messages and documents. Check **Save window state on exit** to have the same window tabs you had open when you exited Notes last. To have Notes automatically save your open documents at a specified interval, check **AutoSave every _n_ minutes**.
Logout (and lock Notes display) if you haven't used Notes for _n_ minutes	A security measure that prompts you to type in your password if Notes has been inactive for a designated number of minutes.
Additional options	Contains a list of options that control how you use Notes. A checkmark appears beside active options. Click an option to select or deselect it. Use the scrollbar on the right of this window to see all available options.
Customize Logout Screen	Enables you to select an image to appear on the logout screen.

If you're unsure of an option's meaning, read about the option in the Notes Help system before you activate it. Also, check with your system administrator or Notes Help Desk before you make advanced settings if you are unsure of the results. If you do check an option and you don't like the results, open the **User Preferences** dialog box and deselect it. Your system administrator can implement policies that may override user preferences. If so, preferences you select today might be reverted in a day or so. If that is the case, consult with your system administrator.

Most of the International settings are determined when the Domino server or your workstation are set up. For the most part, you should leave the settings as they are pictured in Figure 19.2. Table 19.2 explains some of those options. Click the **+** sign next to International to reveal three subsections: General, Spell Check, and Calendar.

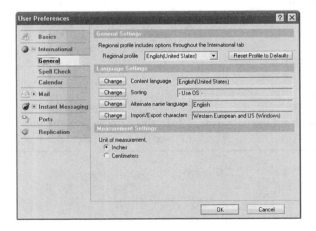

FIGURE 19.2   Most International options never need changing because they are set when Notes is installed on your workstation.

TABLE 19.2 International Options

Option	Description
General	Select the default language and unit of measure settings for Notes.
Spell Check	Select your dictionary (language), and when you need to edit your personal dictionary, click **Edit User Dictionary**. Editing the user dictionary enables you to view words you've added to your user dictionary during spell checking. You can add, update, and delete any of these words. (For more information on using spell check, see Chapter 3, "Email Basics.") You can also install specialized dictionaries here.
Calendar	By default, the Calendar View starts on Monday as seen in Chapter 9, "Using the Calendar." You can select a different day of the week if your work week does not begin on Monday. You also can set defaults for the date picker here, or select a secondary calendar. If you want a second time zone to display in your calendar, you set that here.

As seen in Figure 19.3, you can change Mail options by clicking the **Mail** icon in the User Preferences dialog box, which opens two subsections: **General** and **Internet**. Table 19.3 describes some of the mail options you might want to change.

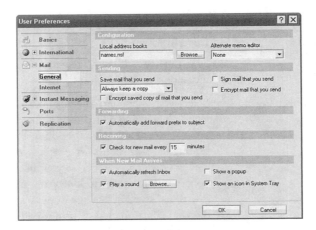

FIGURE 19.3   Mail options are changed in this section of the User Preferences dialog box.

TABLE 19.3   Mail Options

Option	Description
General—Configuration	**Local Address Books**—By default, Notes uses your local address book, called names.nsf. You can add more than one address book so Notes uses two or more address books, but this requires you to name the address books differently; for example, names.nsf, names2.nsf, and so on. For more information on how to do this, search the Help database for "local address books."
	Alternate memo editor—This advanced Mail feature enables you to use either Microsoft Word or Lotus WordPro to create mail messages. In order for this option to

TABLE 19.3   Mail Options

Option	Description
	work, you must have Word or WordPro installed on your workstation.
General—Sending	**Save mail that you send—** Controls whether Notes always keeps a copy of the mail messages you send, never keeps a copy, or prompts you so you can decide at the time you send the message whether to keep a copy of the message.
	Encrypt saved copy of mail that you send—Tells Notes to always protect the mail you save so others cannot view it.
	Encrypt mail that you send— Encrypts all the messages you send.
	Sign mail that you send—Tells Notes to always add a digital signature to your mail.
General—Forwarding	**Automatically add forward prefix to subject**—Fills in the subject line using text from the original memo preceded by "Fw."
General—Receiving	**Check for new mail every (fill in) minutes**—The default value for checking for new mail while connected to the server is 15 minutes. Change this value if you need to.

continues

continued

TABLE 19.3   Mail Options

Option	Description
General—When new mail arrives	**Automatically Refresh Inbox—** Choose this option so Notes dis plays new messages in your Inbox upon receipt. If you deselect this option, a refresh icon will appear in the header of your Inbox and you'll need to click the Refresh button or press F9 to display new messages.
	Play a sound—Controls whether Notes sounds a beep or any other sound upon receipt of new mail. You can select a different notifica- tion sound by clicking on the **Browse** button and then selecting the sound from the list. Notes or Notes Minder must be running for audible notification to work.
	Show a popup—Choose this option so Notes displays a pop-up message on your screen when you receive new mail. Notes or Notes Minder must be running for visible notification to work.
	Show an icon in System Tray— Choose this to have Notes notify you of new mail by placing an icon in your Windows system tray. Notes or Notes Minder must be running for visible notification to work.

TABLE 19.3 Mail Options

Option	Description
Internet	Internet options control the behavior of mail with regard to sending mail through the Internet. Consult the Help database or your system administrator before you change settings in this section.

The **Instant Messaging** options set up how chat works for you, what messages people see when you invite them to chat or join an instant meeting, what messages appear when people check your online status, and how you are alerted when a chat message appears (to learn more about instant messaging, see Chapter 18, "Instant Messaging").

The **Ports** options determine how your workstation connects to the Domino server. Do not change these setting unless you are instructed to do so by your Domino system administrator.

The **Replication** section of the User Preferences dialog box controls how Notes behaves during replication. Some of these options are discussed in Appendix B, "Understanding Replication," and Chapter 17, "Using Notes Remotely."

When you finish changing settings in the User Preferences dialog box, click **OK** to close it.

Setting Toolbar Preferences

Notes toolbars are *context-sensitive* by default; that is, they change as the tasks you perform in Notes change.

The first seven icons to the right of the first toolbar grip are always available. They will not change as you move from task to task in Notes.

To help you understand the function of each icon, Lotus Notes has a feature that shows the icons' descriptions. To see this brief description, hold your mouse over an icon. If the description does not appear, you might need to turn this feature on. Here's how to turn on the icon descriptions:

1. Open the **File** menu and click **Preferences**, and then click **Toolbar Preferences**. The Toolbar Preferences dialog box appears, as shown in Figure 19.4.

2. Click the **Basics** button and, in the **Toolbar Appearance** section, select **Show pop up description text** to display descriptions.

3. Click **OK**.

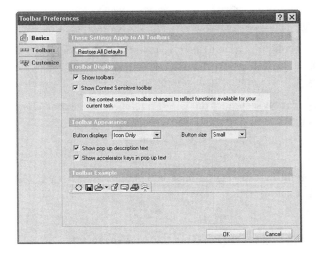

FIGURE 19.4   In the Toolbar Preferences box, you can change the way icons appear on your toolbar by changing Button Displays to Icon Only, Text Only, or Icon and Text. You also can change the size of icons in the Button Size field.

To see or change the available toolbars, click the **Toolbars** button in the Toolbar Preferences box. Select the toolbars you want displayed by placing a checkmark next to the toolbar name.

To customize or modify a toolbar, click the **Customize** button in the
Toolbar Preferences dialog box and follow these steps:

1. Select the toolbar you want to modify in the **Select the Toolbar
   to Modify** drop-down field (see Figure 19.5).

2. In the **Available Buttons** list, click on the icon you want to add
   or remove and click either **Add Button** or **Remove** button. Do
   this for each icon you want to change on the toolbar.

3. (Optional) The icons (buttons) displayed in the box are sorted by
   function. If you want to see them in order of description, click
   the **Sort Buttons** button and choose **by description**.

4. As you add or remove icons, they appear in the **Toolbar
   Contents** section along with all the other icons contained in that
   toolbar. To change the order of the icons in the toolbar, highlight
   the icon you want to move and click the **Left** or **Right** buttons in
   the Reorder section.

5. When you're finished, click **Save Toolbar** or **Restore Defaults**,
   and then click **OK** to close the dialog box.

FIGURE 19.5   You can modify toolbars and add new buttons in the
Customize tab of the Toolbar Preferences dialog box.

Instead of anchoring a toolbar to your work area you can float a toolbar (see Figure 19.6). A floating toolbar appears in its own window rather than being anchored on the edge of the screen (as in Right, Left, Top, or Bottom). To float a toolbar, place your mouse on the toolbar grip and drag the toolbar to the area of the screen you want. To anchor a toolbar, place your mouse on the toolbar grip and drag the toolbar to the edge of the screen where you want to anchor it.

Click the separator bar to drag

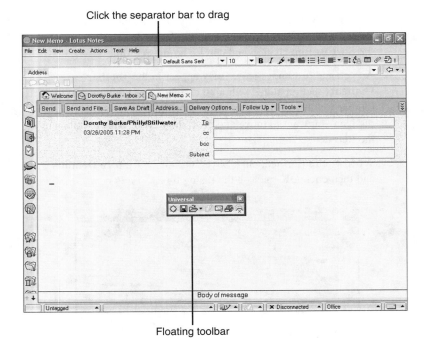

Floating toolbar

FIGURE 19.6 Float toolbars in your work area by dragging them to a desired position. To return a toolbar to its original position, click and drag it to that position and release the mouse button.

Customizing the Welcome Page

You can customize the appearance of your Welcome page. Options for customizing the Welcome page are

- Choose from a list of available styles
- Customize an available style by changing its template
- Create your own page
- Use a bookmark as your Welcome page
- Customize a Welcome page background or contents

> No options? No templates?Your Welcome page is cus-
> tomizable by your Notes administrator. It's entirely
> possible that a corporate Welcome page has been
> designed for your use and you may find that options
> mentioned here do not apply to your Notes desktop.

To create your own page or to customize a Welcome page style, open the customize area by clicking the arrow next to **Click here for Welcome Page options** on your Welcome page (see Figure 19.7).

In the **Current Welcome Page selection** field, use the drop-down menu to select a style for your Welcome page. The default selection for this page, unless changed by your administrator, is the **Basics** page (shown in Figure 19.7). **Basics with Calendar** is similar to the Basics page, except that your calendar displays in the bottom portion of the screen. **Basics Plus** displays a Welcome page that includes your Inbox, Notes search options, your Calendar, and hotspots for Mail, Calendar, Address Book, and To Do list (see Figure 19.8). Choose **Headlines with My Lycos**, **Headlines with my UK Lycos**, or **Headlines with Terra** for a Welcome page that includes the Lycos or Terra home pages.

Click the triangle to open or
close the Welcome Page options

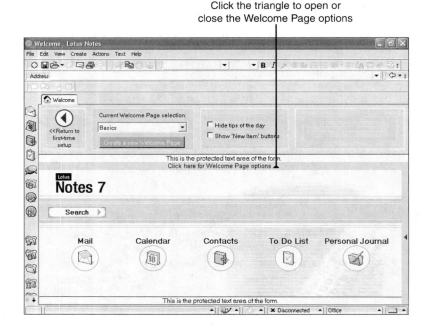

FIGURE 19.7   Customize, change, edit, or create a new Welcome page by opening the Welcome Page options.

When you select the **Workplace** option, the Welcome screen displays three tabs on the left side of the screen (see Figure 19.9). On the Today tab you see three panes: Recent Messages, Today's Calendar, and All To Do's. On the Collaboration tab you will find your Inbox and your Personal Address Book. The Team tab displays your team website and team database and is customizable. You can even add more team tabs. Consult the Lotus Notes Help database or consult with your system administrator or corporate help desk if you want to learn more about customizing team options. The Instant Contacts (if you have instant messaging set up), Search, and Launcher panes appear on the right side of the screen. Table 19.4 provides a brief description of the panes in the Workplace.

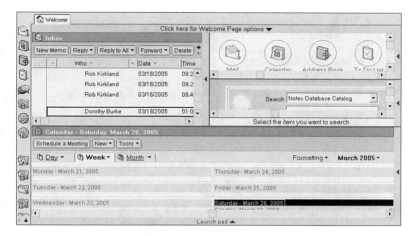

FIGURE 19.8 The Basics Plus Welcome page displays many areas of Notes, including your Calendar and Inbox.

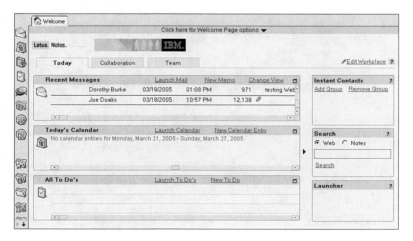

FIGURE 19.9 The Workplace Welcome page is designed to help you organize and manage your work tasks and communication with co-workers. You can change the configuration of the tabs and panes by clicking Edit Workplace.

TABLE 19.4   Workplace Panes

Pane	Description
Today—Recent Messages	Read recent mail, start new memos, change to another mail view, launch Mail (opens your Inbox)
Today—Today's Calendar	See today's calendar entries, create new entries, launch the full Calendar view
Today—All To Do's	See all your To Do items, add new items, launch your full To Do list, display Follow Up or New Notices instead of To Do's
Collaboration—Inbox	Use your Inbox without leaving the Workplace, except for the ability to filter junk mail (you must open your full Mail Inbox to do that)
Collaboration—Bottom Pane	By default this opens with your Personal Address Book, but you can switch it to the Domino directory, your Calendar, your database subscriptions, your favorite website, or your Personal Journal using the links at the bottom of the page
Team—Top Pane	Set it to display a team website, such as a Lotus QuickPlace, or a team Notes database, such as a Team Room or discussion database

TABLE 19.4 Workplace Panes

Pane	Description
Team—Bottom Pane	Set it to display a team Notes database or an existing group calendar
Instant Contacts	Add one or more groups from your Instant Messaging Contact List, see who is online, initiate a chat by double-clicking on a name, start instant meetings by double-clicking on a group name
Search	Search the Web using the Google search engine or search your Notes domain for databases
Launcher	Drag applications, databases, Notes documents, or web pages to this area to start them; book-mark databases to start from the Launcher

To create a brand new Welcome page, click the **Create a new Welcome Page** button located under the **Current Welcome Page selection** field. When you create a new Welcome page (see Figure 19.10), the New Page Wizard walks you through the design of your new page. You can set up your new page in three possible ways. If you choose **Frames**, you work with resizable rectangular areas to which you assign content. **Workplace** uses components that you assign to the Today, Collaboration, and Team tabs. **Personal Page** offers several layouts that you fill with pictures, links, applets, and so on. You can customize the colors and background graphics with Personal Page.

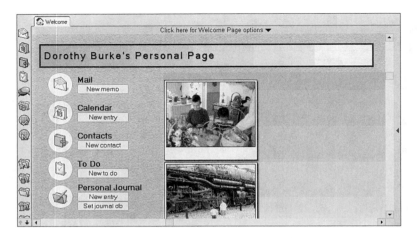

FIGURE 19.10   Using the New Page Wizard and using layout "H" from the Personal Page layouts, we created this new customized Welcome page. To change the page contents, such as adding new pictures, open the Welcome Page options and select **Edit this page.**

In this chapter, you learned how to customize user preferences, change your Welcome page, and customize toolbars.

Appendix A

Understanding Security and Access Rights

Notes security is a powerful, important tool for your company. Lotus Notes and Domino security are multi-layered and comprehensive. Domino and Notes security have three main goals:

- Domino server security—securing the data on the server
- Mail security—protecting mail from prying eyes
- Notes workstation security—protecting your workstation from malicious programs

Domino Server Security

The Domino server's job is 1) to store data, 2) to accept data only from users authorized to submit data to it, and 3) to send data only to users authorized to receive it. To achieve these goals, Domino server security involves the following considerations:

- Who can authenticate with the server
- Who can access the server
- Who can access each database
- Who can access views, forms, and documents within a database
- Who can access fields within a form

Authenticating with the Server

To do its job, therefore, the Domino server usually needs to know who the
users are when they make requests for data. To learn its users' identity, it
requires them to *authenticate*. Domino supports three authentication
modes:

- **Anonymous**—If you're accessing Domino using a web browser
  client and you request access to data that is not restricted,
  Domino won't require you to authenticate. You will be *anonymous* to Domino. An example of unrestricted data would be the
  information on your company's home page. It's freely made
  available to the public at large. The server doesn't care who you
  are and just sends it to you.

- **Name and password**—If you're accessing Domino using a web
  browser client and you request access to data that is restricted,
  Domino will require you to authenticate. You'll have to enter
  your name and password, which your browser will submit to the
  server. If the server can match your name to a Person document
  in the Domino Directory, and your password matches the password recorded there, the server will consider you authenticated.
  It assumes you are the person named in the Person document.

- **Certificate-based**—If you're accessing Domino using the Lotus
  Notes client, you will authenticate with the Domino server by
  sending a *certificate* to it. The certificate is a signed document
  stored in your Notes ID file. It states that you are the owner of a
  public key contained in the certificate. By analyzing the signature, the server can determine whether to accept the certificate. If
  the server does accept it, it will use the contained public key to
  encrypt a session key, then send the encrypted session key back
  to you. If you really are the owner of the public key, you will
  possess a private key in your Notes ID file that can decrypt the
  encrypted session key. Your private key is unique to you and is
  the only key that can decrypt data encrypted with your public
  key. By possessing it and therefore being able to decrypt the session key, you prove to the server that you are the person named
  in the certificate. The server now knows who you are; you are
  authenticated.

While you may use the same password when accessing your mail in a browser as when opening your Notes client, they are not in fact the same password. The password you enter in a web browser is your Internet password, which is recorded in your Person document in the Domino Directory. Your Notes password is recorded in your Notes ID and unlocks it so you can extract your private key from it. To change the first, you have to edit the Internet password field in your Person document (or choose Change Password in Domino Web Access, see Chapter 16, "WebMail and Domino Web Access"). To change the second, you choose File, Security, User Security in Notes, then choose Change Password. Your administrator can optionally set up synchronization of the two passwords, so that changing one causes the other to be changed as well.

Because authentication depends on your private key, it is password protected in your Notes ID file. It is very important that you keep your Notes ID password secret. If I could obtain a copy of your ID file and I knew the password, I could masquerade as you. I could gain access to data that only you are supposed to see. I could sabotage you by sending malicious emails while logged in as you. *Don't reveal your Notes ID password to anyone!*

If you cannot authenticate with a Domino server, Notes may display one of the following messages: "You cannot log in using the supplied User ID file, smartcard or password" or "The server's Domino Directory does not have any cross certificate capable of authenticating you". If you can't authenticate from a browser, you will receive an "Error 401 User Not Authenticated" message.

Server Access

Having authenticated with the server, you may still not be authorized to do business with it. You must also be in the server's list of users who can have access to that particular server. Just because you can authenticate does not mean you have authority to access all the servers in the organization.

If, when you try to open a database that resides on a Domino server, an access list blocks your access to the server or the database, you will see a message such as this: "You are *not authorized* ... ." (The words *not authorized* will appear in the message.)

If you see such a message, and you think you *should* be authorized to access the server or the database, tell your administrator the exact wording of the error message. The administrator controls the server access lists and usually the database access lists as well and should be able to correct the problem.

Access Control Lists

After you establish access to the server, the next step is to gain access to databases on that server. Database access is determined by settings in the Access Control List (ACL) for each database.

When you open a database, the Security button on the status bar displays a symbol representing the level of access you have to that database. Click the **Security** button on the status bar and the Groups and Roles dialog box appears, indicating your access level.

Each person is granted one of seven levels of access to a database:

- **No Access**—This denies you access to the database. You can't read any of the documents in the database, and you can't create new documents.

- **Depositor**—You can create documents but can't read any of the documents in the database—including the ones you create yourself. You might be granted this access level to cast a ballot in a voting database, for example.

- **Reader**—You can read the documents in the database, but you can't create or edit documents. You might have this level of access to a company policy database so that you can read policies but can't create or change them.

- **Author**—You can read documents created by others. You may be able to create documents. You may be able to delete some documents. You may be able to edit some documents or parts of them. Whether you can create or delete documents depends on privileges that must be assigned to you along with the assignment of Author access. Which documents you can edit or delete and which parts of a document you can edit depend on the design of the database. Most commonly, though, you will be able to create documents and to edit and perhaps delete only the documents you created.

- **Editor**—Editors can edit every document in a database, except ones that they can't read. Typically only one or two people, who are generally in charge of keeping a database, have Editor access.

- **Designer**—A designer can do everything an editor can, and can create or change any design elements of the database. To change the design of a form in a database, you must have designer access. Designers can also control some replication settings of a database.

- **Manager**—A manager can access everything a designer can. A manager also can assign and modify the Access Control List (ACL), modify replication settings, and delete a database from the server.

Additional permissions in the ACL control whether you can create documents; delete documents; create personal views, folders, and agents; and replicate and copy documents. Also, some databases may have a class of documents called "public documents." You can have read or write access to public documents independently of your level of access to regular documents. The most notable example of such a database is your mail database. All calendar and to-do documents in the mail database are "public documents." This makes it possible for you to give other people access to your calendar and to-do list without letting them read your mail.

Access Controls within the Database

The database access control list isn't the only control over database access. Within a database, there are additional access lists that control who can use certain views and forms, who can read certain documents, and who can edit what parts of documents. In addition, certain fields within a document may be encrypted so that only some people can read their contents.

In general the designer of the database controls these features. But users can control who is permitted to read documents which they created (or can edit). If you have the right to edit a document, you can limit the authorized readers of that document in its Reader Access List. To do so, follow these steps:

1. Open the document or select it within a view or folder.

2. Press Alt+Enter to open the Document Properties box.

3. Select the Security tab.

4. Deselect **All readers and above**, then click the **Add read access** button to the right of the reader list. The **Select Names** dialog box will open.

5. Select the names of the people who you want to be able to read the document. Click OK. Then press Alt+Enter to close the Properties box. Save and close the document if it is in Edit Mode.

Mail Security

Because mail crosses the network between your workstation and server, and between servers, it is vulnerable to being read by eavesdroppers and to being altered by them en route. To protect against these vulnerabilities, Notes allows you to encrypt and sign messages.

Encrypting Mail

When you encrypt a message, you encrypt it in such a way that only the named recipient can decrypt and read it. You do this by encrypting it with the recipient's public key. You can obtain another Notes user's public key from his/her Person record in the Domino Directory. You can obtain a non-Notes user's public key (if one exists) from other directories (Domino or LDAP) that your administrator may have made available to you for that purpose. And you can store copies of people's public keys in their Contact documents or in Cross-Certificate documents that Notes may have created for you in your Personal Directory.

Text encrypted with one's public key can only be decrypted with one's private key. In a well-secured Notes domain, the only useable copy of one's private key is in one's own Notes ID file. So, as long as each Notes user does not share with others the password of his/her Notes ID file, only your recipients will be able to read encrypted mail you send to them.

Signing Mail

To assure your mail recipients that messages you send to them were actually sent by you (and not some imposter) and have not been altered en route to them by some interloper, you can sign your messages. When you sign a message, you create a "digest" of your message, encrypt the digest with your private key, then send the encrypted digest along with the message to the recipient.

Don't confuse the mail signing discussed here with the written "signature" that Notes permits your to place at the bottom of your email messages. Use the electronic signature we are discussing here for security purposes. Use the written signature (see Chapter 5, "Using Mail Tools") to append "boilerplate" information about yourself to the ends of your messages.

Your recipient decrypts the digest with your public key. That assures the recipient that you must have created the digest, because a digest encrypted with your private key can only be decrypted with your public key, and (in a well-secured Notes domain) yours is the only useable copy of your private key. In addition, the recipient can create his/her own digest of the message. If the recipient's digest comes up identical to the one you created, the message can not have been altered en route.

Mail encryption and signing are enabled by default for Notes mail, but not for Internet mail. You can use them whenever you want when sending mail to other Notes mail users. But you can only send and receive signed and/or encrypted Internet mail if your Domino administrator has implemented Domino's Internet mail security features, known as Secure MIME (S/MIME). See Chapter 3, "Email Basics," to learn how to send signed or encrypted mail.

Workstation Security

One of Notes's most attractive features is that it protects us from malicious software being run on our computer. This is no small benefit in a computing world where spam and phishing messages arrive in our mail every day and where users' computers are being infected by viruses and Trojan horses and taken over by those programs to be used as "zombie" computers to spread even more spam, phishing messages, viruses, and Trojan horses.

The Notes feature that protects us from these things is the Execution Control List (ECL). When a program tries to execute within a running Notes session, Notes checks to see who "signed" the program, then checks the ECL to see what sort of things the programs signed by the signer are permitted to do. Most malicious programs aren't signed at all (because their authors don't want you to know who they are) and, by default, Notes doesn't permit unsigned programs to do anything that could possibly harm your computer or data.

Other programs may be signed by Lotus itself or by some developer or other entity within your own company. Again by default, Notes trusts Lotus-signed programs to do anything, no matter how potentially danger-

ous. How much it trusts programs signed by entities within your organization (or other third-party signers) depends on how your administrator may
have preconfigured your ECL when setting up your workstation and what
changes you or your administrator may have made or allowed since that
time.

You can see your ECL and examine its settings by doing the following:

1. In the File menu, choose Security, User Security. Enter your
   Notes password. The User Security dialog box will open, looking much like the example in Figure A.1.

2. Expand **What Others Do** in the outline. Examine **Using
   Workstation**, **Using Java**, and **Using JavaScript**. Select each
   listed entity to see the actions that programs signed by that entity
   are permitted to take. Click OK, Close, or Cancel when finished.

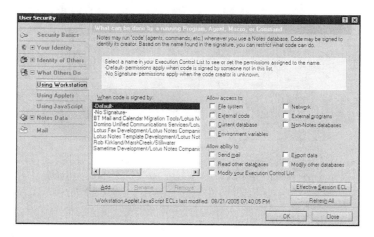

FIGURE A.1   All of the actions listed to the right of the list of signers are potentially dangerous and shouldn't be granted to
untrusted signers.

You can make changes directly in the ECL, but generally you will not and
should not. Typically your ECL will change, if at all, as a result of two
other kinds of action. First, your administrator can make changes to orga-

nization-wide ECLs and push them down to user workstations. Second, you might be able to make changes indirectly, depending on how you react when a program tries to take an action that it hasn't been pre-authorized for in the ECL. When that happens, you will see an Execution Security Alert. This dialog box warns you of the impending action (see Figure A.2) and presents options for dealing with it.

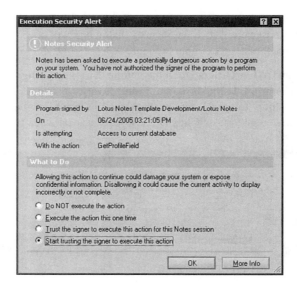

FIGURE A.2 Notes uses this dialog box to warn you that a program is trying to take an action that it isn't authorized for in the ECL. If you aren't sure whether to allow it, contact your administrator.

The choice you make may cause Notes to update the ECL with new rights. Specifically, if you choose the last option, **Start trusting the signer to execute this action**, in the dialog box, the ECL will be updated such that the signer named in the Execution Security Alert will have the right in the future to perform the action named in the dialog box. If you do choose that option, then later wish you had not, you can open the ECL directly (as described above) and reverse your decision.

Depending on how your administrator has configured your workstation, the option **Start trusting the signer to execute this action** may not be available in the Execution Security Alert on your workstation.

APPENDIX B
Understanding Replication

Replication is something unique to Lotus Notes. This appendix explains

- What replication is
- How replication works
- How to replicate your databases to and from the server

How Replication Works

Domino data is stored in databases that are usually hosted by Domino servers, but which may also be hosted by your own Notes client. A given database might be hosted by a single Domino server or Notes workstation or by multiple machines—one or more Domino servers and possibly multiple users' Notes workstations as well.

The primary reason why a database may exist on multiple machines is so that users can gain access to the data more quickly and conveniently. Notes can deliver locally stored data to you more quickly than data stored on a Domino server. It can deliver data stored on a nearby server more quickly than data on a server half-way round the world.

But there's a problem with permitting databases to reside on multiple computers, which is that the content of the databases changes from time to time and somehow the changes have to get copied to the other copies of each database. The process of copying such changes is called *replication*. It is actually a special copying process. Replication does not overwrite the entire database, as copying a database would in your file system. Instead, it updates only the documents that have been modified (and, in fact, only the changed fields within those documents).

Although many programs use replication to move copies of data closer to the users, Notes is unusual in that, by default, it allows users to make changes to the data in any copy of the database. If you and I both change the same piece of data on two different copies of a database, we create a *replication conflict*. The servers will do their best to resolve the conflict, but may not be able to do so, in which case a human being will have to do so. Most other distributed database applications avoid this problem by requiring all changes to occur on a single *master* copy of the database, all others being *read-only* copies.

As a user, you need to know two things about replication. First, a given database might reside on multiple servers; you want to access the database on the closest one. Generally, your administrator can configure Domino so that, when you go looking for a database the first time, you will only find the one closest to you. But if you travel a lot, you might occasionally want to connect to a different copy of the database than the normal one.

Second, you may need to know how to create and maintain replicas on your own Notes workstation. If you travel a lot or work from home and have to use a modem to connect to other computers, you will really appreciate Notes's ability to store local replicas of your server-resident databases. Not only will it be painfully slow to retrieve in real time each bit of data over the slow telephone connection, but the telephone connection might be costly. On the other hand, even if you only ever use Notes in your office at work, you might still find yourself using a local copy of your mail database if the network administrators need to conserve network resources. If so, you need to know how to initiate replication with your server.

> *Home Server* is the term used for the Domino server
> on which your mail database resides. If you can access
> several Domino servers at work, the one containing
> your mail database is your *home* server.

When you are ready to replicate a database, you'll connect to the server in your office. After the two computers "shake hands" and recognize each other, your computer begins sending updates you made to your database replicas. Then your computer receives any modifications made to the server's replicas since you last replicated.

Now look at replication with regard to your Mail database. To receive your mail, you connect to the server from home (or from the road) and replicate your Mail database. After you disconnect from the server, you read your mail, reply to some messages, delete some messages, and file some messages in folders. During this time, Mary Jones sends a new mail message to you, which is waiting on the server replica of your mail database. When you finish reading and replying to mail, you reconnect to the server and replicate mail again. During this replication period, the changes you made while disconnected (new replies, deletions, and so forth) are sent to the server copy of your mail database, and Mary's new message is sent to your replica of the database.

Each database has a unique *replica ID* that identifies it as a genuine replica and not just a copy of the database (you can see it on the Info tab of the Database properties box). If the database on your computer does not have the same ID as the one on the server, replication won't occur.

Before replicating, the server also checks to see when the replica copy of the database on your computer was last modified. If that date is more recent than the date the database was last successfully replicated, the database replicates. The server also looks at the modification and replication dates on the server replica. If that replica was modified since the last replication, replication occurs. Domino maintains a replication history of each database you replicate (choose **File, Replication, History** to view the replication history of the database you have open).

When the database replicates, it updates only those document fields that have been changed since the last replication, and adds any new documents. Each document has its own *unique Notes identification number* (UNID) assigned to it when it is first saved (you can see it on the Document IDs tab of the Document properties box). Part of that number is a document-level sequence number that increases each time you modify the document. If the number is higher for a particular document than in the database on the server, it is replicated to the server. Any documents that you deleted or that were deleted from the server replica leave a *deletion stub*, and that is replicated so the document is deleted from other replicas of the database, unless *Do not send deletions* was checked in the replication settings dialog box.

When replication is complete, you disconnect. You now have an updated copy of the database on your PC.

Setting Replication Preferences

You can control the replication process by specifying what type of files you want to receive, how old the files can be, and the priority of the database replication. All this is controlled under Replication Settings. There are three ways to open the Replication Settings dialog box for the database you have open or selected:

- Choose **File, Replication, Settings** from the menu.

- Right-click the bookmark and select **Replication, Settings** from the shortcut menu.

- Click the **Replication Settings** button on the Database Properties box.

The Replication Settings dialog box has five pages of settings—Basics, Space Savers, Send, Other, and Advanced. You click the appropriate tab to change pages.

On the Basics page, you enable a replication schedule, decide how much of the database you want replicated, and select a preferred server for replication. The purpose of the options on the Space Savers page is to limit the amount of space the replica takes up on your hard disk. The Send page includes options about what types of items you want to send when replicating with the server. On the Other page, you can disable replication temporarily, specify the priority of the replication, and enter the CD-ROM publishing date. The Advanced page has options to control server-to-server replication, which is beyond the scope of our discussion. Table B.1 quickly summarizes the important features of the dialog box that you might need to use.

Check with your Domino administrator before you begin changing replication settings or try to create a mail replica. The administrator may have set that up for you when your Notes client was installed. If not, the administrator may want to walk you through the steps or do it for you.

If you work with local replica databases, be sure to take advantage of streaming replication. In Replication Settings, under Basics, in the **Receive documents from server** field, choose **Smallest First**. This will enable you to start reading your earliest incoming documents while the later, larger ones are still being replicated to your computer.

TABLE B.1   Important Replication Settings Options

When You Need To	Set This Option (On This Page)	Description
Delete documents on your replica without deleting them on the server copy	Do not send deletions made in this replica to other replicas (Send page)	Setting this property will allow you to delete messages from the local copy of a database without deleting them from

TABLE B.1 Important Replication Settings Options

When You Need To	Set This Option (On This Page)	Description
		the server's copy of the database. The purpose is to keep the local copy from eating up too much disk space.
Eliminate documents created before a certain date	Only replicate incoming documents saved or modified after (Other page)	Specify the beginning date. The purpose is to keep the local copy of the database small.
Limit the number of large attachments or memos you receive	Receive partial summary only and limit attachment size (Basics page)	Only receive the beginning of the mail memo (To, From, Subject) or specify how much of the document and attachments you receive. The purpose is to keep replication times short. You can always retrieve the remainder of any document when you need it.
Remove old documents	Remove documents not modified in the last [specified number] days (Space Savers page)	Enter how old (in days) a document is when it's dropped from your replica.

continues

continued

TABLE B.1 Important Replication Settings Options

When You Need To	Set This Option (On This Page)	Description
Receive only part	Replicate a subset of documents (Space Savers page)	Check this item and then select the views and folders you want to replicate on the database (hold down Ctrl to click more than one).
Stop replication	Temporarily disable replication (Other page)	If you are stopping replication because of a problem with the database, call your system administrator for assistance.

Creating a New Mail Replica

People who use their computers outside the office and away from the network are referred to as *mobile users*. If you're a mobile user, it's a good idea to replicate the important databases you need to your laptop *before* you take the laptop out of the office. This will save you time on the telephone lines (if you use a modem). Of course, the most important of the databases you want to replicate is your mail database. Before you begin, confirm with your Domino administrator that you need to make a new Mail database replica. There could be a copy on your laptop that doesn't have a bookmark associated with it. To find out if a replica is on your computer, right-click the bookmark for your mail file and choose **Open Replica**. If **local** appears in the list of replicas, you already have the replica on your laptop. Notes is smart enough to place local replica information on the bookmark when you have opened the server copy, if the local replica exists.

Making a new replica is a straightforward process. Later in this appendix, the section "Using the Replication Page" shows you how to update this replica (or replicate) on an ongoing basis.

1. Open your mail database, and then choose **File, Replication, New Replica** from the menu (or right-click the bookmark, and choose **Replication, New Replica** from the menu).

2. The **Create Replica for Database [database title]** dialog box appears (see Figure B.1).

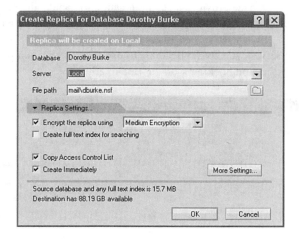

FIGURE B.1 Click the twistie by Replica Settings to encrypt the replica, create a full text index for searching, or have the replica created immediately (versus the next time replication occurs).

3. Make sure the Server displayed is **Local**. Notes automatically fills in the Database and the File path. You can change the path to put the file in a different location if you want, but if you are making a replication of your mail database, you should not change the target location. If you do, your mail bookmarks won't work correctly.

4. Click the twistie by Replica Settings, and then select **Create Immediately**.

5. Click **OK**.

After this, any time you want to replicate (update) your mail, use the Replication page, as shown in Figure B.2.

Using the Replication Page

The Replication page provides a central location to handle all your replication needs. By using the features available on the Replication page (see Figure B.2), you can set options to control which databases replicate and with which servers you are replicating. To open the Replication page, click the Replication bookmark on the Bookmark bar.

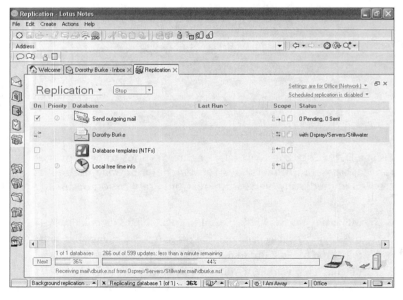

FIGURE B.2   While you are replicating, you can see the progress of the replication at the bottom of the Replication page.

There are several rows, or entries, on the Replication page:

- **Send outgoing mail and Send outgoing Internet mail**—Sends all pending messages from your Outgoing Mail databases. These databases hold your outgoing mail when you work offline. When you use the Replication page, the outgoing mail gets routed to the server.

- **Databases**—For each local database replica that you have, such as Mail, there is a database entry on the Replicator page.

- **Database templates**—Templates are used to create new databases and to refresh the designs of any template-based databases you have. You probably will not need to replicate your templates with the server. (You need to do this only to update your templates.)

- **Local free time info**—Your mail server keeps track of its mail users' calendar entries so that, when we want to schedule a meeting, we can see when potential attendees are free. When working offline, we don't have access to that information on the server. By right-clicking this entry and setting appropriate options, we can store other people's busy times locally, so as to gain this same benefit while working offline.

- **Call server** and **Hang up**—These entries automatically appear when you choose any location configured for connecting to servers via a modem. When you activate replication, these entries place the phone call and then hang up automatically when replication is completed.

Each entry row also has a check box. To include an entry in the replication, click the check box (a check mark appears). When you click the **Start Now** button (select **Start Mail Only Now** from the drop-down menu to replicate the mail files only), Lotus Notes performs the functions of each checked entry row in the order of the rows.

The Status bar at the bottom of the page shows information about the current replication, letting you know when Lotus Notes is attempting to call a server, what database is being replicated, the progress of the replication, how many minutes are left, and when the replication is finished. After replication, the status bar displays statistics for individual entries.

Scheduling Replication

If you regularly work with local copies of databases, you may want to set up scheduled replication, so that you don't have to remember to initiate replication all the time. This would be beneficial to you if you regularly work from home or if your administrator requires you to work from a local replica of your mail database.

You can set up scheduled replication in two places—your location document (under the Replication tab) or the Replication page. All you have to do is choose to enable it. Notes will thereafter attempt to replicate with each appropriate server every 60 minutes as long as Notes is running. You can further refine this, again in the location document or the Replication page. In the Replication page, you can choose Set Replication Schedule on the Replication page to open a dialog box of replication settings. In the location document the same replication settings appear directly when you enable replication.

The available replication settings are described below:

- **Create new replicas**—The options are **Immediately** and **Next Replication**. This sets the default behavior for whenever you create a new local replica. If you choose Immediately, the new replica will be created then fully populated with documents from the server while you wait. If you choose Next Replication, the new replica will be created immediately, but it won't be populated with new documents until the next time replication occurs with the server from which the replica was created.

- **Replicate when Notes starts**—If you select this, you can choose two further options: **Prompt before replicating** and **Don't prompt**. Either Notes will replicate with appropriate servers when it first starts or it will prompt you to tell it whether or not to do so.

- **Schedule**—Selecting this reveals the next three listed options, allowing you to refine the replication schedule.

  - **Replicate daily between**—The default is 8:00 AM–10:00 PM, meaning that scheduled replication will take place between those hours. You can change the time range. You can also set multiple time ranges, or you can set individual times. Separate individual times or ranges with semicolons.

  - **Repeat every**—The default is 60 minutes, meaning that replication will repeat every 60 minutes. You can change this time interval. If you chose individual times in the previous field, this number has no effect.

  - **Days of week**—You can choose on which days of the week scheduled replication will take place. The default (all or none selected) is every day of the week.

- **Replicate when Notes ends**—Select this if you want Notes to replicate when you shut it down. If you do select this, two other options will appear, permitting you to tell Notes to replicate on shutdown only under the following circumstances: **If anything is waiting to be sent** and **If outbox is not empty**.

- **High priority replication**—Selecting this checkbox reveals a second set of scheduling fields (**Replicate daily between**, **Repeat every**, and **Days of week**), permitting you to define a different replication schedule for *high priority* databases. You can set a database as high priority in the Replication Settings dialog box. The benefit here is that you could have high priority databases replicate frequently, others less frequently. You could, for example, retrieve new mail every 15 minutes but other data every few hours.

INDEX

H

I

J-K-L

Java applets, 245
junk mail, blocking, 71-73
Junk Mail view, 24, 72

keyboard hotkeys, 211

Language button, 89
Launcher pane, 313
length of day, setting, 115
less than or equal to sign (<=), 107
less than sign (<), 107
letterhead, 65-66, 111
Letterhead tab (Mail preferences), 111
line spacing, 210
Link Hotspot command (Hotspot menu), 222
link hotspots, 222-224
Link Message mail memo, 219
links, 214
    anchor, 215, 218-219
    creating, 214
    database, 215, 219
    document, 215-216
    hotspots, 222-224
    types of, 214
    view, 215, 219-220
    viewing, 217
list fields, 206
List Icon, 212
lists
    Instant Contact List, 278, 281-283
        adding people to, 278, 281
        removing people from, 281
        showing/hiding, 278
    mailing lists
        creating, 184-187
        deleting, 188
    To Do, 12
loading searches, 109

local databases, 83
Location button, 91
Location documents, 193-194, 200, 264-267
    choosing, 8
    editing, 200
    folders, 59
Lock Display command (Security menu), 19
locking User IDs, 19-20
Log Off Instant Messaging command (Instant Messaging menu), 278
Log On Instant Messaging command (Instant Messaging menu), 276
logging on/off
    instant messaging, 276-278
    WebMail, 248
Logout option (User Preferences Basics), 299
Lotus Applications command (Programs menu), 125
Lotus Applications menu commands, Notes Minder, 125
Lotus Instant Messaging and Web Conferencing User's Guide, 296
Lotus Notes Minder dialog box, 126

M

Mail, 11. *See also* Domino Web Access; WebMail
    accessing
        access rights, 119
        access to others' Mail, 124
        shortcuts, 124
        WebMail, 244
    Action bar, 26
    Auto Save feature, 4
    compared to WebMail, 242-244
    displaying, 24

Restore Default Calendar Colors
button, 137
results (searches), displaying, 99
Return receipt, 45
rich text fields, 29, 38, 68, 206
Roles view (Mail), 25
rooms (meetings)
    canceling, 161
    reserving, 158-159
    searching for, 159-161
Rooms and Resources tab (Calendar
preferences), 118
rules
    creating, 74-76
    defining actions, 76
    editing, 76
    selecting conditions, 75-76
    setting exceptions, 76
    turning on/off, 76
Rules folder, 75

S

Sametime Connection, 12
Save and Send Invitations button,
153
Save As Draft button, 42, 153, 253
Save As File command (Meeting
menu), 288
Save As Stationery button, 253
Save as Stationery command (Tools
menu), 67
Save Attachment dialog box, 237
Save Window State command (File
menu), 4
saving
    attachments, 237
    meeting invitations, 153
    memo stationery, 67
    messages, 42, 57-58
    searches, 108
    web pages, 197-198

Scale all graphics to 100% option
(Print dialog box), 63
Schedule a Meeting button, 132, 148,
294
scheduling
    meetings, 147-149, 152-153
        checking availability, 149,
            152
        creating invitations, 147
        delivery options, 152-153
        options, 152
        saving invitations, 153
    replication, 336-337
Scheduling tab (Calendar prefer-
ences), 116
Search Bar, 96
    condition buttons, 102-103
    expanding, 101
search box, 99
Search button, 11, 197
Search For text box, 99
Search pane, 313
Search within option, 101
searching
    case-sensitive searches,
      enabling, 98
    databases, 99-100
        conditions, 101, 104
        Fuzzy Search option, 101
        loading searches, 109
        operators, 104-107
        Quick Search, 100
        saving searches, 108
        Search within Results
            option, 101
        sorting results, 107
        Word Variants option, 101
    folders, 4
    for meeting equipment, 161
    for meeting rooms, 159-161
    search results, displaying, 99